Rock
Formation

FOUNDATIONS OF POPULAR CULTURE

Series Editor: GARTH S. JOWETT
University of Houston

The study of popular culture has now become a widely accepted part of the modern academic curriculum. This increasing interest has spawned a great deal of important research in recent years, and the field of "cultural studies" in its many forms is now one of the most dynamic and exciting in modern academia. Each volume in the **Foundations of Popular Culture Series** will introduce a specific issue fundamental to the study of popular culture, and the authors have been given the charge to write with clarity and precision and to examine the subject systematically. The editorial objective is to provide an important series of "building block" volumes which can stand by themselves, or used in combination to provide a thorough, and accessible grounding in the field of cultural studies.

1. **The Production of Culture: Media and the Urban Arts**
   by **Diana Crane**

2. **Popular Culture Genres: Theories and Texts**
   by **Arthur Asa Berger**

3. **Rock Formation: Music, Technology, and Mass Communication**
   by **Steve Jones**

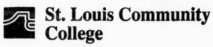

Rock Formation

Music, Technology, and Mass Communication

Steve Jones

Foundations of Popular Culture Vol. **3**

SAGE Publications
International Educational and Professional Publisher
Newbury Park   London   New Delhi

For information address:

 SAGE Publications, Inc.
2455 Teller Road
Newbury Park, California 91320

SAGE Publications Ltd.
6 Bonhill Street
London EC2A 4PU
United Kingdom

SAGE Publications India Pvt. Ltd.
M-32 Market
Greater Kailash I
New Delhi 110 048 India

Printed in the United States of America

Library of Congress Cataloging-in-Publication Data

Jones, Steve, guitarist.
    Rock formation: music, technology, and mass communication / Steve Jones.
        p.   cm.—(Foundations of popular culture; v. 3)
    Includes bibliographical references and index.
    ISBN 0-8039-4442-X.—ISBN 0-8039-4443-8 (pbk.)
      1. Rock music—History and criticism. 2. Mass media and music.
    3. Popular culture—History—20th century. I. Title II. Series.
ML3534.J68   1992
781.66—dc20   92-2237

92 93 94 95 10 9 8 7 6 5 4 3 2 1

Sage Production Editor: Astrid Virding

Credits

The research for this book was made possible in part by grants from the University of Illinois, Urbana-Champaign and the Association for Recorded Sound Collections.

For Jodi

Contents

Series Editor's Introduction

Music is central to the cultural practices of all societies. We know that, starting in the earliest period of recorded history, music in its many forms was an important source of self-expression, as well as being a staple form of popular diversion. It was used in the home for family amusement, and as formal entertainment by professionals outside of the home. It provided one of the sole sources of merriment for a significant portion of the population throughout most of human history, and it was used as a carrier of news and propaganda as well as simple declarations of love and romance. On occasion, such as in religious ceremonies, it is used as a means of creating cultural and social cohesion. Music has also been accused of inciting people to wild and lascivious behavior, as well as fomenting racism and violence. Increasingly in the twentieth century, it is music that has become the central pivot point around which much of our popular culture revolves. Particularly since the mid-1950s, rock music, and the attendant "rock culture" have become significant factors in all facets of modern cultural practice, shaping the political attitudes and the aesthetics of youth worldwide. It is surprising therefore that before this study, there has not been a serious, book-length examination of the influence of technology on one of our most important forms of popular culture.

In this study, Steve Jones examines the significant role played by technology in the emergence of popular music as a major cultural form of the 20th century. While the author has concentrated the bulk of his discussion on the specifics of rock music, the book provides a detailed history of the various technologies which have shaped modern popular music. In fact, Jones sees technology as the central force behind the evolution of popular music, and each new technical development has allowed the emergence of a "new sound." It is this constant search for new sounds which has brought about changes in the styles and content of popular musical forms.

In a clear, accessible style, Jones provides a history of recorded sound, and lays out the arguments surrounding the question of "authenticity" of performance. The author poses several key questions which open up for discussion such issues as: How does technology alter the actual performance of the artist? What role does the record producer play? What do audiences know and expect from artists and their recordings? Other important issues such as copyright and sampling are also examined. In the end the reader is forced to confront the question of what is "authentic" in this popular culture form? Ultimately, this book makes a major contribution to increasing our understanding of the interrelationship between the public and music.

—GARTH S. JOWETT
Series Editor

Preface

This book is in some measure organized by my experiences as a record producer and engineer, and to some extent by my experiences as a fan and critic of popular music. During recording sessions, I often wondered about occasions when aesthetic decisions were made because of available recording equipment. There was a constant compromise between the recording artist, producer and engineer, based on the ability of a technological object to perform a given function. The issues raised here are based on ones that arose during some of those sessions.

The writings of Simon Frith and Lawrence Grossberg are particularly influential in my thinking about popular music. Their ideas, coupled with broader issues of technology and electronic media that can be found throughout the work of James Carey and Clifford Christians, form the core of my thinking. I am greatly indebted to them, not just for their work but for their encouragement.

Though intended as a social history of music recording, it is quickly apparent that recording devices could not be considered apart from musical instruments, sound reinforcing equipment and sound processing equipment. They are intimately related to recording. Synthesizers, computers, and other electronic devices are now virtually synonymous with recording, and leaving them out of the analysis would be foolish. Discussing recording without discussing auxiliary equipment would be like analyzing chess by looking only at the board and leaving out the pieces.

One of the most difficult problems to overcome is the reconciliation of popular music, aesthetics, and recording. Discussing the aesthetics of popular music is not easy. Most such discussion takes place over a few beers, at a friend's house, while listening to records, or at a concert. But even if the conversation is about the latest Springsteen LP and its production values, it is, at root, a defense of one's own aesthetics and not only Springsteen's (or those of his producer, group, etc.). Popular music's elitism permeates all talk of aesthetics, and as a fan of popular music I cannot pretend to transcend that elitism. I do hope, though, that an awareness of it has prevented me from overindulging in personal tastes.

Acknowledgments

Many people assisted with the research, development and writing of this book, people to whom I am indebted and hope to repay.

The University of Wisconsin-Eau Claire Department of Journalism provided a happy home for several years while work on this book was in progress. I am particularly indebted to Dr. James Fields for his support, Gloria Wilson for her friendship, and Laura Jasper for her ability to recast even the gloomiest of outlooks as a shining opportunity. Ron Satz and the office of Graduate Studies and Research provided funding for travel to conferences where many ideas were reshaped and refined. Bert Spangler and Larry Glenn helped keep me abreast of the latest developments in the audio field.

I have been blessed with colleagues in the University of Tulsa's Faculty of Communication who are not only bright, sharp thinkers, but friends. In particular Dr. Robert Doolittle has provided sterling guidance, and John Pauly has set many a derailed thought back on track. Frank Christel's advice and friendship are much appreciated. Jan Reynolds and her assistants, Amanda Smith, Matt Landis, Rachel Reynolds, and Juliette Tays provided help when time was of the essence, as did graduate assistant Barbara Buckley.

I am obliged to Garth Jowett and Ann West for their encouragement and guidance during the book's writing and revision.

The Association for Recorded Sound Collections provided funding for research at a critical juncture in the book's life.

The University of Illinois College of Communications must be singled out for special thanks, especially for the intellectually nurturing and nourishing environment it provided while I attended graduate school. Julian Halliday and Keya Ganguly made that period of time most valuable and memorable.

Steve Higgins's and Linda Strong's support and friendship made it possible for me to finish this book. They gave unflagging research assistance and opportunities to draw my mind in different directions at the most appropriate times.

April Filak endured many weeks of writing and revising with nothing but kind words and support, and to her I'll always be obligated.

I must acknowledge The First Things, who provided me with my first experience in a recording studio, and all the groups and musicians I've subsequently worked with and upon whom I've imposed my own sounds as they imposed theirs on me. In particular Mel Eberle, Lynn Canfield, Nick Rudd, and Henry Frayne have been most influential, as well as most companionable and warm-hearted. Scott Wyatt tutored me in the recording studio, providing for an apprenticeship I'll not forget and hope to pass along to another. Glenn Graham, Marian Kuethe Wyatt, Tim Hanafee and Jill Graham are, to this day, inspiration itself.

Paul Marszalek, too, has been an inspiration and a valuable source of information about the music business, and Bill Cone gave the "inside poop" on the latest in the musical equipment trade. Perry Leopold and the Performing Artists Network (PAN) provided a gateway to the music business that let me be everywhere at once, and make many, many contacts—and friends. Those interviewed for this book deserve special praise for taking time out of busy schedules to return phone calls and correspondence, and to put up with prying eyes and ears during recording sessions. The staff at Paisley Park Studios, the Living Room, Faithful Sound and Private Audio have been most accommodating.

The support and assistance of the following people is greatly appreciated: George Athanasopoulus, Elisa Becker, Norm Denzin,

Woody Dumas, Earl Gray, Vicki and Stan Holden, Bill Knight and the *Prairie Sun*, Tucker Robison, Debbie Senn, Eileen Sohn, Martin Sorger, Diane Tipps, the Whites (each and every one), John Joyce, D. Charles Whitney, David Horn, Mandy Crane, Tim Vear, and the Eau Claire Thursday night club.

The International Association for the Study of Popular Music, its U.S. branch and its members, have been a forum in which I could talk about my ideas about popular music when it seemed no place else welcomed any such discussion.

Among the most significant people in my life I count; Steve Winner, who asked me to review records for the school newspaper and led me astray from life as a biologist; Joli Jensen, who made me understand that it is possible to pursue knowledge about that which I desire to learn; Richard Hildwein, for encouraging me to pursue that learning; Ted Peterson, who taught a goofy young journalist just how much more he needed to learn about writing and editing as well as to appreciate jazz; Joel Rutstein, who taught me to be myself; Kris Simonson, who taught me about friendship; and my mother and father, who have never left my side no matter the distance that has separated us. Without these people the thoughts embodied in this book would not have crystallized.

Sound is a very special modality. We cannot handle it. We cannot push it away. We cannot turn our backs to it. We can close our eyes, hold our noses, withdraw from touch, refuse to taste. We cannot close our ears though we can partly muffle them. Sound is the least controllable of all sense modalities, and it is this that is the medium of that most intricate of all evolutionary achievements, language. We are therefore looking at a problem of considerable depth and complexity.

—Julian Jaynes
The Origin of Consciousness
in the Breakdown of the
Bicameral Mind

"I won't give you up,
I won't let you down.
Gotta have some faith in the sound,
It's the one good thing that I've got."

—George Michael
"Freedom 90"

1

Technology and Popular Music

Without technology, popular music would not exist in its present form. Obvious as it may seem, such a statement (like many other obvious ones) deserves closer scrutiny. On the surface, it would appear obvious that without tape decks, stereo systems, CD players and the like, we could not listen to popular music. Fair enough. But, as I will argue throughout the course of this book, it is the technology of popular music production, specifically the technology of sound recording, that organizes our experience of popular music.

Without electronics, and without the accompanying technical supports and technical experimentation, there could not be the mass production of music, and therefore there would not be mass-mediated popular music, or its consumption. But beyond production and consumption, there would also not be the composition of popular music, for popular music is, at every critical juncture of its history, determined by the technology musicians use to realize their ideas. Of equal importance, without technology there could not be the creation of sounds that are today intimately associated with popular music. This is particularly true in the case of rock and roll, as technology often drives innovation in composition.[1]

Chapple and Garofalo (1977) note the importance of rock and roll as the primary form of popular music:

TABLE 1.1 Type of Music Purchased Expressed as Percentage of Dollar
              Volume

Music Type	Percentage of Dollar Volume
Gospel	2.5
Jazz	4.7
Classical	3.5
Other	6.0
Country	7.4
Black/Urban	13.3
Pop	15.2
Rock	46.2

SOURCE: *1989 Update*. (1989). Washington, DC: Recording Industry Association of America.

Rock music is the most important cultural expression in the United
States today. Rock music, which accounts for more than 80 percent of
all record and tapes sold, is also the core of a $2 billion business that
dwarfs other entertainment industries. (p. xi)

Of the types of music purchased, rock music far outstrips every
category defined by the Recording Industry Association of America (Table 1.1). Most professional recording studios are used for all
types of music, from classical to rock. But popular music, in the
form of rock recording, keeps most (nonjingle/advertising) studios
booked, and most music technology is used and designed for it.

The bulk of the popular music industry revolves around and is
financially sustained by the production and sale of recordings.
Record and tape sales in 1972 accounted for $1.924 billion in
revenues and expenditures, according to Chapple and Garofalo
(1977, p. 172). By contrast, in 1972 live popular music production
accounted for approximately $150 million (pp. 149, 172). By 1975
record and tape sales accounted for $2.36 billion (Sterling, 1978,
p. 38). In 1972, 968,828,500 recordings were manufactured in the
United States and in 1976, 600 million recordings were sold in the
United States (pp. 40, 190). By 1988, when total sales included
compact discs, the number of recordings sold in the United States
reached 706.8 million, for a gross sales of $5,567,500,000 (*1988
Update*, 1988, p. 9).

Moreover, popular music is the music of television, of radio, of advertising—of everyday life. Many claims are made for its economic primacy, or for its power as a social force. But its power lies in its pervasiveness. Few people in industrial and developing nations are unaware of it. Most media and public events, from film and television to sporting events and fashion shows, include popular music as (at least) a subtext.

It is most often the consumption of recordings that is studied, and rarely popular music production. Both are, of course, profoundly technological. But most writers have pointed out the dependence of popular music on technology by examining the technological objects that mediate recorded music, usually from the point of view of the popular music listener. Edward Kealy (1982), though writing about the work performed in recording studios, predicates his analysis by viewing music as "an impersonally mediated experience. Instead of being with musicians and hearing them sound an instrument in an aesthetically pleasing way, they (the audience) listen to a speaker system" (p. 100).

Though true for the audience, this is not necessarily the case for musicians themselves.

Occasionally, as in Geoffrey Stokes's (1976) *Starmaking Machinery*, the relations of production are examined as they apply to creation of recordings. The emphasis remains, however, on popular music consumption rather than production. Of the 13 articles in *The Phonogram in Cultural Communication* (Blaukopf, 1982), only two concern the recording process.

Barry Truax (1984) explores the relationship between sound and technology, as mediated by listening, and calls technology an "interface between the individual (listener) and the environment" (p. xii). But it is also an interface between the musician and the environment, and the musician and listener.

Pop music critics like Dave Marsh, Rick Johnson, and Robert Christgau have difficulty reconciling modern technology and the inherent desire for "authentic" music. Marsh's (1979) notion of authenticity is most closely allied to the one held by rock fans. In his first biography of Bruce Springsteen, he writes that over the past decade, rock has betrayed itself. It gnaws at my marrow to recall a hundred sellouts, from the rock opera movies that were all glamour and no heart, to the photos of rock celebrities with international jet-set fugitives. The inevitable result was *records that were made not with feeling but because there was a market demanding product* [italics added], and concerts performed with an eye only toward the profit margin. Rock became just another hierarchical system in which consumers took what was offered without question. Asking who was fake and who was for real used to be half the joy of the thing. (p. 6)

For Marsh, as for many rock fans, it is the idea of *feeling* that is at the heart of experiencing rock music. But how does one determine who is real and who is fake? Lester Bangs (1987) had a view of authenticity similar to Marsh's, but with added insight into the complex interplay between technology and popular music creation. In a review of Van Morrison's *Astral Weeks* LP he wrote that

the whole ensemble—Larry Fallon's string section, Jay Berliner's guitar . . . Connie Kay's drumming—is like that: they and Van sound like they're not just reading but dwelling inside of each other's minds. The facts may be far different. John Cale was making an album of his own in an adjacent studio at the time, and he has said that "Morrison couldn't work with anybody, so finally they just shut him in the studio by himself. He did all the songs with just an acoustic guitar, and later they overdubbed the rest of it around his tapes." Cale's story might or might not be true—but facts are not going to be of much use here in any case. . . . What *Astral Weeks* deals in are not facts but truths. (p. 23)

Bangs's position is not far removed from that of critics like Larry Grossberg, Dave Laing, Simon Frith, Craig McGregor, Franco Fabbri, Chris Cutler and Iain Chambers. Cutler and McGregor distinguish between two forms of popular music: rock as folk music and rock as mass culture. Cutler (1985) distinguishes between the "folk mode" and mass form of popular music, and criticizes the value of recording as "only commercial, . . . leaving the profound and innate potential of the medium for cultural and aesthetic expression still undeveloped" (p. 142). The problem with dividing popular music in such a fashion is that the folk mode is predicated on live performance and mass culture on recording. But the widespread use of inexpensive multitrack recorders and the spread of homemade cassette networks are giving rise to another form of folk music that fits neither category. Likewise the use of turntables and microphones in rap music contradicts the easy combination of recording and mass culture.

Grossberg (1984) puts forth a similar argument, distinguishing between two forms of rock and roll product: music and records. Music, he writes, "is produced locally, out of a local community with a set of shared experiences and perhaps, a shared albeit unconscious ideological representation of the world. Hence, as music, there is a real sense in which rock and roll must be seen as folk art" (p. 228). What "gives rock and roll the appearance of mass art" is its "reproduc[tion] as an object" (p. 229). Grossberg qualifies his argument by adding the word *appearance*, and later writing that the "issue is not mass production and consumption, but the determinations operating upon the production and reception of the music (p. 238).

The distinction between production-consumption and production-reception is difficult to make though, and may not even be useful. For Grossberg concepts of authenticity and creativity are outdated because popular music is constantly technologized. New forms of rock and roll arise from new technology and it is the ability of different audiences within rock and roll to use technology and be empowered by it that Grossberg welcomes. Iain Chambers (1988) sums up this position well.

The fact that the recording studio, with its technology and accompanying financial requirements, is the central site of pop's sonorial production by no means implies a simple technological determinism. This history of pop reveals other, of unsuspected tendencies, among them the story of a continual appropriation of pop's technology and reproductive capacities. This has resulted in diversified cultural investments, involving different fractions of white metropolitan youth taking up guitars and synthesizers and adopting various imported sounds, as well as black youth "resignifying" the use of the microphone and the turntable. . . . Both maintain the fruitful paradox of subordinated, frequently oral-centered cultures mastering and extending the electronic medium of pop and, in the process,

re-presenting their "selves" in the heartlands of contemporary urban
life. (p. 609)

These ideas are especially valid when one considers reggae, rap,
hip hop, and other forms of nonmainstream popular music. Dick
Hebdidge's (1987) analysis of these forms is on target, especially in
regard to issues surrounding the penetration of music technology
into the home.

> When looking at Two Tone (Records), the point to remember is not
> that it was, as some rock and reggae purists have suggested, a
> "media-created hype" (less "authentic" than the original 1960s ska
> movement). . . . [W]hat's important about Two Tone is that Jerry
> Dammers realised that when dealing with the popular music indus-
> try, the important issues for the artist have less to do with staying
> "honest" and "authentic" and refusing to "sell out" than with grab-
> bing and retaining control of the product at every stage and in all its
> forms. (p. 107)

Hebdige is less concerned with what is and is not authentic than
with *who* is responsible for the creative activity. It is thus important
to simultaneously consider the changes in technology that have
blurred the roles of producer, engineer, and musician.

One can categorize these debates and place them along a contin-
uum: Cutler and concepts of folk culture on one end, Hebdige and
acceptance of technology on the other. Simon Frith falls in the
middle of this debate. Frith (1985) best examines the aesthetics of
popular music from both a production and consumption point of
view. He writes that popular music "exist(s) because of a series of
decisions, by both producers and consumers, about what sounds
good" (p. 82). Frith, throughout much of his writings, has tried to
reformulate an understanding of popular music by asking "how
music works to construct a people, a culture, an aesthetic . . . it
creates our understanding of what popularity is" (p. 6). Similarly,
the technology of sound recording creates what our idea of the
popular sound is.

The development of recording technology has run parallel to a
reorientation in popular music production. The goal of getting a

good sound is no different now than it was when the first recordings were made, but the idea of what a good sound is and how it should be achieved are radically different.

Few of these writers thoroughly examine the technological changes in recording equipment over time, and they rarely mention the sonic and compositional limitations of equipment used for the fixation of sound. The effects those limitations have on the composition and realization (fixing of sound in a specific medium for later consumption and/or manipulation) of music play a critical role in the production of popular music. Therefore, it is at the level of composition and realization that one should begin to analyze the relationship of technology and popular music, for it is at that level that popular music is formed. As the printing press enabled production of mass-circulation newspapers, which consequently affected newspaper content (for example, the inverted pyramid news story, the objective account, etc.), music technology affects the content of music during its creation as well as its consumption.

Music technology has also had a far-reaching impact on the music business. First, it has allowed for exploitation of copyright by way of airplay royalties, mechanical royalties (for the rights to manufacture recordings), and sales of rights. Second, it has provided a new source of songs, superseding the pop "factories" of Tin Pan Alley, and, along the way, altering the scheme by which songwriters, musicians and groups are discovered. Today, record company artists and repertoire (A&R) staff, those responsible for discovering and nurturing new talent, spend much of their time working in their car, or anywhere there is a cassette player. New artists come in almost exclusively by way of the demo, or demonstration, recording—which is easier to make thanks to the penetration of sound recording technology into the home.

In the realm of music, technology takes basically two forms. First, it is "an activity which immediately produces artifacts" (Mitcham & Mackey, 1972, p. 2). It includes the creation of music as well as the creation of musical instruments and equipment. The second form of technology to be considered is "know-how" (Jarvie, 1972, p. 54). In music, technology, he writes, "contains within it both pure tools and all knowledge" (p. 61). It both enables and restricts realization of ideas by providing knowledge of how to do things and tools with which to do some things and not do others.

As an example, the musical equipment industry—manufacturers of musical instruments and recording devices—directly affects the options available to a composer, recording artist, or producer by deciding to include or exclude certain options when designing a piece of equipment.

Many of the technological objects in music are initially created as producer, not consumer, goods and follow a very roundabout development. For example, impetus for the development of magnetic tape recording in Germany was not music recording, but Hitler's desire to record his speeches (Chapple & Garofalo, 1977, p. 20). The end result, the tape recorder, eventually found its way into music production, then into the consumer market, and eventually was manufactured to meet the needs of those markets. Similarly, the music industry, from record companies to instrument manufacturers, is currently manufacturing equipment geared toward the western popular music market, even while, ironically, many manufacturers are not based in the West but in Japan.

Musical equipment designers do not include features that are often used in popular music recording and performance. Manufacturers may design equipment in anticipation of its own effect, thereby perpetuating the market's values. Predicting its effect, though, is difficult, especially when that equipment ends up in the hands of creative individuals. The uses equipment is put to are often independent of the uses the manufacturer intends.

Among the compositional considerations affected by equipment used for fixing sound to a medium (including the phonograph, wire recorder, tape deck, and digital recorder) are:

1. dynamic range (the span of volume between the loudest and softest sounds),
2. noise (as measured by the signal-to-noise ratio, the range between a recording device's signal intensity and its accompanying noise content),

3. frequency range (the span of frequencies the equipment will pass or reproduce without substantial loss),
4. noise (such as tape hiss, hum, pops, and clicks),
5. time (length of composition),
6. distortion (audible or measurable differences between the input signal intended for recording and the actual recorded signal),
7. editing (ease of splicing), and
8. multitracking (ability to record more than one discrete channel of sound simultaneously).

Auxiliary recording equipment, such as echo and reverb units, equalizers, mixing boards, and so forth, also play an important role in the recording process. Each of the above parameters and the ways in which sound recording equipment allows for their manipulation play a critical role in the way music sounds during its composition, production, and consumption.

The role of the recording engineer in popular music is very important; the engineer plays a big part in the realization of a composition by deciding what technology should be used and how to use it. Interplay between the musician, record producer, and engineer is critical to the recording process. However, what the recording engineer eventually fixes to tape must first be composed around the limitations of the available technology. Thus the most direct interactions between music and technology occur during composition and realization.

These interactions can best be analyzed by examining the ways that technology has affected compositional technique and vice versa, and by examining the discourse between musicians, composers, engineers, and equipment designers and the culture within which music technology is developed and used. To quote Grossberg (1984) again, the "issue is not mass production and consumption, but the determinations operating upon the production and reception of the music."

Such determinations regarding sound and music are affected by the use and design of technology, and by the culture within which technology is produced and consumed. To borrow from Mumford (1934), "behind all the great material inventions of the last century and a half [there] was not merely a long internal development of technics: there was also a change of mind" (p. 3). A change of mind is currently underway in popular music as new technology both enables and restricts the creation and realization of music. The change of mind includes what Mumford identified as a "reorientation of wishes, habits, ideas, (and) goals," (p. 3) and an understanding of it is critical to a complete awareness of the evolution of popular music.

Such an awareness requires an understanding of the complex and often contradictory roles technology plays in popular music. For instance, it can be at once liberating and restricting. Frith (1981) wrote about the central role of the producer, saying that

> record producers, who are responsible for what happens in the studio, play . . . the crucial rock role: they act as the link, the mediator, between musicians as artists and their music as commercial product. . . . This means musical as well as administrative decisions: in planning a recording session the producer is determining how the potential material will be arranged and embellished . . . it is the record producer who is responsible for getting the sound that is the essence of a record. (p. 111)

Yet with the increased penetration of sound recording technology into the home, and the concomitant increase in home recording studios, the producer's control is challenged; the producer is not the only one with knowledge and experience in the studio. Even so it is technology that enables the producer to play a major part in creation and realization of a piece of music.

It is true that recording sound requires a good deal of knowledge about everything from microphone placement to level setting, equalization, and a myriad of other technical details. Indeed, to compose on any instrument one must know a certain technique. It certainly takes some time to master an instrument, acoustic or electric, ancient or modern, and to master a musical language, and it takes time to master recording equipment as well.

But now the representation of music is changing through technology—from standard music notation to visual representation by digital means. Therefore, technological language becomes increasingly important for the creation of music. As a result, it becomes even more difficult for those who simply wish to sit down and improvise music without any formal knowledge of music or of a specific instrument. One now often needs knowledge of a techno-logical nature (such as the language associated with electronic signal generation) as well. And it is people without a great deal of formal knowledge who have traditionally played a large creative part in popular music. Popular music is termed *popular* not only because it appeals to a mass audience but also because virtually anyone can make popular music, even though not everyone can "make it" (financially, creatively, etc.) in the field of popular music. As Donald Hughes (1964) wrote, "It needs considerable imagina-tion today to realize how difficult it was for anyone interested in music at the beginning of the century to follow up that interest" (p. 152).

Following up that interest is simpler now, and people without technological knowledge are using technology in creative ways. It is allowing for creation of sounds, quick and easy editing, and low equipment prices. It may be enabling people to create and realize their music without spending large amounts of money renting time in sophisticated recording studios. And it is central to the birth of new musical forms, including rap.

Some, like the International Communication and Youth Consor-tium, believe that new music technology offers "opportunities for the democratization of popular music production" (Robinson, Buck, & Cuthbert, 1991, p. 55) and the opportunity for "a new era of music production in which musical creativity will flourish" (p. 248). The danger in such statements is that one may believe that the music industry may significantly change. While this book will show that creativity and production are changed and changing as music technology changes, such evolution has so far had lit-tle impact upon the music industry's longstanding policies and practices.

In any case, technology (and its experience by the musician) is changing the relations of production of popular music. As popular music has evolved from the early twentieth century and Tin Pan Alley days to rock music, it has become sound—and not music—

that is of prime importance. Though it will be discussed at greater length in a subsequent chapter, it should be noted at the outset that the primary impact of recording technology has been to make the sound of a recording its identifying characteristic. One can refer to the "Phil Spector" sound, or the "Motown" sound. Prior to the advent of recording, musical passages were the identifying characteristic. In some cases they still are—much of pop music relies on the "hook," the instantly memorable musical phrase. But the overall sound of a record is a means to identify the performer(s) within the first few bars of a song. As Dick Clark once mentioned in an interview, "[The sound is] what the kids listen for . . . the more different, the more original, the more unique the sound is, the more chance a record stands of becoming a hit" (Aronowitz, 1963, p. 91).

Musicians have consistently been interested in the sonic capabilities of technological objects. Recent technology has enabled musicians to create sounds they had previously not been able to create, with a clarity not previously possible. However, as music technology has become more complex, the mastery of it has become as important for the composition and realization of music as musical knowledge. Although one need not know the operating system of a synthesizer to be able to make music with it, one must understand it to create timbres with it. Currently, a class system with three categories is developing—performer, programmer, and performer-programmer. Performers play synthesizers, programmers create sounds with them, and performer-programmers do both. Stratification has come with this class system, and the ideas and ideals that permeate popular music permeate its technology too. The concepts of authenticity, honesty and sincerity, long used by pop fans and critics, become woven into the mesh of music and technology. This book is, therefore, not only concerned with the interaction of music and technology but also more broadly with the evolution of popular music, its ideology, and capacity.

It is the technology of sound recording, the instruments used for fixing sound, that is the driving force behind this evolution and the concurrent change of mind among musicians, composers, producers, and all involved in the creation (and consumption) of popular music.

Note

1. I define popular music as music that is mass-mediated, that reaches a large number of people via specific electronic media, be it radio, records, tapes, television. In *The Politics of Youth Culture: Some Observations on Youth Culture in America*, an unpublished paper, Lawrence Grossberg avoids the distinction between *rock and roll*, *rock* and *rock 'n' roll* because he is "concern[ed] . . . with identifying the broad range of historical experiences, functions and effects of the music." Throughout, I use *popular music, rock music* and other terms interchangeably, because they signify an artistic, aesthetic medium as much as a musical form. Music technology is designed and marketed for popular music, but the technology is used for virtually all forms of music. My focus is primarily on the music for which it is designed, although I will draw from other forms of music to illustrate the effects and uses of music technology in music at large.

2

The History of Sound Recording

The growth, persistence in our culture, and technological improvement of sound recording reflect its evolutionary, not revolutionary nature. Sound recording technology is one of the cornerstones of communication. The technology of sound recording dates back to the late 1800s. The wax and tin foil cylinders, precursors of the modern phonograph, were among the influential inventions that heralded the end of the nineteenth century and the start of the twentieth century. Communications technology was coming into its own, with initial development of the telephone, telegraph, radio and phonograph occurring during the late 1800s. These inventions were not unrelated.[1] Thomas Edison, who, it is generally agreed, invented the phonograph in 1877, was in some measure involved in the research and development of all of them, as were Alexander Graham Bell and Emile Berliner (Read & Welch, 1976).

That these inventions were related is not surprising. The driving force behind these communications technologies (and the radio) was the desire to transmit the human voice. Their subsequent use, though, reflects the social and economic relations in which they evolved.

Before the Phonograph

Prior to the phonograph, music notation was the only means of preserving a composition short of memorization. That it is still used testifies to its simplicity and usefulness, as well as its ability to define "music." Still, music notation was a method of preserving notes, and not sound.

The first technological method of sound recording dates back to 1857 when Leon Scott, a French scientist, developed the phonautograph. This instrument used a hog's bristle, attached to a diaphragm located at the small end of a conical horn, to cut lateral grooves into a cylinder of heavy paper coated with lamp black. One could shout into the horn and rotate the cylinder by hand, thereby enabling the "writing" of sound (hence the term *phonautograph*). Scott, however, had no provision for playing the sound back.

Another French inventor, Charles Cros, never raised enough money to build his Phone-Graphos, though in April 1877 he deposited an envelope containing plans for it with the Academy of Science in Paris. The plans described a method of recording on a flat glass disc, with suggestions as to the reproduction of sound from the disc. Though never realized, his plans provided the inspiration for Emile Berliner to invent the Gramophone, the first practical machine for recording and mass reproducing sound some ten years later.

Music boxes had been popular since their introduction in the early nineteenth century, and the player piano predated experiments with the phonograph by almost 20 years. Neither device qualifies as an instrument for sound recording, however, because they do not fix and store sound. They produce sound, they do not *re*produce sound. Interestingly, computer-based electronic sequencers, currently in heavy use throughout modern commercial and home recording studios, operate in a similar fashion. The phonograph was the first machine to fix sound in a medium for subsequent retrieval.

The Phonograph

Several excellent histories of the phonograph and other recording devices have been written,[2] and I will not discuss its technical
development in detail. I wish to tease out of these existing histories
the uses to which these devices were put, the uses foreseen for
them, and the quality they were perceived to have as instruments
for sound recording and reproduction. They are ultimately devices
for the realization of music, and contain within their development
traces of the influence of musical values, as machines for both the
consumption and production of music.

In July 1877, Thomas Edison filed for a patent for a telephonic
repeating device with the British patent office. The method was
similar to Scott's and Cros's though Edison used tin foil as the
medium upon which grooves were cut by a stylus.

Apparently, the immediate use that Edison foresaw for the phonograph was recording the human voice. A quotation from Edison's
lab notebook from July 18, 1877 reads:

> Just tried experiment with diaphragm having an embossing point
> and held against paraffin paper moved rapidly. These speaking
> vibrations are indented nicely and there is no doubt that I shall be
> able to store up and reproduce automatically at any future time the
> human voice perfectly. (Hughbanks, 1945, p. 6)

Edison had at the time been working on the telephone and telegraph, and it is quite reasonable that in pursuit of improvements
for those inventions he envisioned the phonograph as one such
improvement. If Hughbanks is correct in asserting that Edison's
first glimpse of the possibility of sound recording came when he
rotated a device for converting telegraph clicks to sound and heard
a musical note, then there is no doubt that Edison oriented his
experiments toward the reproduction of speech and not music.
Hughbanks also claims that Edison told one of his workmen that
he designed a machine "that would record and reproduce speech"
(p. 11). It is no wonder that the phonograph was then commonly
referred to as a talking machine.

Hughbanks writes that the early phonographs were "tinny and very unmusical" (p. 12). Even its reproduction of speech lacked fidelity. "The reproduction it made was little better than a parody of the voice" (p. 14). The early phonograph was used to both record and reproduce sound by means of a large acoustic horn (familiar to many people from the RCA/Victor "His Master's Voice" logo), thereby necessitating strong sound sources to provide adequate levels of loudness. Yet the sound could not be too loud, in that the stylus carved pits into the cylinder (then termed *hills and dales*) and could not be allowed to cut too deeply lest it damage the medium.

The early phonograph was far from perfect in any respect. A court document quoting one of Edison's lawyers states that

> the original phonograph, although a very wonderful philosophical apparatus, was not suited for practical use, since the sounds obtained were distorted and the tinfoil surface became quickly destroyed. Furthermore, the tinfoil record of the original phonograph, owing to its fragile nature and to the fact that when applied in place a joint was formed between the meeting edges, could not be removed and again replaced in position on the same or other instrument. Consequently, with the original phonograph, the practice was to apply the foil in place, make a record therein, reproduce it a few times and tear the foil off, in doing which, of course, the record would be destroyed. (*Proceedings of the 1890 Convention*, 1974, p. vii)

The mass produced recording was a long way off. Shortly after inventing the phonograph, Edison turned to inventing the incandescent lamp, and did little to improve on the phonograph's basic design over the next several years. Before he did so, however, he filed patents for the phonograph and improvements on it. Those documents clearly show that Edison had thought out possible uses for the device. In a patent filed April 24, 1878, Edison (1878b) mentions that for

> amusement and instruction . . . for instance, a revolving cylinder containing phonograms of the letters of the alphabet . . . can be used in teaching the alphabet . . . [or it can reproduce] a dog's bark . . . [to be] used in a toy animal . . . clocks may be provided with phonogram cylinders or wheels to call off the hours, to give alarms.

Further on in the patent, Edison makes mention of a musical application: "Fig. 29 shows a single phonograph adapted to receive the voices of three persons as in singing." Edison also wrote an article for the *North American Review*'s May/June 1878 issue in which he listed letter-writing, dictation, phonographic books, education, music, family records, toys, clocks, advertising, and speech recording as the primary applications of the phonograph (1878a, p. 527). His phonograph patent even includes a method by which phonograms may be reproduced by plating and pressing, a method that is strikingly similar to that currently employed in the manufacture of phonograph records. Though the patent contains a description of the method, Edison did not test it. Indeed, Edison's primary goal with this patent was to ensure that it attended to any unforeseen uses of the phonograph. His business acumen was sharp, but it gives further weight to the idea that, because music is mentioned only later in the patent, its recording was an afterthought and not a driving force behind the phonograph's invention.

The phonograph enjoyed startling popularity from the day of its first public exhibition. The Edison Speaking Phonograph Company was established to market the phonograph, backed by the same group of men who financed Alexander Graham Bell and the Bell Telephone Company. The two companies even shared office space. Unlike the telephone, however, the phonograph was commercially successful from the start. According to Read and Welch (1976), the Edison company at first leased the phonograph to demonstrators. Some machines were outfitted with coin slots and sets of hearing tubes with which up to 17 people could listen to a recording.

But several problems lingered. In that the phonograph was initially developed for reproduction of the human voice, with its limited frequency and dynamic range, lack of fidelity limited the phonograph's popularity—as did the short supply of recordings. The novelty of hearing a recording of the human voice wore off quickly, and technical improvements became necessary if the phonograph was to become an instrument for recording music with any degree of fidelity.

Of equal importance, there was not a means for mass producing recordings. Phonographs came to be manufactured by furniture companies (Columbia, which evolved into Columbia Records, being the most well-known and notable) but manufacturers of recordings were slow to gear up. Eventually phonograph manufacturers themselves began producing recordings, but the problem of software lagging behind hardware is one that has plagued the consumer electronics industry continually, most recently with compact disc and digital audio tape hardware.

Until recordings came to be mass produced, however, the following process, described by Chew (1967), was employed.

> Suitable records were made either by the (demonstrator) himself, or by the subsidiary company or by the parent company. Since no means of duplicating records was yet available, it became an arduous matter to meet the demand for pre-recorded cylinders; to produce a batch of 200 records of a march it had to be played 20 times in front of a battery of ten recording horns. It became clear that if the phonograph was to prosper in its new role of public entertainer, the recording process must be centralized, some form of record duplicator must be produced, and the instrument itself must be simplified and cheapened to put it within reach of the average citizen. (pp. 14-15)

That Chew mentions the recording of marches is no coincidence. In that the grooves were cut into the cylinder by the sheer force of sound pressure necessary to cause the stylus to vibrate, it was precisely such loud pieces that were easiest to record, pieces that had loud sounds forceful enough to ensure reproduction. Consequently, the hardware dictated the music that would be available to the consumer.

The next step in the phonograph's evolution came, ironically, from Edison's archrival, Alexander Graham Bell. The reason for Bell's switch to experiments on the phonograph are unclear. Perhaps, as Read and Welch (1976) speculate, Bell became upset with Edison's delivery of the carbon transmitter to Western Union (Bell Telephone's competitor). Whatever the reason, Bell, using funds from an award given him by the French Academy of Science, brought his brother Chichester and Professor Charles Sumner

Tainter to a laboratory in Washington D.C. in 1881 for the purpose
of electrical and acoustic research. Tainter's notebooks reveal that
the three scientists were working on improving the phonograph.

> Very early in the work of the associates their attention became di-
> verted almost exclusively to the phonograph. Rather significantly,
> Tainter's first recorded notes are upon experiments with the phono-
> graph. (Read & Welch, 1976, p. 28)

The three men were meticulous about documenting their work,
and deposited notes and drawings in sealed containers with the
Smithsonian Institution (where they are still available for viewing).
The device they created was later called the Graphophone in
advertisements for the Dictaphone Corporation. It was virtually
identical to Edison's tin foil phonograph, except that it used wax-
covered paper and not tin foil. Instead of indenting grooves into
tin foil, the Graphophone cut grooves into the wax. The Graphophone patent, issued in 1886, included this distinction between
indenting and incising, and Read and Welch (1976) call it "the one
important concept that made possible the establishment of the
commercial phonograph industry" (p. 36).

Bell, Bell, and Tainter also developed a system whereby a jet of
compressed air amplified sound reproduction, as well as a mechanism by which the cylinder could be rotated at a variable speed.
Moreover, though some were immediately struck with the Graphophone's potential as a dictating machine (hence its later adoption
by the Dictaphone Corporation), the inventors were more interested in the Graphophone's ability to reproduce music (p. 37).

In 1887, Edison resumed working on the phonograph, possibly
because of the warm reception received by the Graphophone. The
first change to his original design came in January 1888 when he
substituted a wax cylinder for the tinfoil one. By using a very thin
bamboo needle for playback, the wax cylinder could be replayed
many times without damaging its surface. By 1895, with the help
of inventor Ezrah Gilliland, Edison developed an improved, spring
motor driven phonograph. Gilliland, however, had been working
on another invention he called the *spectacle*. This device allowed for

immediate switching between recording and reproduction on the phonograph. The spectacle was important for the phonograph's use as a dictating machine, but the principle of immediate repro-duction/recording remained central to subsequent recording ma-chines like the cassette deck.

During this time German-born inventor Emile Berliner, inspired by Scott's phonautograph, was working on the Gramophone, the direct ancestor of the phonograph as we now know it. Berliner used a method of photoengraving to etch grooves onto a metal plate. In that he had to first make a metal cylinder for recording, straighten it out for photoengraving, then roll it up again for reproduction, Berliner eventually did away with the cylinder and opted for the convenience of recording on a flat disc instead.

He also did away with the photoengraving process, replacing it with a method of plating and duplicating discs similar to the one used today. In 1888 he was ready to demonstrate the Gramophone.

> The Berliner recording process included the coating of a zinc plate (with grooves initially recorded by a stylus) with a very fine layer or film of acid resisting material. The plate was then subjected to an acid bath, the acid eating out a groove in the zinc of sufficient depth to pilot and to vibrate the stylus of the reproducing machine. This zinc plate was used as a master record, from which, by suitable processes, duplicates, which we know as commercial records, were made in hard material (ebonite) having similar laterally undulating grooves; which caused the stylus and diaphragm of the reproducing machine to vibrate and reproduce the sound. The reproducing machine was called the gramophone. The reproduction from these hard records was quite loud. However, as the etching process left the walls of the groove quite rough, considerable extraneous noise or scratch was added in reproducing, which detracted materially from the enjoy-ment of the listener. (Hughbanks, 1945, pp. 16-17)

Berliner solved several problems the early phonograph industry faced. First, he enabled duplication of records from one master record. The result was the mass production of recordings which set the scene for the rise of the recording industry. Another result, however, was the separation of recording and reproduction. No longer were they one and the same process. Second, the recording of discs was no longer a directly acoustical process. Though the master record's grooves were cut by the stylus, each subsequent record's grooves were not. The grooves were etched by the acid bath, and not cut into the disc by the acoustical energy acting upon the stylus. Third, Berliner's method used grooves that spiralled around the disc and moved laterally, not up and down, increasing fidelity.

> [The Gramophone] record was made horizontally and parallel with the record surface. By itself it formed the screw or spiral which propelled the reproducing sound-box, so that while the needle was vibrated, it was at the same time pushed forward by the record groove. As the sound-box was mounted in such a manner that it was free to follow this propelling movement, it made the reproducer adjust itself automatically to the record. The horizontal record of the gramophone was more capable of recording sound in its entirety. In the vertical record of the phonograph-Graphophone, there was a certain distortion which became more pronounced the deeper the sound waves indented or engraved the record substance. (Hughbanks, pp. 25-26)

The result was that louder sounds could be recorded and correspondingly louder volumes reproduced. However, this still imposed a limit on the loudness of sounds in that the louder the sound the wider the groove, and grooves could not overlap. Lower, bass frequencies created the widest grooves and were, therefore, more difficult to record.

There was also a restraint on the length of a recording. This was based not only on the size of the disc, as is obvious in either cylinder or disc method, but on the dynamics of the recorded material. The louder the material, and the more low frequencies it contained, the less of it would fit on a disc, because the grooves would be correspondingly wider. For example, it would be possible to fit ten minutes of a piccolo solo on a disc, whereas it would be possible to fit only five minutes of the same part performed on bassoon. The largest Berliner discs, 12 inches in diameter, could hold up to three-and-a-half minutes of music. Edison's standard cylinders could contain up to two minutes of sound, which he later was able to increase to four minutes by narrowing the grooves. The relationship between length, loudness, and dynamic range remains in the manufacture of modern vinyl recordings.

Like Bell and Edison, Berliner had begun work on the telephone in the 1870s, invented a microphone, and his goal with the gramophone was to "provide an accurate record of human speech" (p. 24). At the Gramophone's first demonstration, though, Berliner chose a program consisting of five musical pieces and one recitation.

It was shortly after this demonstration that the operator of a machine shop, Eldridge Johnson, became interested in the Gramophone. Johnson undertook to improve the machine, developing a spring motor and a better sound box. He eventually became the manufacturer for the Berliner Gramophone Company, and in 1901 Johnson organized the Victor Talking Machine Company.[3] By that stage in its development the Gramophone did not allow consumer recording—it had become an instrument primarily for the reproduction of sound, from recordings made by professionals.

The cylinder phonograph did not disappear immediately, and Edison continued to manufacture it. One of Edison's rivals, Thomas McDonald, had developed a method by which one cylinder could be copied from another. However, cylinders could only be copied one at a time, in real time. There was also some deterioration of sound from generation to generation, as there is today when one copies cassette tapes. Edison had also discovered that larger cylinders were better able to reproduce high frequencies, because they could rotate more quickly (about 160 rpm) and thus provide more space for rapid vibrations. He could then dub smaller cylinders for public use from the large one, with better clarity than dubbing from a small cylinder. The large cylinders did not catch on with the public, despite their better fidelity. They were too big, taking up the space of fifty discs, and unwieldy, requiring a special lifting device to be removed from their carton. With improvements in disc recording, the large cylinders faded away.

Cylinder recordings continued to be sold by Edison until 1929, but Edison himself helped bring about their demise by introducing the diamond disc phonograph in 1912. This machine, whose stylus was made of diamond, closely resembled modern phonographs.

The fidelity was quite good, and at public demonstrations of the diamond disc phonograph the audience could not distinguish between a recording and a live performer (Read & Welch, 1976). The phonograph and record industries were well on their way to becoming a significant force in the entertainment business. The phonograph, however, was still chained to acoustic reproduction and amplification. It would not be until the 1920s, when radio became popular, that electronic amplification came to the phonograph.

It is surprising that the phonograph came to be a primarily musical device, in that there was nothing in its technical development that vigorously pointed in that direction. Perhaps the only intimation of its future development appeared during initial testing. Though the intentions of its inventors were geared toward reproduction of the human voice, most of the fidelity tests they performed included singing. It is perhaps only natural that musical accompaniment followed. But there may be other reasons that music predominated.

First, the amount of time one could record was limited. This meant that recording instructions, dialects, dictation, and the like would involve several discs or cylinders. Though the same could be true of musical recordings, it was generally the case that the musical material was chosen to fit the time limit of the phonograph. Short popular songs were typical of the recordings of the time.[4] Second, as the phonograph developed, recording became divorced from reproduction. The phonograph became primarily an instrument for listening, and separate machines were used for each process. It was not until the reel-to-reel tape recorder was invented that practical, good fidelity home recording became possible. The stage was thus set for an industry to provide content for the phonograph. Edison's National Phonograph Company, established in 1896, did just that, with Edison himself selecting what would be made available to the public. Hughbanks (1945) claims it was "[t]he ardent desire of the inventor . . . to bring into the American home music that would be beautiful and sweet" (p. 62).

Third, until Berliner's disc was perfected, the phonograph was mainly used for novelty purposes, recording the human voice. Any musical recording had to be done in front of a battery of several phonographs, and even then only about 20 or so cylinders could be made. The performance would have to be repeated for the next 20, and so on. Berliner's duplication process paved the way for recorded music as it is now known in that it allowed the same performance to be transferred economically and with little or no loss of fidelity to hundreds and thousands of discs.

Fourth, the marketing of phonographs pushed their use toward entertainment. The Edison company, and others, leased the phonograph and some of the machines were outfitted with coin slots. These were prototypes of the juke box. As Read and Welch (1976) perceptively point out, "here was the origin of the penny arcade" (p. 51). One out of every three phonographs was coin operated (p. 50). The Graphophone was originally marketed as a business machine, and Edison's desire was to exploit the phonograph as a business tool, but the machines failed for a lack of means of locating messages and proven starting and stopping mechanisms. It was due largely to the phonograph's demonstrators that the phonograph industry took notice of the instrument's potential for entertainment:

> [The Columbia Phonograph Company's] purpose was to exploit [the phonograph] as a dictating machine for office use. In this respect, however, it proved a failure. I remember some hundred of the instruments being rented to Congress and all being returned as impracticable. The Columbia Company seemed headed for liquidation at this failure, but it was saved by a new field of activity which was created, almost without their knowledge, by showmen at fairs and resorts demanding records of songs and instrumental music . . . in general the preferred fare seemed to have been comic songs, monologs, whistling and band records . . . the receipts from some of these early slot-machines were amazing, especially in view of the mediocre quality of entertainment offered and the fact that there was no selection offered. (Read & Welch, 1976, pp. 108-109)

Fifth, the phonograph was too bulky for any form of portable use. It was difficult to develop its potential for preservation of sound for scientific purposes or ethnography. Read and Welch note that there were numerous attempts to extend the phonograph's

uses, and papers on the phonograph as a tool for language instruction were presented at the 1893 Convention of Local Phonograph
Companies (p. 54). The British Parliament used the phonograph in
1909 to record a debate on the budget, but the phonograph's cost
and size blocked its potential.

The phonograph was most easily marketed as an entertainment device, and ultimately gained favor as "a serious musical
instrument," not as a business, scientific or educational machine
(Hughbanks, 1945, p. 34). Indeed, in Britain individual speeches by
Churchill, Lloyd George, and others were sold to the public via the
Gramophone Company/HMV label. The company stated, "the
issue of these bills must not be taken as any indication the Gramophone has departed from its neutral political standpoint. The
Gramophone has no politics" (*Talking Machine Review*, 1969, p. 7).
This issue also reprints advertisements for a record of drill instructions for use of the six-inch Howitzer, to help men commit the drill
to memory. The practice of using sound recordings for instructional
purposes persists (especially in the development of CD-ROM technology, discussed later in this chapter). But sales of hardware and
software for instructional purposes make up a very small portion
of the market for audio recordings.

Tape Recording

Between 1879 and 1885 the Bell, Bell, and Tainter team, while
working on the Graphophone, attempted magnetic recording and
succeeded in recording on tape. Perhaps due to Edison's moderate
success with the phonograph, however, Bell abandoned magnetic
recording in favor of cylinder recording.

The first practical magnetic recorder was invented by Danish
inventor Valdemar Poulsen in 1898, and patented in America in
1900. Its connection to the phonograph is unmistakable, as it employed a cylinder wrapped with magnetic wire. A recording head
revolved around the cylinder, magnetizing the wire. Even the name
Poulsen chose for the device, the Telegraphone, places it alongside
the phonograph and telephone.[5]

The general principle of magnetic recording rested on the polarization of metallic particles on a piece of wire (later a length of tape). The orientation of the particles could be altered by passing the wire before a magnetic recording head (itself magnetized by an electrical current resulting from acoustical energy), thereby encoding a signal on the wire. Passage of the wire before a playback head, one sensitive to the particles' orientations, resulted in a reversal of the process. The magnetized particles would set up an electrical current which could be converted into sound.

Several important differences from the phonograph are apparent. First, the wire could be erased by passing it through a strong magnetic field, and recorded over without difficulty. By contrast, the wax on a cylinder or disc had to be melted before it could be rerecorded upon.

Second, the recording was of a strictly electrical nature, as opposed to the phonograph's mechanical form of reproduction. The phonograph took sound and converted it into mechanical energy to encode the sound in the form of grooves on a cylinder or disc. The signals encoded onto the magnetic recorder's wire were converted from mechanical energy to electromagnetic energy. Though it is possible to see the metallic particles under a microscope, it is impossible to see the manner in which they represent sound. Under close examination, a record's grooves reveal something about the sound they contain. Magnetic recorders offer no such information to the eye.

Third, the magnetic recorder's wire was more suitable for editing and splicing. A phonograph record could be edited only in crude fashion, by starting and stopping it during recording, or by attaching different cylinders. Audible pops and clicks would give away the edit points, however. A wire could be cut and reattached with greater ease and better fidelity. And, importantly, minute sections of wire could be cut and reassembled.

Still, there were several problems with wire recorders that prevented its widespread use. For example, the wire could not be rewound or forwarded at a speed greater than that at which it played. This meant that to reach a certain section of the wire, one had to wait for the spool to wind in real time. In addition, threading the machines was much more difficult than putting a disk or cylinder in place.

Work on magnetic recording proceeded slowly, in part because there was a concentration of work on improving the phonograph in the early 1900s and because the phonograph's acceptance as a device for both recording and reproducing sound meant that there was no concentrated research effort into new methods of recording.

It was in the 1930s that the next major advance in tape recording came about, albeit indirectly. One of Edison's plans for the phonograph was to combine it with film, and he and others developed means of synchronizing records to film. The problem was, of course, that precise synchronization was difficult not only to achieve but to maintain through the length of a reel of film. A photoelectric means of reproducing sound was developed in the late 1930s that enabled sound to be recorded onto motion picture film in synchronization with the images. This method of recording sound on film or cellophane was also used for the recording and reproduction of music. It prefigured two-track stereo and other multitrack tape recording methods, in that it employed as many as 60 parallel grooves on a one-inch wide tape, but played one groove at a time, somewhat like the 8-track tape cartridges that were rivals to the cassette in the early 1970s.

When recording, the cellophane units more closely resembled the phonograph than the magnetic recorder. The tape was recorded by a sapphire stylus that traced grooves into it. Playback, however, foreshadowed the advantages of magnetic tape. *Newsweek* reported the benefits:

> The "playing" of the film—a continuous performance—thus avoids the scratch and damage of a needle, and unlimited replayings are possible. Other advantages . . . a musical program can be cut and edited like a movie film; an endless number of copies can be made from the master film, which loses none of its fidelity through constant playing; weight is greatly reduced and breakage is entirely avoided during shipment. (Transmission by Tape, 1938, p. 27)

Editing, duplication, durability, and mobility were immediately advantageous to magnetic recording. It also allowed for up to eight hours of sound on one spool of cellophane, as opposed to the approximately 15-minute maximum offered by the phonograph.

One of the most often mentioned advantages was the ability to reproduce a recording immediately. There is no mention in popular or academic literature of the original phonograph's ability to do the same. Portable phonographs were available for recording. An advertisement in the May 1940 issue of *Radio News* shows the Federal Recorder, a portable recording phonograph with built-in speaker and radio, for $110 including a microphone. The recorder, according to the advertisement, weighed 55 pounds. Still, the phonograph had already become a tool primarily for reproduction of sound.

There are three reasons. First, in that Edison's introduction of separate styli for recording and reproduction, the added expense of purchasing a recording stylus divided the two processes economically. Second, a large body of prerecorded material existed. Third, the phonograph was introduced and marketed as a coin-operated entertainment device that played back prerecorded sounds, not as a recording device. In its early incarnations, the phonograph was used by the public for private recording, and enjoyed some popularity as a means of recording radio programs, but amplification problems due to lack of fidelity prevented widespread appeal. It was not until the vacuum tube was invented that these problems were overcome. The phonograph never caught on as a high-fidelity home recording medium. The apparatus needed for recordings of good fidelity was too large and expensive for home use.

During World War II, the Allies and the Nazis showed an interest in magnetic recording. *Time* magazine reported in 1943 that the U.S. Army and Navy had developed a "Magnetic Wire Sound Recorder" that weighed around ten pounds, could record up to four hours, and could run on batteries. The potential uses the military foresaw were for "pilots [who could] plug it into a plane's electrical system and record what they see—things they might forget to tell

Intelligence when they get home. Signalmen can use the Recorder for intelligence reports. The instrument is, in effect, a simplified portable dictaphone" (Wire for Sound, 1943, p. 58). The parallel between this recorder's association with dictation and the phonograph's is interesting. *Life* ascribed the same function to it some months later, and the device gained acceptance among war correspondents (Magnetic Wire Recorder, 1943, p. 49-50). A smaller, three-pound version, was developed in 1945. The musical uses of the wire recorder were not ignored, as the *Time* story mentions that radio engineers were skeptical about the device, and *Life* carried a caption that read, "Complete symphony, conventionally recorded on seven double-sided 12-in. records may be put on a single spool of wire to yield uninterrupted music in postwar homes" (Magnetic Wire Recorder, 1943, p. 49). In 1947, *Popular Mechanics* carried a brief story on a wire recorder built into a radio/phonograph unit (Wire Recorder, 1947).

Though problems with fidelity were numerous, the wire recorder was soon married to the film recorder, resulting in magnetic tape recorders. Contrary to the assertion in most audiophile histories, magnetic tape recording was not *invented* in Germany to record Hitler's speeches, it was *perfected* there (Fantel, 1973, p. 164). Poulsen had, as early as 1900, mentioned that steel tape would solve the problem of the wire twisting around the magnetic heads.

Marvin Camras, the military's expert on magnetic recording and a student at the Illinois Institute of Technology, initially wanted to record on tape but was unable to get any due to materials shortages during the war. Subsequent problems with the twisting of the recorder wire resulted in its substitution in the United States with tape well before the end of World War II.

In 1927 J. A. O'Neill received a patent for paper tape coated with a magnetic liquid, and German inventor Fritz Pfleumer developed a metallic oxide formula that adhered to paper. The stage was set for inexpensive magnetic tape. Paper magnetic tape was also extremely easy to edit and splice. It was not until the end of the war, however, that U.S. engineers became fully aware of the work that had been done in Germany. According to *Business Week* of July 10, 1954, what spurred Ampex Corporation president, A. M. Poniatoff, to develop tape and tape recorders as the company's main product was his use of one of the German-built tape recorders that the U.S. Army recovered.

Consumer tape recorders manufactured in the late 1940s were not up to high fidelity standards, though some were able to reproduce sound very well. Most cellophane film recorders had a frequency response of about 100 Hz to 6500 Hz, and, it is claimed, some wire recorders had a frequency response up to 15 KHz. A professional wire recorder, the Magnecorder, had a response from 50 HZ to 12 KHz, and a special motor to drive the wire past the heads at a constant speed. The recorders were generally coupled with radios to permit recording of broadcasts, and mass production of recordings was still impractical. The home taping controversy, which raged in the late 1970s and early 1980s and was rekindled by digital tape recording can trace its origin to this period. Magazines such as *Musical America* advocated copying records to tape to preserve their sound quality. However, sound quality was behind that of phonograph records, prompting *Consumers' Research Bulletin* to state on page eight that "tape is no substitute for disk records" (Brush Sound Mirror, 1947, p. 25). Nonetheless, there was concern that tape recorders would make the phonograph obsolete.

Expensive, high-end tape decks were available for commercial use, and tape recording had a significant impact on the broadcasting industry. Until the late 1940s, radio stations used 16-inch discs that cost approximately $8 for a half-hour program. By contrast, tape cost $4.50, and could be reused. The ABC network purchased 24 Ampex tape machines and 2.5 million feet of tape in 1948. Ampex was being distributed by Bing Crosby Enterprises, Inc., after Crosby discovered that he preferred the reproduction of his voice on tape over that of discs (Tape for the Networks, 1948). The tape machines were expensive compared with the phonograph, and considering that some networks and independent stations had already invested considerable capital into disc recording and reproduction, it is not surprising that their switch to tape was a gradual one. One of ABC's engineers wrote that

prior to 1948, (ABC) did none of their own recording. . . . Tape machines have the advantage of requiring little service except routine
maintenance, and the tape may be used over and over, with a very
low cost per recording, and no storage problem. The fidelity of tape
greatly exceeds that obtained with the best disc equipment, and
recordings of almost any length can be made with no interruption . . .
[though] it [was] difficult to time [a] disc to place the end of a
recording at a point where the continuity is not disturbed. (Speirs,
1950, p. 41)

Other advantages of tape were immediately apparent to those
involved in radio production, as portrayed in this incident:

Recently, announcer Ken Carpenter inadvertently read his Crosby-
show commercial as "Philcos gives" instead of using a singular verb.
On the playback the producer caught the error and sent for Carpenter
to correct it. While the announcer was on the way the engineer went
to work with the shears. He simply clipped out the "s" on "gives"
and spliced the tape. Not even the most alert listener could tell the
difference. (Tape for the Networks, 1948, p. 52)

The savings were important to radio stations at a time when
television began to draw advertising revenue away. Magnetic recording quickly found its way into the film industry too, in that
"with optical sound a take has to be expensively (4 cents a foot)
processed before it can be played back. The magnetic system
permits monitoring during the actual shooting and thus eliminates
the expense of remaking scenes because of sound defects" (Sound
Goes Magnetic, 1949).

The problem of mass production of tape recordings was solved
in the early 1950s, when Ampex developed a high-speed tape
copying system that could dub as many as 10 tapes at a time
running at 16 times normal speed. *Business Week* reported that the
copying system "sells for about $20,000, compared with about
$25,000 for a (record) press that, in the same time, makes discs
carrying only half as much recorded material." The system was
purchased immediately by RCA and Capitol Records. Ampex's
sales rose from $968,000 to $5.4 million in a year (Hi-Fi, 1954,
pp. 162-165).

Stereo

As refinements continued to be made to tape recorders, different recording formats appeared. The first tape recorders could record only monophonic sound in one direction. By the early 1950s tape heads were developed that could record on half the width of the tape, so that it could be reversed and the other half recorded on as well. This, in turn, led to the development of two-track stereo tape recording. Several technical problems had to be overcome before this was possible. First, the less tape covered by the tape heads the less dynamic range that could be recorded and reproduced. Second, the speed of the tape was crucial to sound quality. The faster the tape speed the more tape would pass by the heads and therefore be available for the magnetic signals to be imparted. This is analogous to photo screening for printing. The fewer dots a photo is made up of the better it looks, the better the resolution. Similarly, the more tape available for a sound, the better the audio.

Stereo eventually became the high-fidelity standard. Read and Welch (1976) write that "introduction of the stereo tape recorder for the home in 1955 heralded the most dramatic increase ever seen for a single product in home entertainment" (p. 427). In 1954 RCA began issuing high fidelity reel-to-reel tape recordings. According to Read and Welch, that event was "looked upon . . . as signalling the beginning of a grand new era in the seventy-five-year history of sound recording. To others, concerned sentimentally or financially with the existing disc industry, it seemed more like the portent of doom" (p. 441).

Because of mechanical difficulties, the stereo disc was not introduced until 1958—and then it caused some confusion, primarily due to questions of its standardization and compatibility with monophonic equipment. A method of cutting stereo discs had been invented in 1931, but it involved cutting two separate grooves for two needles. It was not until the mid-1950s that a method of single-groove stereo record cutting was perfected. The phonograph had not seen such innovation since the switch from acoustic to electrical phonographs in the 1920s, when the vacuum tube enabled efficient amplifier design. With the addition of an electrical amplifying circuit as a transducer between the acoustic sound and the mechanical action of the stylus, electrical recording and reproduction made it possible to control loudness. Improvements in disc materials made phonograph records both quieter and more durable, and the advent of microgroove recording by Columbia and RCA in the late 1940s meant that records could contain up to 20 minutes of music per side; the LP was born. But the three-dimensional illusion created by the stereo disc insured that the phonograph would at least keep pace with the tape recorder.

Controversy arose surrounding the advantages and disadvantages of tape versus disc and stereo versus mono. The argument was over consumer playback equipment, but applied to record and tape production as well. A reporter for *Fortune* magazine summed it up saying that "realistic reproduction of sound is what the engineers are after, but it is hard to find two experts who agree as to what is realistic" (Boehm, 1958, p. 165). There is no doubt, however, that the illusion of reality is what engineers aim for. Roy Allison, an engineer at Acoustic Research in 1959, said, "The day is coming when we will be able, finally, to produce a consistent illusion of really 'being there'" (Hodges, 1978a, p. 26). Stereo was a crucial part of that illusion.

The popularity of stereo discs was foreseen by the recording industry, and the shift to stereo was without doubt a move by record companies to capture part of the stereo tape market. "At this stage many [record company executives] frankly admit they fear stereo will catch on too fast," Boehm wrote, "'Why, in a year,' one of them says, 'we may be out of the monaural business'" (1958, p. 110).

Read and Welch (1976) write that "acceptance of stereo discs by the American public in the early months of 1958 was so rapid that within a year the publishers of Schwann's catalogs found it necessary to integrate the new stereo discs as they were issued with the monophonic releases" (p. 442). For a time, record companies released both mono and stereo versions of records to avoid cutting out of the market those people who would not immediately purchase stereo phonographs. The disc and tape markets would coexist, though not without clashes over quality and piracy. LeBel

(1958), in a perceptive article in the *Radio and Television News*, wrote that

> the [stereo] disc will enjoy mass acceptance, due to low cost and the convenience of the record changer. . . . The [stereo] tape will enjoy good acceptance, due to low cost and the freedom from ticks and pops. . . . The serious listener, truly interested in quality, will have a great deal of difficulty in choosing between the convenience of disc and the quality of two-track tape. *He will end up by owning both.* [italics added] (p. 41)[6]

This was certainly a reasonable expectation given that record companies were able to produce both records and tapes. However, one company rarely manufactured both phonographs and tape decks (RCA was a notable exception, and a producer of recordings as well). It was the hardware manufacturers that became competitive with their products, and the software manufacturers (the record companies) who eventually became concerned with copying and piracy of their recordings. And, it was not until prerecorded tapes became readily available that piracy of recordings by way of taping was perceived by the record industry as a problem. Initially it was piracy of live performances that worried record companies.

Tape Cartridges

Recording cartridges were developed in 1930 to make threading wire recorders less difficult, but were not incorporated in tape recorders until the late 1950s, as a means of ensuring the continued acceptance of tape despite the popularity of the stereo disc. Tape companies' research teams, like the one at Ampex were also at work developing videotape in the 1950s, which had a significant impact on television production but slowed work on audio tape development.

RCA announced in 1958 that it had developed a tape cartridge that played 32 minutes and would retail for about a dollar more than a stereo disc. RCA's cartridge was the precursor to the 8-track cartridge. Although it was mass produced in the 1960s and 1970s, it did not find acceptance among consumers. It was difficult to use for recording and it did not have an efficient means of fast forwarding and rewinding the tape. A form of the 8-track became standard equipment in the radio industry, for announcements, station identifications and advertisements.

The most widely accepted tape cartridge format to date, the cassette, was introduced by the Philips Company in 1963. To ensure standardization of the cassette format, Philips gave up manufacturing rights to anyone wanting to produce cassettes, provided they used Philips' specifications. By 1965 several companies were making cassette recorders, and reviews were favorable. Eisenberg (1965) wrote that it "achieves real portability by using a miniature self-loading cartridge rather than by merely duplicating in condensed form the basic design of larger, conventional machines . . . it is hard to imagine how operation could be simpler" (p. 46). Again, dictation was seen as an important use for the machines, as was the ability to play tapes in the car.

Much like the wire recorder, cassette recorders were used for newsgathering. One reporter noted in a *Newsweek* article that the recorders were especially good for dealing with politicians. The story goes on to say that

> newsmen are somewhat belatedly plugging into the main current of the American tape culture, which seems determined to record every noise and utterance. Mrs. Johnson tapes her diary; wives and girl friends are now mailing taped holiday messages to their men in Vietnam; and "oral historians" at no less than 100 universities and research centers have taped for posterity conversations with everyone from Judge Learned Hand to Bennett Cerf. Industry spokesmen say more than 5 million tape recorders have been sold this year and claim one out of every seven homes now has one. (Tapeworms, 1967, p. 74)

Cassettes were relatively inexpensive compared with both LPs and reel-to-reel tape recorders (a 60-minute tape cost approximately $1.50 in 1968), and, as shown by the wide variety of people reportedly using them, were easy to operate. Recording was no

TABLE 2.1 Tape Recorders—Sales in Units

Year	Open-Reel	Cartridge	Cassette	Total
1963	1,800,000	——	——	1,800,000
1964	1,800,000	100,000	——	1,900,000
1965	1,650,000	250,000	——	1,900,000
1966	1,700,000	500,000	200,000	2,400,000
1967	1,650,000	1,200,000	600,000	3,450,000
1968	1,600,000	1,600,000	1,700,000	4,900,000
1969(est.)	1,500,000	1,800,000	3,400,000	6,700,000
1970(est.)	1,400,000	2,000,000	4,700,000	8,100,000

SOURCE: Angus & Eisenberg, 1969, p. 53.

longer solely in the domain of the hi-fi enthusiast. *Business Week* in 1968 called cassette decks a "music maker for the masses." Cassette sound quality was good, with most cassette decks able to reproduce from 50 to 10000 Hz. In 1969 the Dolby noise reduction system was adapted for use with cassettes, reducing tape hiss and improving dynamic range.

The rapid acceptance of cassettes prompted renewed concern from record companies that the phonograph may be doomed. *Business Week* noticed the reason for concern stating that

> the teen-ager, the major market for recorded music, no longer has to thread a tape through a bulky and costly piece of equipment in his living room to make his own music. Instead, he can snap a blank cassette (cost: about $3 vs. $6 for a prerecorded one) into his tiny portable recorder . . . and copy two hours of music. (Music Maker, 1968, pp. 108-109)

What *Business Week* left out of its article was that the cassette could be played in the car, which was essentially home to many teenagers. The same article quotes an executive of RCA's record division as saying, "there are indications that the cassette sales have adversely affected record sales" (p. 109). Cassette decks far outsold other tape recorders by 1970, as Table 2.1 illustrates.

It is during this period that the division between hardware and software manufacturers becomes clear. The article quotes an executive of Columbia Records: "[We aren't] in the hardware business, [and we don't want to help GE, Norelco] or any others sell their equipment by telling the public they can play our music on cassettes" (p. 109). The recording industry called for a change in copyright laws, and hardware manufacturers marketed play-only cassette machines (which did not catch on with the public). In the late 1980s, though, the trend quickly reversed, most notably when Sony purchased Columbia Records, and hardware manufacturers realized, perhaps from observation of the computer industry, that their hardware (compact disc players, digital tape machines) would sell more rapidly if prerecorded music were available to consumers.

In the late 1960s, during the cassette's rise to popularity, records were still cheaper to mass produce than prerecorded cassettes, and in that cassettes were duplicated at high speeds, their quality was at best variable compared with records. Angus and Eisenberg noted in 1969 that they "doubt (records) will be displaced, except possibly by some fantastic technological breakthrough which—if it occurs—will make all present forms of recorded material obsolete" (p. 53). That breakthrough was to come in the late 1980s by way of digital recording.

Multitrack Recording

To increase the amount of sound that could be recorded, cellophane tape recorders encoded sound on as many as 60 parallel grooves or tracks. Magnetic tape recorders soon employed similar methods, first to increase the amount of sound that could be recorded, then to reproduce stereo sound by encoding sound on two separate tracks. In 1958 a four-channel tape recorder was introduced by the Shure Brothers company. It allowed recording and playback of two separate stereo programs, one in each direction.

By 1970 engineers adapted the four-channel system for playback in one direction, creating four-channel, *quadrisonic* or *quad* sound.

The process was difficult to duplicate with discs (like stereo it was first available only on tape), and required special encoding and decoding equipment. The cost of a quad system was much greater than of a stereo one, involving added expense for at least two extra speakers, and usually for additional amplifiers, preamplifiers, and so forth. Quad sound did not catch on with the public, and was not well supported by the recording industry.

The four-channel recording system remained however, and became the backbone of the recording industry. Tape recording found its way into professional music production rapidly, from the moment Bing Crosby used it in 1947. The first Crosby show recorded on tape was October 1947. Prior to that his shows were recorded on discs. The radio network was not convinced that tape would work well, and insisted that discs be made from the tapes. Crosby's recording engineer, John Mullin (one of the people responsible for shipping German magnetophones to the United States after the war) said, "When the show was finally assembled on tape, it had to be transferred to disc because nobody—including me—had confidence that this newfangled thing could be relied on to feed the full network" (Wallerstein, 1976, p. 61). It is now standard practice to press records from studio-recorded tapes. The effect of the introduction of this intermediate step between recording and pressing will be discussed in a subsequent chapter.

By the early 1950s most recording studios were using tape for the same reasons that broadcast studios were. Tape was inexpensive, reusable, and easily manipulated (edited, spliced, and so on). Even a relatively small studio such as Sam Phillips' Memphis Recording Service, where Elvis Presley cut his first records, had tape, albeit side-by-side with a disc cutting service "where anyone could go in and make a record for two dollars a side" (Miller, 1980, p. 25). Multitrack recorders added even more flexibility to studios. Woram (1981) writes that

beyond the editing process, little could be done to modify the recorded music. Nevertheless, the luxury of tape editing represented a major advance over earlier recordings, made directly to disc. Here,

the performance was permanently cut into the groove at the moment
of recording, and there was no practical way of making even a simple
edit later on.

Once magnetic tape became the standard studio recording medium, it was only a matter of time before musicians began adding
accompaniments to their recordings by playing along with a previously recorded tape . . . this technique is known as overdubbing. At
about the time it came into wide use, studio tape recorders with three
or four separate tracks were pretty much the industry standard.
(p. 371)

Tape radically changed the way recording was done in studios,
with consequences for both musician and audience. By 1967 the
8-track recorder became the studio standard, followed by 16-, 24-,
32-, and 48-track.[7]

By 1980 prices dropped on most multitrack decks, and companies like Tascam and Fostex were aiming products like the Tascam
Portastudio—a small, inexpensive four-track recorder that used
cassettes—at amateur and semi-professional musicians. These
units usually included a small mixing console for combining the
sounds from the four tracks, and their list price was in the $1,000
to $1,500 range. In 1985, Fostex introduced an eight-track deck at a
list price of $1,600. Studio recording was no longer confined to the
studio, and the home recording studio became financially possible.

Disc recording was briefly repopularized in the early 1970s as an
audiophile medium. The Sheffield Record label in particular released several audiophile recordings. In essence, the method was
a throwback to the pretape recording era, but with the advantage
of modern electronic equipment. Recording was done live, no
overdubbing or editing. The expense of the records (usually double
that of standard LPs), and mechanical problems with record cutting lathes, which could not track the wide dynamic range of a live
recording, slowed the acceptance of direct-to-disc records. The
introduction of digital recording and compact discs made disc
recording virtually obsolete.

Digital recording

Though a seemingly recent phenomenon, digital audio recording's history goes back to the invention of magnetic tape. A common use of magnetic recording was for computer data storage and instrument recording. Camras (1985), writes that

> digital recording, which is universal in computers, has already penetrated deeply into instrumentation recording and is now used for the finest audio recordings. . . . For digital recording we can show the oldest reference of all: Morse's telegraph patent of 1838. Morse didn't think that people could recognize his on-off codes rapidly enough to translate them back to the alphabet, so he recorded the coded characters before transmitting, and after receiving. The complex digital codes that were recorded could then be decoded at a more leisurely rate. (p. 1319)

Morse code was the first practical digital code, consisting of dots and dashes (that is, binary ones and zeros, just as digital code for audio and data recording consists of a stream of ones and zeros). According to Monforte (1984), "The process of digitization was developed at the Bell Telephone Laboratories in the 1920s with the aim of overcoming the limitations of analogue recording" (p. 78). Again, the links between sound recording, the telephone, and telegraph are apparent.

Digital recording was not practical until the microprocessor was invented, primarily because of the enormous amount of data that had to be sorted for conversion from analog to digital and back again. White (1985) writes that "in the digital world, the need . . . [developed] for a data storage system that offered 'random access,' that is, rapid access to data at any location in a file" (p. 1). Magnetic disk drives were developed in the early 1950s to fill this need. By the late 1970s, though, microprocessors were abundant and inexpensive enough that the recording industry could begin to use them, and combinations of disk drive and tape recorders made their way into recording studios.

The audio quality of digital recordings is remarkable. Both standard (analog) tape recording and disc recording had an inherent amount of noise in the background; tape hiss for the former, and pops and clicks for the latter. Digital audio, however, is free from noise. Though professional digital recording machines such as Sony's use tape to store the digital signals, in that it is not the signals on tape that are reproduced (instead the *information* is processed) the sound is not bound to the tape's limitations. Len Feldman (1978), contributing editor to *High Fidelity*, wrote that "analog . . . signal[s] . . . [are] converted to a series of pulses . . . [and] every pulse can be recorded at a level well above the residual noise level of the tape and well below the saturation level. Thus, the system's dynamic range is no longer limited by the parameters of the tape itself" (p. 58).

The critical areas affecting sound quality are the analog to digital (A/D) and digital to analog (D/A) conversion points, and methods of filtering—not the storage medium. Tape could still be used to store digital code. Sam Borgerson of Studer Revox, a high-fidelity-equipment manufacturer, said "The main problem with audio is the analog to digital conversion and the filtering technique. That's what gives you audio quality. Once you get into the digital realm, it's mainly a problem of storage and what is most convenient" (Pollock, 1985, p. 82).

Tape was often a convenient storage medium, and Borgerson noted that "right now, you can get more storage . . . on audio tape at a good speed with more reliability than you can on some of the newer floppy disk-based recording machines" (Pollock, 1985, p. 82). Digital recording on tape is nonetheless susceptible to drop-outs (areas where the tape's oxide has come off, the tape is worn or damaged, or the head does not come in contact with the tape). It is for this reason that optical storage, such as that used with compact discs is preferable. There is no mechanical contact with the medium.

Digital recording was first used in recording studios, and audiophile records and tapes were created from digital master tapes (effectively making direct-to-disc recordings obsolete). The records were twice the price of analog recordings, and still subject to the pops, clicks and wear and tear of conventional records. But with its absence of noise and wide dynamic range, digital audio more closely fulfilled both the hi-fi enthusiasts' and the engineers' goal of realism.[8]

Feldman (1978) noted that "by introducing digital master tape recording as the initial studio recording technique, the advantages of multitrack recording can be combined with the sound quality of direct-to-disc techniques since the digital master tape system introduces no intermediate degradation of the music signals" (p. 82). 3M was the first company with a professional digital recorder. Released in 1977, the 3M deck was a 32-track system using tape, with a cost of $150,000. Editing was not as easy with the digital machine, however, and much of the work on improving professional digital recording equipment centers around editing. Systems by independent manufacturers that allow one to transfer a digital recording to a microprocessor and edit signals in software, then return them to a storage medium, are also becoming available.

Consumer electronics companies marketed digital audio with the compact disc (CD) at the 1977 Tokyo Audio Fair. The CD is (currently) a playback only medium, consisting of an optical disc scanned by a laser. The CD system does not require contact with the disc. A 1979 *Newsweek* report accurately predicted that "the real boom won't begin until total digital systems and components invade the home—probably sometime in the mid-1980s. Then, a digital playback device will employ a tiny laser to 'read' a digital recording . . . The disks will be impervious to scratches, dust and fingerprints" (Coppola, 1979, p. 65).

In the 1980s CDs have become an important part of the recorded music market. In that they are an optical storage system, CDs are also quickly developing as a medium for random access data storage, by way of CD-ROM (Compact Disc Read-Only Memory) devices connected to personal computers. Consumer models are available that encode digital signals onto videotape (PCM, or Pulse Code Modulation, recorders), and by 1987 digital tape recorders (DATs) were on the market (albeit at very high prices). In 1991 several semi-pro equipment makers, including Akai and Alesis, introduced digital multitrack recorders for the home recording studio.

Digital audio tape has become very popular for professional audio production, and is finding a niche as a data back-up medium in computing applications. As for the consumer market, delays in its introduction due to legal struggles between the record industry and hardware manufacturers (record company executives believed they were living their worst piracy nightmares as visions of digital copying became reality) stifled marketing plans, and in the interim, Philips, who introduced the cassette and CD, brought forth the Digital Compact Cassette (DCC), to be marketed to consumers in late 1991. The advantages of DCC are compatibility with analog cassettes, a lower price than DAT machines, and more stable recording processes that reduce tape wear and speed up high-speed duplication. It is possible that DAT may retrench and become a "pro" medium, and DCC a consumer medium, much as the reel-to-reel and cassette analog formats coexisted.

Digital recording made a significant impact in the recording studio not only for its use in multitracking and mastering, but for its general use as a sound storage and playback device. Digital sampling synthesizers, such as the Fairlight, Synclavier, and Emulator, among others, allow sounds to be recorded and stored in the synthesizer's random access memory, manipulated and played back. Sampling is used prominently in the popular music, is especially prevalent in rap music, and is finding a welcome home among those who view synthesizers as a means of reproducing the sound of acoustic instruments.

Digital workstations have found favor in the audio and video postproduction industries, primarily because they are all-in-one systems that embody sound recording, manipulation editing, and synchronizing all in the digital domain. To call them high-powered samplers is to miss their true usefulness to members of these industries, for digital workstations are to them what desktop publishing systems are to publishers, printers, and typesetters.

Sampling of any sort, though, is not without controversy, in that some recording artists sample sounds they find on other people's records. Copyright law is not equipped to deal with the mixing of authorship that results. The problem is not a new one (a bill was introduced in Congress to copyright electronic sounds in 1959) but, with the ready availability of samplers (Casio Corporation marketed one for under $100 as early as 1986) it is becoming widespread. Some samplers like the Fairlight, Synclavier, and PPG HDU have the capability to act as multitrack digital recorders. Though their cost is still very high ($75,000 for the Synclavier in its standard form), if the price of integrated circuits and microprocessors continues to drop digital recording may soon become quite affordable.

Another form of recording—*sequencing*—developed parallel to digital recording and sampling, thanks to the microprocessor. Sequencing involves storage of data, input from either an electronic keyboard in performance or from a computer keyboard, which is later fed back to sound generating equipment. Sequencing is not a means of recording sound as such. It is a means of recording control signals relating to pitch, tempo, and so forth, which can regulate electronic synthesizers. The synthesizers' sounds are independent of the sequencer. In other words, it is not the sound that is recorded but instructions for the synthesizer, not unlike a player piano. That analogy should not be taken too far, however, in that sequencers offer an extremely precise degree of editing, and are in function, if not essence, recorders.

Like the stereo versus mono and tape versus disc arguments, digital recording has its battles; digital versus analog and DAT versus CD. The former is characterized by vice-president of dbx, Inc., Jerry Ruzicka's comment that "There is [analog] technology available today with which you can make original master recordings equal to or better than today's digital recordings. [Digital] technology, as it has evolved to this point for professional recording, is not perfect" (Peterson, 1983, p. 172). The latter is similar to the controversy surrounding home videotaping and piracy of movies. When videotape recorders became popular, the movie industry was concerned that films would be copied on the machines and the movie companies would receive no money for these pirated copies. Of course, the music industry is concerned that DAT will lead to piracy by way of digital copying. A former head of the FCC said, "Every time there's a new [audio] technology, the instant reaction is that it's a threat to the status quo. . . . What's happened histor- ically is that in the end, it becomes a big new revenue source and a tremendous opportunity for the very people doing the complain- ing" (Block, 1986, p. 206). This certainly seems true of the compact disc.

In 1991 Philips announced another digital tape type, the Digital Compact Cassette (DCC), a hybrid DAT/analog cassette format. DCC machines play back analog cassettes and record and play back digital cassettes. The impetus for DCC's introduction seems to be a marketing strategy that inserts DCC as a go-between from analog cassette to DAT, making it almost literally a medium medium. From the specifications announced for DCC it appears that audio quality is below that of DAT but above that of analog cassettes.

Within weeks of Philips' announcement Sony unveiled a record- able mini-CD (dubbed the "MD") format scheduled for shipment some time in 1993. Though a form of recordable CD was avail- able in the late 1980s (using WORM—Write-Once-Read-Many— technology) it is prohibitively expensive for all but the best- capitalized recording studios and mastering labs, and it was not an erasable format. Sony's MD is erasable. The MD's specifications call for audio quality below current CD levels. Sony may not get out of the gate with the MD as fast as Philips with DCC, but it is likely that Sony's product will have a greater chance to prosper when one considers the potential uses of the MD in personal computers. As CD-ROM devices become more widespread, and magnetic floppies are replaced by hard disk drives, the availability of small *removable* RAM mass storage devices such as the MD are all that keep the personal computer from achieving new levels of miniaturization. The MD's optical disk is even housed in a case that makes it look like a three-and-a-half-inch floppy disk.

The most likely scenario for digital recording is as follows. Connection of DAT decks to computers will make for all-digital editing of master tapes commonplace, and DAT machines will become professional mastering tape decks as analog reel-to-reel decks are currently used. The MD will become the format of choice for the consumer in that it will most closely match what the consumer is already used to using for delivery of music into the home (and because Sony's music divisions will provide the necessary prerecorded fare). Its price will decrease dramatically as computer applications are developed for it. DCC will likely not make much of an impact unless audio quality is greatly improved and price decreased to a level below that of either DAT or the MD.

Record companies were reluctant to manufacture CDs (and had difficulty doing so, in that until 1987 only two CD pressing plants were operating in the world), but CD sales have grown tremendously. New technology is quite profitable for the record companies because it enables them to reissue recordings that have already been paid for, thus creating profit with their back catalog. Still, a too-great profusion of formats is not in the music industry's best interests, in that it requires capitalization of manufacturing facilities for each format. Agreements in 1991 between the U.S. music industry and audio hardware manufacturers signal a new era of cooperation between the two that will no doubt lead to a standardization of format. But, regardless of the controversies and arguments among audiophiles and between software and hardware manufacturers, the quest for perfect sound continues. Current engineering is geared toward an affordable system of optical recording and storage to bring CD recording into the consumer market.

Summary

From the history of recording it is possible to discern three motives underlying user acceptance of a particular medium: cost, realism, and editing. Cost is a significant force in the acceptance and use of virtually any technology, and recording technology is no different. The search for realism and the easy manipulation of sound show, in Innis's (1951) terms, recording technology's bias toward space and time. Recording sound is an attempt at preserving the space and time of a musical event and also altering that space and time. Recording enables sound's subsequent manipulation. The evolution of recording equipment moved both toward greater accuracy in the preservation of the space and time of the event and greater flexibility in subsequent manipulation of that event. Time and space no longer imposed any limits on the creation of music. Instead, both could be manipulated along with the music.

The representation of sound and music has changed from written notes that the eye could see, to phonograph grooves, to magnetic particles, to digital streams of ones and zeros. As each method of recording developed, it required another level of interpretation before it could be heard or seen. The written note requires an instrument for its realization. A phonograph record required a needle to interpret the physical structure of the grooves. A tape recorder requires a playback head to interpret the magnetic particles and convert them to electrical signals, and an amplifier to convert those signals to sound. A compact disc player requires a filter, a D/A converter, error-correction mechanisms which, if sound information is missing, literally recreate sound based on rapid computations, and an amplifier. The digital process, however, is remarkably similar to music notation. "A digital recording is really just a sophisticated musical 'score,'" Turner (1986) writes. "It in no way reproduces the actual shape of the music, the way the grooves in the plastic of a normal record do, any more than [notes] reproduce the sound of music—or indeed, than the letters on a page reproduce the sound of speech" (p. 47). The digital language is extremely good at reproducing music, however, and Turner adds, "It is as if, knowing the right language, you could write the names of foods so that if you ate the paper on which they were written it would be more tasty and nourishing than the foods themselves" (p. 47).

Recording technology did more than liberate music from the constraints of space and time. Along with electronic instruments, it enabled music to be organized around sound and timbre instead of notes. The realm of popular music, which was traditionally not written but memorized, would see the greatest change and utilization of recording. Just as the collective memory was externalized by printing and other forms of mass media, popular music and the collective memory of musician and audience alike was externalized by recording.

Notes

1. The November 17, 1877, issue of *Scientific American*, in an article on the phonograph, contains the following passage on page 304: "The orator in Boston speaks, the indented strip of paper is the tangible result; but this travels under a second machine which may connect with the telephone." The phonograph, like the telephone, was originally viewed as a means of voice transmission as well as storage. Edison wrote in the May/June 1878 issue of *The North American Review* that "the phonograph will perfect the telephone, and revolutionize present systems of telegraphy" (p. 534). Leon Wortman, in a retrospective on magnetic recording in the July 1954 *Radio and Television News*, wrote that "in the latter half of the 19th Century any boy who was interested in electricity considered telephone work to be the highest goal of attainment in an ambitious life" (p. 89). It is no coincidence that development of the telephone and phonograph are connected. What is interesting, though, is the path each took in its evolution: the telephone remained an instrument of transmission, while the phonograph became an instrument of storage, transmission and manipulation.

2. The most complete and concise history of the phonograph is Read and Welch (1976), *From Tin Foil to Stereo*. Krishef (1962) in *Playback: The Story of Recording Devices* provides a short, elementary history of the phonograph and tape recorder. Buttterworth (1977) gives an excellent history of the hi-fi and stereo industry, encompassing the phonograph and radio. Hughbanks (1945) wrote a detailed book about the invention of the phonograph. Gelatt's (1954) *The Fabulous Phonograph* is a look at the connections between development of the phonograph and development of the record business. *The Music Goes Round and Round* (Gammond & Horricks, 1980) contains a chapter on the early history of the phonograph and recording. The two best illustrated books on the phonograph are Chew (1967) *Talking Machines 1877-1914*, a brief, well-illustrated account of the phonograph's invention with many drawings and plans for early phonographs, and Hoover's (1971) *Music Machines - American Style*, a catalog of an exhibition at the National Museum of History and Technology with many photographs.

3. It was Johnson who adopted the well-known "His Master's Voice" dog-and-horn symbol in 1909.

4. In *Talking Wax*, Leroy Hughbanks's personal reminiscences include titles of many recordings, as well as a good account of the wonder of hearing an early phonograph in the late 1800s.

5. Marvin Camras provides a detailed history of the development of tape recording in "Origins of Magnetic Recording Concepts," *Journal of the Acoustical Society of America*, April 1985, pp. 1314-1319. A form of electrochemical recording was reported in the June 4, 1904 issue of *Scientific American*, which used a platinum band passing through an electrolyte in a glass container. The band could be easily and completely erased by washing with an acid. This recording method never caught on, perhaps because of the difficulty in using a liquid electrolyte solution, or because of the expense of platinum. American inventor Oberlin Smith described his own magnetic recorder in a letter to the *Electrical World*, September 8, 1888, and called it a form of "recording telephone."

6. The magazine's editor, in the same 1904 issue of *Scientific American*, wrote that "stereo discs and tape will not be competitive but will augment each other" (p. 8). This was certainly a reasonable expectation given that record companies were able to produce both records and tapes. However, one company rarely manufactured both phonographs and tape decks (RCA was a notable exception, and a producer of recordings as well). It was the hardware manufacturers that were competitive with their products, and the software manufacturers (the record companies) who eventually became concerned with copying and piracy of their recordings. Initially it was piracy of live performances that was seen as a problem, and not piracy of recordings (see *High Fidelity*, August 1966, pp. 45-48, and *Saturday Review*, March 26, 1966, pp. 55-56, 65).

7. The Beatles' 1967 LP *Sgt. Peppers Lonely Hearts Club Band,* and many other classic rock albums, were recorded on four-track tape machines. The 8-track recorder is not to be confused with the 8-track cartridge, which was intended primarily as a consumer-only playback device.

8. Digital recording's inability to reproduce frequencies above 22 KHz represents a stumbling block to some. The high frequency limit is due to the rate at which a digital recorder samples sound. The rate must be at least twice the highest frequency to fully capture the sound. Higher frequencies create digital glitches or noise, so digital systems contain a filter that removes frequencies above a certain point. Audiophiles argue that the filtering removes frequencies that are inaudible but nonetheless essential to faithful reproduction of all the overtones of a sound. However, faster microprocessors and increasing computer memory capacity may push the frequency limit higher.

3

Sound and Popular Music

The ability to record sound is power over sound. If it can be recorded, it can be played back. It can be played forward, backward, faster, slower. Only parts of the recording can be played, sound can be cut out, put together with other sounds and played back, and so on. The fundamental goal of recording technology is to provide this power over sound, and it is a technology within the realm of Harold Innis's (1950) notions of bias and control in communication. It is a technology oriented toward control of space *and* time—control of time by capture and manipulation of sound, control of space by capture and manipulation of the sound's environment.

As Innis notes, different types of media have different biases, and the same is true of recording media. Compared to wire recorders, the inclusion of fast forward and rewind controls on tape recorders shows a bias toward time. Tape recorders save a lot of time when one is searching for a specific point in a recording. Likewise, digital sequencers (and some digital recorders) require virtually no time at all to precisely locate any point in a recording.

But it is the bias toward space, and its acoustic realization, that makes recording technology most interesting. Musicians, producers, recording engineers, and the popular music audience often refer to the sound of a recording as something distinct from the music it contains. One can admire a group for having "a really good sound," despite being musically incompetent. Rock and roll in particular is largely categorized by sound. The *Rolling Stone Illustrated History of Rock and Roll* (Miller, 1980) contains chapters on the "Sound of New Orleans," the "Sound of Chicago," the "Sound of Texas," the "Sound of Memphis," the "Sound of San Francisco," the Motown sound, and so on.

What is the definition of sound in these terms? Essentially, the organization of noise by means of the recording process. But before that process can be examined, the parameters of sound in popular music must be identified.

Noise and Sound

> Sound exists only when it is going out of existence.
>
> Walter J. Ong
> *Orality & Literacy*

Sound is essentially ephemeral, as Ong (1982) notes. It occurs in time, is so bound by time that it cannot, he says, be stopped. To stop sound is to create silence. From this we can glean the difference between sound and music. Sound is that which occurs over time, cannot be stopped, and is irreducible. It cannot be examined in the same way that one can examine music via a musical manuscript, note for note, measure for measure. One can listen to or perform a piece of music, measure for measure, over and over, but as each second passes so does the sound that has occurred. Sound cannot be frozen in space for close examination like notes on a page of sheet music. Its experience takes place over time, while reading sheet music is not time-bound. Musical notation, sheet music, allows us to capture music. Recording allows us to capture sound.

Popular music is primarily mediated via electronics, via sound, and not by means of written notes. Folk music and popular music are transmitted by means of performance, they are traditionally not written. As Paul Willis (1978) explains,

The ascendancy of pop music marked the decline of sheet music as the main distributed form of popular music. Sheet music could be played in very different ways by different groups at different times. The essence of music, the common denominator between groups, was the notation on the sheet. In the age of pop music, the only text is the actual record. This makes the precise style and intonation of the singer very important. (p. 8)

I will examine Willis's emphasis of the singer later. For now, it is important to note that the distinction between sound and music in popular music is most clearly embodied in the way pop musicians copy each other's songs. They listen to recordings, play along with them, and decipher the music from recordings. Most groups do not read sheet music, and many pop musicians cannot read music. Music is organized sound, but music notation is not the image of sound—it is the organization of instructions for the creation of sound.

The ability to preserve or modify organized sound by way of recording is a means of controlling sound independent of its creation and creator. Therefore the recording of sound is a profoundly political act, as Jacques Attali (1985) identifies:

Recording has always been a means of social control, a stake in politics, regardless of the available technologies. Power is no longer content to enact its legitimacy; it records and reproduces the society it rules. Stockpiling memory, retaining history or time, distributing speech, and manipulating information has always been an attribute of civil and priestly power, beginning with the Tables of the Law. But before the industrial age, this attribute did not occupy center stage: Moses stuttered and it was Aaron who spoke. But there was already no mistaking: the reality of power belonged to he who was able to reproduce the divine word, not to he who gave it voice on a daily basis. Possessing the means of recording allows one to monitor noises, to maintain them, and to control repetition within a determined code. In the final analysis, it allows one to impose one's own noise and to silence others. (p. 87)

Deciding what is recorded, what song or what sound, and how it is manipulated during all stages of recording, is the critical political struggle in popular music production, not only because

most people's experience of popular music is mediated via recordings (and therefore sound is the means by which the audience
identifies music and the recording artist) but also because it is the
site of power, the area where one can "impose one's own noise
and . . . silence others." For instance, rock producer and engineer
Tony Visconti recalled that in the 1960s and 1970s recording engineers rarely shared their power with drummers and other musicians. "If the sound was wrong (on the drums) you changed the
mics or moved them about a bit," he said. "If a drummer was really
respected, he might be allowed to move his own overhead mic!"
(White, 1987, p. 32).

Visconti's use of the word *respected* illustrates the confused nature of the politics of sound recording. The drummer's musical
ability or popularity as a performer may have little to do with his
or her ability to make a recording sound good. On the other hand,
Visconti's remark proves that musicians do have some measure of
control in the recording studio. Another of Visconti's remarks
illustrates Attali's (1985) idea that sound can be imposed:

> When I really decided to make a big move technically, I was working
> with T Rex and we were simply not getting the sounds we wanted
> from the engineer. He was a great engineer but he was the sort of guy
> who would add EQ or reverb without telling you, so we ended up
> with his sound, not ours. (p. 32)

In Dick Hebdige's (1987) book *Cut 'n' Mix*, a Rastafarian drummer succinctly stated the political nature of sound recording. "At
that time we wasn't really checking fe recording," he said. "We
were only into the music, letting it go free as it come to us" (p. 59).
I will return to Hebdige's analysis of reggae, rap and hip-hop
recording. For now, though, it is important to realize that recording
is a distinctly different activity from musical performance.

The first articulation of the power of recording sound comes
from the early twentieth-century avant garde, within which futurism and dadaism took root. In 1909 Marinetti (Berman, 1982) wrote
the first futurist manifesto, paving the way for musique concrete
and electronic music, only now being commercially realized in the

mainstream with the widespread use of digital synthesizers and digital sampling technology. Marinetti wrote that

> we will sing of great crowds excited by work, by pleasure and by riot; we will sing of the multicolored, polyphonic tides of revolution in the modern capitals; we will sing of the nightly fervor of arsenals and shipyards blazing with violent electric moons; greedy railway stations that devour smoke-plumed serpents; factories hung on clouds by the crooked lines of their smoke; bridges that stride the rivers like giant gymnasts, flashing in the sun with a glitter of knives; adventurous steamers . . . deep-chested locomotives . . . and the sleek light of planes. (Berman, 1982, p. 25)

The music of such 1980s groups as Throbbing Gristle or Einstuerzende Neubauten, and many of the groups on Chicago's Wax Trax Records, which uses samples and background tapes of mechanical and industrial sounds, is a direct descendant of Marinetti's decree.

Futurism and dadaism fostered a spirit of adventure among artists, most evident in Busoni's "Sketch of a New Aesthetic of Music" in which he declared, "the creative artist does not follow laws already made, but . . . he makes laws" (Appleton & Perera, 1975, p. 5). This spirit, along with futurism's embrace of the modern, meant that new music technology such as the phonograph, the electric organ, and the Dynamophone would find a place with composers and artists, and become more than machines for the reproduction of sound but machines for the creation of new and previously unheard sounds.

An important influence on avant garde music was the publication in 1913 of Russolo's "The Art of Noises," in which he "suggested fixing the pitch of noise sounds" (Appleton & Perera, 1987, p. 7) This opened the door for musique concrete, forged a direct link between futurism and music, paving the way for everyday sounds—industrial noises, traffic sounds, and so forth—to be used as the raw material of music. The moment was a crucial one especially when viewed in light of the use of digital samplers. Samplers record external sounds and allow them to be played back anywhere on a keyboard, essentially realizing Russolo's desire for a machine to fix the pitch of any noise. Any number of recordings released since the mid-1980s, when the purchase of samplers became affordable for many musicians and recording studios, feature the use of noise or "found" sounds. One of the most popular was Paul Hardcastle's "19," a top ten single. But perhaps the most creative was De La Soul's *Three Feet High and Rising* album, which included snippets of game shows, popular songs, and conversation to create an audio collage linking the group's rap songs.

On a deeper level, publication of "The Art of Noises" was the point at which music theory ceased to be dictatorially controlled by traditional western musical ideas such as pitch and rhythm (which lent themselves to notation). Avant garde music by its very nature lent itself to technology and to recording. It was difficult to write down in a systematic manner, and it relied on sounds that, in some cases, were not perfectly repeatable (the screech of a train's brakes, for example, or the sound of a factory). The connection to sound recording technology is direct. As Frank Biocca writes, "no longer would black marks on paper be the only manner to hold still a fleeting melody, now sound itself could be captured. The link between music, sound, and technology became fused in the mind of the avant garde" (Biocca, 1985). In other words, one could now notate, by means of recording, the *significance* of music, the "grain of the voice" as Barthes (1977, p. 188) calls it.

This is not to say that composers had been unaware of sound up to this point, or that pitch and rhythm have been abandoned, for that is clearly not the case. Early twentieth-century avant garde composers became more aware of sound as a malleable form, adaptable to their needs or whims. The difference was one of perception. Recording technology allowed for control over sound by means of editing, tape manipulation, and the like. Consequently, the sounds produced by musical instruments could take on a new role, as the raw material for composition rather than the means for realization of a composition.

As importantly, recording allowed for repetition of sound so that composers could hear their own (and other) pieces over and over again, with no need for performers. Biocca (1985) states that the phonograph and radio participated in the process of musical change by preparing the audience, musicians, and composers for new forms of aural experience, by shifting the sensory ratio in favor of greater cognitive attention to hearing, and also by diffusing the new experiments in sound. (p. 16)

By the late 1930s and early 1940s, sound had become the organizing principle in music. Electronic instruments were available, as were relatively inexpensive recording devices. Composition was redefined, as "composers were beginning to think in terms of timbral relation; oscillators and instruments capable of controlling timbre had been perfected" (Ernst, 1977, p. xxiv). A new relationship between composer, musician, music, and musical work emerged, confusing, in terms of the realization of music, labor and production, and in terms of the composition of music, the perception of sound itself.

Sound and Popular Music

It was not until the late 1960s that many of the innovations of avant garde music found their way into mainstream popular music, most notably in the Beatles' music, on records like *Sgt. Pepper's Lonely Hearts Club Band*. Contemporary pop and rock groups have continued to mine this territory (Cohen, 1991, p. 174). However, the seeds for the intersection of the avant garde and the popular were planted well before the Beatles, in several ways. First, as mentioned earlier, recording technology added power over sound and permitted reconfiguration and juxtaposition of sound. During the 1950s, popular musical parodist Spike Jones relied on recording sound effects to create humor in his music (perhaps not coincidentally, Jones' producer was George Martin, who later produced the Beatles' recordings). Much like film editing, sound editing and recording enabled the construction of a sort of narrative impression, via the collision/juxtaposition of sounds.

Second, and more importantly, recording enabled the fixation, and therefore repetition, of music based on improvisation. The implication for popular music is remarkable. The following paragraph by Jones and Rahn (1981) illustrates the relationship between repetition and improvisation (albeit in a backhanded way).

> In accord with Adorno's view of popular music as a standardized product subject to variation, Howard Brown asserts that a popular piece retains its germane characteristics despite considerable deviations from the original version. Rearranging and improvisation play a large role in popular music. This range of variability is probably related to aural transmission and to the audience's and performer's lack of concern about the composer's intentions. In this regard, popular music resembles traditional folk music, which has also circulated in an oral tradition and whose composers have largely been forgotten. Groups such as Liverpool, which imitate Beatles' arrangements note for note, are closer to classical performance practices than to those that we usually associate with popular music. (pp. 46-47)

Jones and Rahn are correct in identifying improvisation as one of popular music's most important characteristics. Recording technology's reconciliation of popular music as a standardized yet improvised product is what makes it the site of struggle and creation of popular music. For successful musicians to maintain popularity they must repeat and reconfigure the elements that made their music a hit in the first place, without overtly copying their previous hits. The classic example is that of the Rolling Stones' "(I Can't Get No) Satisfaction" and "Jumpin' Jack Flash," the latter simply inverting the melodic hook while retaining the sound of the former.

Jones and Rahn's mention of Liverpool is interesting because the group is identified as being within the realm of "classical performance practices" because of their note-for-note imitation of Beatles' songs. Few popular groups perform even their own compositions note-for-note. However, in live performance most do attempt to achieve a *sound* close to the one they achieved in the recording studio.

Bennett (1990) provides an example of the way in which a recording is used by a band to learn to cover another group's song.

The upshot for the group is that, after three-days of rehearsals, they were able to execute the song "just like the record" (p. 226).

The reasons for this dedication to the recording are not quite clear, and may be dominated by economics as much as aesthetics. Perhaps the group feels the studio sound best realizes its compositions' potential (that is, maybe they simply *like* the studio sound). It could also be that the group wants to imitate its recording so that the audience will purchase the recording, or the group feels it may alienate the audience by not adhering to a sound with which it is already familiar. The reason the phrase "all you need is a guitar and three chords" became a cliché is that it is not how one *plays* an instrument but how one *sounds* that matters in popular music.

And so the authenticity of rock 'n' roll is closely connected to the distinction between live and studio performance, in that what can be achieved in the studio by a performer is often difficult for her or him to reproduce. Rock groups often state in interviews that the stage and studio must be kept distinct—in any case it is difficult to exactly reproduce a studio recording on stage. Punk groups valued live performance as the best means of expression because it was a direct link to the audience, and *therefore the most authentic expression.* Studio trickery has been a matter of contention among musicians, fans, and critics from the days of the earliest recordings.

However, it is currently quite difficult, given the abilities of digital samplers and other sound reinforcement equipment, to discern whether even a live performance is indeed live or pre-recorded. The result has been a debate concerning whether or not it should be mandatory for concert tickets to shows using pre-recorded material to include mention of the use of such material. The issue temporarily came to a head when in 1991 it was discovered that Whitney Houston used a back-up tape for her vocal during an appearance on a network television special in the United States.

Indeed, recording technology has greatly affected live performance and the recreation of studio sound in a performance setting. At one time it would have been difficult for a group such as Pink Floyd, for instance, to exactly reproduce its studio sound on stage.

Now, however, it is common for a group to make a digital sample of the sounds created in the studio and use those in performance (as used by the Philip Glass Ensemble and Howard Jones, among others). Live performance is thereby linked both to the studio and to the technology of recording via sound. It is now possible to sample the sound of a 40-piece orchestra that was employed in the studio and include that as part of a live performance, with no need for an actual orchestra. Its sound has been extrapolated from its creators and power over the sound has changed hands. It is likely that an orchestra was *not* used in the studio, but that a sample was, not solely for economic reasons but for the increased control a recording engineer has over a sampler as opposed to an orchestra. Such use of the recording studio also results in a tremendous savings of time and money for producers, engineers, record companies, and so forth, who do not have to hire and record the orchestra. But it is no wonder that musicians' unions are having difficulty coping with and accepting much of the new recording technology. Not only can it take jobs away from musicians; it can wrest political control over their sound away from them. There is little (at this time) that can stop someone from sampling the sound of a philharmonic orchestra from a CD for use in a studio.

Although the contradiction between repetition and improvisation in popular music may be reconciled in the recording process by way of the mass production of a unique event, the contradictions of sound and originality in popular music are not, especially in rock and roll. Groups attempt to forge a unique, individual sound, yet one not too far removed from an established framework. Their sound serves both to place them within a given social, cultural, and political area and to set them apart from others in that area.

Bob Dylan placed himself in an interesting situation at the 1965 Newport Folk Festival when he switched from acoustic to electric guitar, in one stroke (strum) alienating much of his folk audience and proving the political power of sound in popular music. The experience and ideology of folk music were based on the acoustic guitar, an instrument that could be played anywhere and was designed to be heard by a small group of people. The electric guitar carried the image of rock music and amplification intended to increase its reach to a large audience. Dylan's folk audience was well aware of this and considered his switch to electric guitar a form of selling out.

Thus sound serves as a means of establishing cultural, musical, and political boundaries, and the production of music is the point at which such work takes place. Groups negotiate their way among the sounds available, adding some, discarding some, and modifying others, until their sound is one slightly different from, but within the limits of, a sound they like and believe will be accepted by their fans. Recording engineers and producers are hired to help bands achieve that sound, to help them find a sound, or to add their sound to the band's. Yet as much as sound is a way for musicians to align themselves with fans, with subcultures, it is also a way for record companies to exploit marketing techniques. For example, the Charlatans UK achieved considerable success on U.S. radio with their song "The Only One I Know" because, though hardly a mainstream group, their sound, a contemporary combination of 1960s organ and 1991-era Manchester-style shuffle drumming, did not seem out of place bookended by other bands' songs.

Rock: Sound and Culture

The following examples are typical of the cultural function of sound in popular music. The first is that of the Sun sound.

Epitomized by the early recordings of Elvis Presley, the Sun sound was the creation of Sam Phillips, owner of Memphis-based Sun Records. Several histories of Sun exist and I will not recount its history here.[1] Suffice it to say that many consider the Sun Records studio to be the place where rock 'n' roll was born. What is important to the matter at hand is that Sun had a unique sound, identifiable (a combination of white country and black blues styles) yet uncharacteristic of other recordings of the mid-1950s. Peter Guralnick (1971) describes Phillips' style.

His production methods were instinctive and almost always appropriate. Like Leonard Chess he was one of the first to go for a heavy echo effect, but the overall sound was crisp, clean, and full of life. (p. 174)

Chambers (1985) goes further to pinpoint Sun's uniqueness:

Listening to the recordings that Elvis made for Sam Phillips in Memphis in the mid-1950s and comparing them with those made a little later for the same Sun label by Carl Perkins, the magisterial power of Presley's performance is unmistakable. With Perkins there are similar musical currents at work, but the respective country and blues elements remain less integrated; his voice tends to cut across and over the instrumental backing. Presley's voice, however, has a "voluptuous" presence within the music. This is particularly evident if we compare the two singers' respective recordings of "Blue Suede Shoes." It indicates Elvis's greatest debt to the blues. *It is an aural difference that permits us to appreciate both Presley's fundamental importance in white popular music and Roland Barthes' point that in the "grain" of the singing voice it becomes possible to locate a cultural sense* [italics added]. (p. 37)

The Sun sound was dictated by the available recording technology as much as by Phillips's production values (which were, in turn affected by technology, both for production and consumption of music) and Presley's talent. In the mid-1950s Phillips had available a tape machine capable of capturing a live performance in a monaural recording. There was no capability for overdubbing (layering of tracks) and it is likely that some of the spontaneity that comes across in the Sun recordings is due to the live performance turned in by the musicians grouped together in the same room. The "live" quality also stems in part from the microphone placement—microphones were not isolated (in that the musicians were in the same room), but could pick up some of the ambient room sound as well as adjacent instruments.

The "cultural sense" to which Chambers refers is crucial to popular music. It creates a space within which popular music can operate, and a space within which audience discourse concerning popular music takes on meaning, in terms of sound. Conversation among popular music fans often includes a discussion of a group's sound, or of a sound in particular. Articles regarding sound are a common feature in most music magazines, including those aimed at musicians themselves. And radio programmers consistently target a recording's sound for consideration during meetings with staffers at which station playlists are compiled.

Dick Hebdige (1987) points out how sound affected reggae throughout its history.

> In the early days, when the sound system operators first began making records, the studio facilities had been very primitive. Usually the music was played by session musicians and the recording was made in one take. Before long, vocal tracks were added too. The instrumentals were recorded on one track of the tape and this was later pressed as a record. But as the industry evolved and became more sophisticated, so too did the recording equipment. Soon it became possible to mix together a number of musical tracks to build up a more complex and interesting sound. At the same time, the engineers experimented by mixing the tracks together on the final tape in different ways. For instance, ska and rocksteady records were mixed differently. In ska, the vocal track had been given prominence, and this is still the case with most forms of modern pop music where the lyrics are considered important. But on the new rocksteady records, the singers' voices tended to be treated like any other instrument. Instead, pride of place was given to the bass guitar . . . new "dread ridims" were called *rockers*. As with every other shift in Jamaican pop music, the new sound can be traced back to the way the drums and bass guitar were featured on recordings. (pp. 71-72, 82).

Different reggae styles were identified by their sound—and made possible by studio technology. Recording played a prominent role in the development of these styles by enabling the engineer and producer to control individual elements of the songs. The technology also enabled reggae to cross over into the rock marketplace, as Hebdige relates:

> To get through to the wider audience, the Wailers' LP had to be remixed so that the overall sound was brought into line with the expectations of the white rock audience. Many of the reggae LPs

produced with the foreign market in mind are still remixed in this
way. For example, some producers speed up the tapes slightly for
reggae records destined for the American market, because the American rock and soul audiences who are likely to buy reggae prefer the
faster rhythms. (p. 82)

Recording is used in this instance as a marketing tool in addition
to the typically musical uses to which it is put.

A recent critical example of the importance of sound to popular
music comes from British punk rock. Punk created a climate in
which anyone could form a band and many wanted to. This
sudden explosion of new groups, forming and breaking up seemingly overnight, caught the recording industry off guard.

One of punk rock's aims was to disavow mainstream rock as a
corporate farce, removed from its fans, by pointing out what a farce
rock had become. But in so doing it pointed out that it too had to
be a farce, as caught up with the music business as mainstream rock
(the Clash signed to CBS, the Sex Pistols to EMI, then Virgin). Punk
rock sneered at and simultaneously exploited the music industry,
which in turn exploited it. And the do-it-yourself alternative that
punk offered, though still an inspiration to many aspiring musicians (and music businesspeople) has become a small-scale mirror-
image of the music industry as a whole, while losing its tenacious
grip on the industry's financial merry-go-round (independent record label Rough Trade's demise in 1991 is particularly telling).

The emphasis in punk was on the live performance. Groups with
little or no musical training performed in small, crowded bars, in
direct opposition to the elaborate staging and musicianship of
mainstream groups such as Genesis, Electric Light Orchestra, and
Queen. Despite the emphasis on performance, though, punk bands
desperately wanted to release records (and many started their own
record labels to do so). It is one of the many contradictions of punk
rock that, despite denying connections to rock's history, it nonetheless articulated itself within the standard medium of rock music.
Ultimately it had no choice, because records were both the medium
through which groups communicated with an audience beyond
their immediate area and the medium favored by radio stations.

Few, if any, groups could reach an audience large enough to sustain them without releasing a record, and most groups wanted to go beyond mere sustenance and reach as many people as possible.

Punk groups were not keen to go into recording studios, in that many viewed the studio as the place were rock had become stagnant, where bands would hole up and shut themselves off from their audience. In an interview with Caroline Coon (1979) Johnny Rotten of the Sex Pistols said, "Everyone is so fed up with the old way" (p. 18). Caroline Coon added, "For three years we accepted the situation, almost stunned. Theatrical bands like Queen, Roxy Music and 10cc tried to anaesthetize us with dollops of romantic escapism and showbiz gloss . . . there is a growing, almost desperate feeling that rock music should be stripped down to its bare bones again" (p. 19). Punks wanted nothing to do with any of those showbiz trappings, including the standard process of recording, which took anywhere from several weeks to several months, with a producer in strict control of the proceedings. Part of the political struggle of punk against mainstream rock took place over sound— "stripped down" versus "gloss(y)." Dave Laing (1985) describes mainstream recording as it developed in the 1970s.

> Since the rewards from a global hit were potentially vast, the (major labels) were willing to invest large sums in the preparation of both artists and recordings. Most of that money was spent on and in recording studios, whose technology had become increasingly sophisticated. In particular, the exponential increase during the decade in the number of tracks, or channels of sound, into which the music to be recorded could be separated, allowed musicians and producers to manipulate the sounds to an unprecedented degree.
>
> In the popular music sphere of 1976, the expert manipulation of that technology . . . had become accepted as the precondition for successful and competent music. Although punk rock was soon to prove that exciting and valid recordings could be made for a fraction of the cost, the generality of musicians in 1976 identified good records with expensive ones. And since the only source of adequate finance for the studio costs of a good recording was the major or large independent label, the only path to artistic success musicians could imagine lay through convincing those labels that one's own work would prove commercially viable. (p. 3)

Punk groups regarded studio recording as an extension of live performance, and recorded in a fashion not unlike Phillips used at Sun Records. As Phillips recorded and released records on his own label, so punk bands released self-made records on their own labels. Most punk recordings were made in small four- or eight-track studios, using recording equipment left over from the 1950s and 1960s. For the many bands that did not sign to a record company, recording in technologically sophisticated studios was not only aesthetically unacceptable but also economically out of the question. However, as large studios bought new equipment and sold the old, some smaller studios were in a position to buy up the used equipment and offer recording time at rates affordable to most punk bands. These smaller studios were not equipped to do much more than live recording, on a kind of do-it-yourself basis (which suited punk aesthetics). However, had it not been for technological development that forced down the price of old technology, it is likely that punk bands would not have been able to do very much recording at all. A group like Generation X (whose singer, Billy Idol, went on to international popularity in the late 1980s) was able to rent recording equipment, set it up in their apartment, learn how to use it, and record their first album.

What was ultimately at stake was authenticity. The punks felt that, by doing things themselves, they were more direct, more honest than the "pre-fab" rock stars that had dominated popular music in the 1970s. They boldly articulated what had become a tradition in rock 'n' roll since the 1950s. As Mike Stoller, of the Leiber and Stoller songwriting team (responsible for many 50s hits by the Coasters and Elvis Presley, among others) said about Presley's artistic decline, "he no longer appeared in public . . . he wasn't getting the feedback. He was insulated. There was none of the go-for-broke situation that creates exciting performances" (Tobler & Grundy, 1982, p. 16). The punks wanted, more than anything else, to be in touch with their audience; most of them had, at some point, been audience members.

Technology is intimately connected to rock's notions of honesty and directness. It lets one reproduce and manipulate sound, and the development and design of sound recording equipment (and sound reproducing equipment—witness the development of digital media for home use) is biased toward easier manipulation of sound and more faithful (i.e., high-fidelity, more true-to-life, authentic) reproduction. Frith (1988) notes the relation of technology and authenticity in popular music, saying that

> Each . . . [moment] in rock history fused moral and aesthetic judgements: rock 'n' roll, rhythm 'n' blues and punk were all, in their turn, experienced as more truthful than the pop forms they disrupted. And in each case authenticity was described as an explicit reaction to technology, as a return to the "roots" of music-making—the live excitement of voice/guitar/drum line-ups. The continuing core of rock ideology is that *raw sounds* are more authentic than *cooked sounds* [italics mine]. (p. 266)

Of course, raw sounds must themselves be cooked—to the point that they sound raw.

New Sounds/Old Sounds

As already mentioned, popular music production has traditionally been concerned with finding new sounds and reconfiguring old ones. As Glyn Johns, record producer and engineer for the Rolling Stones, the Who and others, commented about studio work, "the [recording] engineer [is] being asked for something different, please, because we've heard this one before" (Wale, 1972, p. 65).

The search for new sounds is at the heart of modern musical instrument technology. Instruments such as the Kurzweil 150 synthesizer are marketed with their sound-creating and sound storage potential as their biggest selling point. An advertisement for that instrument reads, "The Kurzweil 150 . . . can create infinite numbers of sound combinations . . . sound layering techniques enable you to create distinctive sounds with remarkable ease" (Kurzweil 150, 1987, p. 18). A similar trend is evident in sampling and recording technology. The Korg DSS-1 sampler is advertised as being able to bring the performer "into new dimensions of sound," and the

Otari MX-70 is advertised as "the perfect multitrack for the synthesizer oriented studio."

The manipulation of sound has never been easier than it is now, nor has it been as vehemently pursued. In fact, a division has arisen between those who create sounds and those who perform them. Synthesizer programmers, such as Bo Tomlyn and Larry Fast, create sounds for their clients and have spawned an industry based on the trading of sounds via tape or computer disk. In April 1987, *Keyboard* magazine's five-page classified advertising section contained 111 advertisements, 74 of them selling sounds for synthesizers or instruction books detailing how to create one's own sounds. A typical advertisement reads,

> Ensoniq ESQ-1 Owners, Buy the Best. Volume 1: 40 exceptional sound programs. Only $19.95 for data cassette and program sheets; also tips for effects processing, splits/layers. CZ-101 owners: Affordable, recordable, 32 devastating patches (sounds). Only $13.95 for program sheets and demo cassette. (Classified Ads, p. 141)

A computer network and database, the Performing Artists Network (PAN), contains hundreds of sounds in its files section that can be accessed via computer modem. The sounds can be downloaded by subscribers and programmed into their synthesizers. For most purchasers of modern electronic musical equipment, sound, and the availability of sounds for an instrument, is the first priority. Synthony Music, a large musical equipment retailer based in the Southwest United States, recently polled their customers and found that 88.6% of the respondents thought sound was the most important consideration in a purchase, followed by price and features (The Results Are In, 1987, p. 2).

Authenticity is at stake here too, for there is a rift between those who create their own sounds and those who buy others' sounds. Creating one's own sounds is currently perceived as more authentic than buying sounds. As stated in *Electronic Musician* magazine, "Some people are beginning to complain that the extensive use of instruments with the same factory presets (sounds), sampling instruments that use the same (sound) disks, and the wholesale sampling of other people's sounds is producing an objectionable similarity in current music" (Anderton, 1986a, June, p. 58). By listening to U.S. top 40 radio for a moderate length of time, one can tell which groups use the same sounds, as a certain sonic sameness creeps into top 40 songs. Rock producer Peter Wolf stated his dislike of using the same sounds over and over again.

> I'll get incredible drum sounds and then only use them on [one] record. After we're done with them, that's it, they go into the rock 'n' roll museum. I know some people think that certain sounds become a trademark, but who cares? When all this stuff starts melting into a big pot and you turn on Power 106 [an LA top 40 station] and everything sounds like Janet Jackson, I could puke, I can't believe it. In my own little way I'm trying to change that by not ever using the same sounds. (Peter Wolf, 1987, p. 34)

Still, the identity of a group or artist is associated with sound and changing that sound can often prove disastrous. Composer Scott Wyatt, after hearing a sound effect at a recording session, remarked that, "it's a bad cliche, but that's the biz" (Wyatt, 1987e). The ability to rapidly identify a group is critical to success in the music business and one important way to establish that identity is to establish a sound. Record producer Mickie Most noted of one group, "They've always had a little color in their sound which I think has given them an identity" (Tobler & Grundy, 1982, p. 136). Record producers can also be associated with a sound. Glyn Johns said, "[Phil] Spector came up with a sound, and a Spector record could come on the radio now that you and I have never heard before and we'd know it was Phil Spector" (Wale, 1972, p. 77). Producers are often hired for their ability to get a certain sound on a recording. Recording engineers are likewise hired for their knowledge of recording equipment and talent for getting a sound. Glyn Johns was asked about his production and engineering contribution to the Who's *Who's Next* LP, and his reply was, "First and foremost the sound" (Wale, 1972, p. 75).

Simon Frith (1981) places sound and individuality/authenticity in rock music in the context of artistic creation. "For many fans,"

he writes, "it [is] this sense of individual creation that first distin-
guished rock from other forms of mass music" (p. 53). Frith argues
that one of the contradictions of rock 'n' roll revolves around the
struggle between individuality and commercialism. That struggle
is articulated in most successful rock groups' attempts to reconfigure their old sound, the sound that made them successful, with new
sounds. The difficulty lies in finding the proper mix of old and new,
of avoiding overt repetition, emphasizing progression, without
enacting a change so great that the audience will not recognize the
group. For some groups this is not hard, and relates to Barthes's
(1977) concept of *significance*. In the Rolling Stones, the Beatles,
U2, Madonna, Talking Heads, and others, one has vocalists whose
voices are so recognizable that the instrumental backing can
change dramatically from song to song, or record to record, without doubt of the group's identity. Moreover, the instrumental backing can sound *the same as* that of other groups' but the singer's voice
stamps the song with its identity. Perhaps this may also account for
the claim that particularly innovative instrumentalists make their
instruments "sing."

Of course, up-and-coming groups will often imitate the sound
of a successful group to be identified as a hit group, and hire
producers and engineers who can recreate already famous sounds.
Blondie's use of producer Richard Gottehrer for the 60s-ish "In the
Flesh" is a case in point, as is the Go-Go's hiring of Gottehrer for
the same reason. Bill Szycmczyk, commenting on his relationship
with the Who, said, "Your reputation (as a producer) goes before
you, and it's like, 'You hear the way that sounds? Do that to me'"
(Tobler & Grundy, 1982, p. 89). Television critic Ron Powers (1987)
once said that "clearly the test of prime-time greatness is not
originality but taste in imitation." The same holds true for pop
music greatness (p. 170).

A terrific example of the recombination of music and sound into
a new and popular song can be found in Dave Rimmer's (1985)
semi-biography of Culture Club. In it, he describes Boy George's
delight at wearing his musical influences not only on his sleeve,
but in his songs.

"Listen," George touches my elbow when the opening Motown beat of "Church of the Poison Mind" belts out. He grins, waits for the cue and then sings Stevie Wonder over the top: "Uptight, everything is already, outta sight . . ." It fits perfectly.

Jon, sticking his head over the top of a nearby seat, raises an eyebrow. "I'd keep quiet about that if I were you."

But George has no intention of doing any such thing. He points out a bit of the melody of "It's a Miracle" that comes from Gilbert O'Sullivan. When the flute comes in at the beginning of "Storm-keeper," he smiles and says "that sounds like Men At Work." George is not ashamed of borrowing. Far from it. He seems positively proud. As we listen on, the names of those to whom Culture Club have accorded the sincerest form of flattery continues to tumble out. (p. 80)

It would seem that most groups, and virtually all record companies, know that audiences are well aware of sound. Part of the reason for the audience's reaction to Dylan's switch to electric guitar was because of the radical change to his sound, and part of the reason that groups are signed to record companies is based on their sound's proximity to current hit sounds.

The association of sound and individuality exists not only among singers but also with musicians. Rock guitarists are identified by their sound (Jimi Hendrix being one of the first to experiment with the electric guitar's sound potential), and similarly, users of synthesizers, digital samplers, and recording equipment are identified by sound. The fragmentation of sound into discrete, tradeable and saleable units has created a climate in which the musician who can create sound is valued over one who does not. *Electronic Musician's* editor, Craig Anderton, (1986b, September) writes that

sound is a very personal thing. . . . The question that concerns me is that if more and more musicians forsake programming, how will those musicians express their individuality with synthesizers and samplers? Samplers in particular offer the promise of using the entire world as a sound source, although many musicians seem content to use their samplers simply to copy the "sounds du jour." (p. 6)

Pressure to maintain a sound distinct from others' but within the range of current sounds creates tension when the means to create and reproduce an extremely broad range of sounds is readily available. Just as there is, in rock 'n' roll, a qualitative distinction between live performance and recording, based on authenticity and directness, so too is there a distinction between acoustic and electric sound. Currently another distinction, between electric and electronic sound (electric guitar versus synthesizer), is apparent. The ideology of rock, and therefore its meaning, revolves around sound. Recording technology, as the means by which sound is manipulated and reproduced, is the site of control over sound, and therefore the site of musical and political power in popular music.

Note

1. The best is the chapter on Sun in Peter Guralnick's (1971) *Feel Like Goin' Home*.

4

The Design and Marketing of Music Technology

Design

The musical equipment market is dominated by large corporations. Many musical equipment makers are subsidiaries of still larger conglomerates, ones with interests in a vast array of consumer goods, including electronics. Of these, the best known—Yamaha, Roland, Casio, Akai—release several new products each quarter. Most manufacturers produce a startling variety of equipment. Yamaha, the largest manufacturer of electronic musical equipment, makes cassette multitrack recorders, synthesizers of all kinds, personal computers specifically designed for use with digital sequencers and synthesizers via MIDI (the Musical Instrument Digital Interface), and signal processing equipment. It is quite easy, in fact, to put together a small recording studio with only Yamaha equipment. The design and marketing philosophies of most manufacturers are intricately bound together, and they will often produce complete sound systems.

In that most modern music technology relies heavily on electronics and the integrated circuit for its operation, it is not surprising to find that most equipment is manufactured in Japan. Though this has not always been the case (Ampex and Scully, to name two, were long the primary suppliers of professional tape recorders) it is beyond the scope of this work to trace a complete history of the manufacture of musical and sound recording equipment. Such a task merits its own book, and would, I think, prove quite interesting and revealing. It is an industry in which a company can become a giant overnight (as the Linn Corporation did) and go out of business almost as quickly (again, as Linn did).

For several reasons, my focus is on recent music technology, primarily on sound recording devices, instruments, and associated recording studio equipment that has been manufactured since the 1970s. First, very little equipment that was manufactured before 1970 is in use (the reasons for this will be explained shortly). Second, the pace of technological change has recently increased. Equipment obsolescence is a significant problem for anyone purchasing recording equipment. Third, the decrease in the price of computer chips has led to a reduction in the price of electronic musical and recording equipment, and fueled the tremendous expansion of recording in the home, forcing a change in marketing strategies. Fourth, increases in computer memory have led to the design and manufacture of digital recording equipment and digital samplers that have had a significant impact on composition and realization of music. And fifth, these conditions have acted to determine a radical rethinking of the production and subsequent consumption of sound.

Few composers, musicians, producers, and engineers know much about the design and marketing of musical equipment. It is not that they are not interested, but that unless they work directly for a manufacturer they are not let in on trade secrets. For example, during a conversation with an employee of a major synthesizer manufacturer, mention was made of a new synthesizer under development. The employee would not say when it would be released or even when its release would be announced. A curtain of secrecy is placed over most manufacturers' research and design departments for fear of industry spying. Nonetheless, according to composer and programming consultant Paul Lehrman (1987), "A certain amount of industrial espionage is going on."

Manufacturers often preview equipment to certain people, though. Many use musicians and recording studios as "beta-testers," people and places to whom they send equipment that is almost ready for production. By using beta-testers the manufacturer gets an idea of how the product will perform in the field, and can change or modify the product as necessary. Computer software designers regularly employ beta-testers to discover problems in their programs, and this is common practice among designers of software-based sequencers. Oftentimes user interfaces in the form of menus and screens are redesigned based on the suggestions of beta-testers. Beta-testing not only saves money that could be lost from equipment that fails to meet market demands but also allows the manufacturer to discover major design flaws. Beta-testing can virtually save the life of a piece of equipment (and perhaps even a company). Steven Cox (1987), a computer analyst and musician who works for the International Music Company (distributors of Akai products in the United States), gave an example of beta-testing's use.

> For instance, Oberheim's instrument that reads everybody else's sampling disk. It was going to have one output. And ... before it was on the market (people) said you've got to have as many outputs as you have voices for studio use. And before it hit the market it went through that change and had that added.

Additionally, beta-testing is useful to musicians and recording studios. Though it can be time-consuming, as when reporting back to the manufacturer, or even costly, as when a problem with the product causes trouble during a recording session, beta-testing gives access to equipment that no one else has. Just as the search for new sounds can inspire musicians and synthesizer programmers to get new sounds from their instruments, so it can drive studio engineers to acquire the latest piece of equipment to achieve a new sound. What could be better than having the latest piece of equipment that is not yet on the market? And quite often beta-testers are allowed to keep the product they are testing, which may include features not found on production models.

Some studios are offered equipment because they are often written about in consumer and trade publications like *Keyboard* and *Mix*. Dan Dryden (1987), sound engineer for Philip Glass, commented that the Living Room, Glass's New York studio, gets equipment and, "do[es] a lot of evaluation. Since we get published in these magazines a lot of people come to us and say, 'We've got this system and we want you to plug it in and see if it works for you the way you want.'" Most equipment design involves some kind of feedback from musicians and other users. A relatively common situation is the one described by John Senior (1987), a software engineer and designer for Ensoniq Corporation.

> Most of the engineers here [at Ensoniq] are musicians, and I have a studio at home. I use our stuff during the development cycle at home, to see if it holds up. In addition we do solicit feedback from beta testers and outside people we have contacts with. We receive a fair amount of unsolicited response. We're definitely open to it.

Tony Gambacurta, co-owner of ART (Applied Research and Technology, makers of digital reverbs and other signal processing equipment) and formerly with MXR, echoed Senior's remark. "In the case of MXR, about half the employees were musicians," Gambacurta (1987) said. "We had quite a range, anywhere from rock to jazz, all kinds. Musicians who weren't making it financially as musicians worked at MXR."

Manufacturers also get feedback from salespeople who keep in close touch with equipment dealers. "Salespeople keep their ears to the ground," Gambacurta said, "and hear about what the competition might be doing, find out where they're weak." In some cases dealers will get jobs with manufacturers. David Oren started working for Tascam Corporation in 1972, after being an equipment retailer. He too believes design is accountable to user feedback (Oren, 1987). In some instances musicians will be retained by a company as spokespersons, and will endorse certain products. In return, the musician gets perks similar to those of a beta-tester— free equipment, free consultations, and so on.

Product design is, according to most manufacturers, similar to design in other fields. Gambacurta (1987) described the procedure:

The first thing is product idea. These come from two places. First, seeing what competitors do. The other is original creative ideas which are drawn out of the ether. Another area is related to competition, only taking a concept that others have done, for example flanging, and making it for lower cost . . . [it's] the same as any product, whether it's a camera, computer, same basic process. You develop a prototype, and timelines in terms of date of introduction, and then you work everything back to when the case has to be done, the schematic has to be finalized, various parts put together, and put it on a timeline. During that process you develop prototypes that are closer and closer to the final product, letting other people see it and interact with it, make changes. It's usually an evolutionary process, from a crude prototype. What you're doing is putting together specifications it'll have, its limitations, and ways you can expand upon [it], add some little feature that'll cost very little but may be a selling point. You interact with people who are involved in marketing the product, salespeople and so forth, so you get ideas. You're thinking about the whole process of merchandising. Sometimes you're getting feedback from the field too.

Though the process varies somewhat for each product, the idea-prototype-production scheme is common for virtually all products. To some extent the equipment industry operates like the record industry, producing variations on a theme and little that is completely new. As Simon Frith (1987b) wrote:

> the music industry finds out what the public wants by seeing what it has already got—hence the importance of "guaranteed" stars and "tested" formulae; hence the essential *conservatism* of an enterprise in which the new always means more of the old. (pp. 5-6)

As certain sounds and types of equipment become popular, more manufacturers create equipment incorporating those sounds.

An offshoot of equipment design is software design. Software creation is often related to equipment design, in that most modern equipment is microprocessor based. In effect, engineers design hardware and programmers design software for it. Such is often the case for production of sequencers, digital reverberation units, and synthesizers. For example, software for many signal processors, like Lexicon's digital reverberation units, is constantly being upgraded, as programmers discover new features to implement. The owner can purchase a microchip with new software to replace one already in the unit, or returns the unit to the manufacturer for upgrade installation for a nominal fee. The owner saves money by not having to buy a new unit altogether, and the value of the unit increases both financially and creatively. Software updates are especially common with software based sequencers for personal computers. Many companies specialize in creating software only.

Paul Lehrman (1987), formerly a programmer for the South-worth Company and co-creator of Total Music, once a widely used sequencer for the Apple Macintosh, explained the software design process for Total Music.

> I would look at it and say "what do I want this thing to do" [as a musician]? Also, we would present it to studios and user groups. We'd ask "what's missing, is there anything you don't like?" This guy in New York came up with an edit screen. We had it designed and he said "why don't you have a play button at the bottom of the screen?" and we thought, that's brilliant! I put it in. [We use c]onstant feedback from people who are using it, telling us how they want to use it.

According to Robert Moog, who now works at the Kurzweil Music Systems, Inc. and whose name (at least until Yamaha came along) is virtually synonymous with the synthesizer, the ideal instrument is designed with as few restrictions as possible. Moog (1987) said,

> I don't think any two electronic musical instrument designers ever had the same idea of how their instrument would be used . . . what's most productive is that the instrument designer assumes as little as possible and builds in as few restrictions as possible.

Restrictions *are*, however, built into equipment, and for most manufacturers the primary design constraint is cost. Design depends on acceptance by the board of directors, according to Stanley Jungleib (1987), who works for synthesizer and sequencer manufacturer Sequential Circuits. There is thus a constant give-and-take between what Gambacurta (1987) calls "selling features" and "user features."

> A user feature is something that the final user will find useful, they will be glad it's there. Unfortunately sometimes it's not obvious that the feature is there at the point of sale. They will learn about it in use, after some time. A selling feature is something that sells the product but is not that important to the final user, may not be important to actual use. For instance, quite often flashing lights get somebody's attention in a store, but they're not going to help a guy use it, necessarily. They're going to help sell the product. A user feature might be something like pressing a button and getting a special mode. . . . As someone who would like to provide the end user with the best product possible I wouldn't like selling features. As someone who would like to sell as many products as possible and make as much money as possible, selling features are important.

As Cohen (1991) points out, "[i]nstruments [are] valued not only for their sound but for their visual qualities, particularly in relation to the image the band members wanted to present" (p. 135).

Reliability is as important as the most sophisticated design features. Though recording studios usually place equipment in a permanent rack fixture, musicians demand equipment that is going to withstand abuse on the road. Scott Wyatt (1987c), director of the University of Illinois' Experimental Music Studios and an internationally recognized composer, laments most equipment's lack of road worthiness. Dryden (1987) also criticized the lack of durability of much equipment, saying that

> we put . . . stress on reliability. We choose things that are durable, simple. Sometimes we have to take a chance on an unproven piece of equipment. For instance, we learned by taking the Emulator II [sampler] on a limited number of outside jobs that it wasn't constructed with as heavy steel as the Emulator I. Once you have the voices programmed, even though the Emulator I is more difficult to manipulate, in terms of software and editing voices . . . it's quite reliable in terms of calling up voices and playing. We ended up using the Emulator I because we've had it for two years, we know it's reliable, so we're not going to replace it with an Emulator II.

Reliability is crucial in the studio as well, in that many large studios charge anywhere from $100 to $200 an hour for recording time. Don Christensen (1987), an engineer at the Living Room, emphasized the cost of time as well as money lost by an equipment failure.

> You always look for reliability. We'll work continually, every day. Reliability is probably the most important factor, next to the [effects] box being able to do what it says. Which is amazing. A lot of boxes advertise that they do things which they don't do very well. A lot of it verges on fraud, it seems to me. I mean, you can always return a piece of equipment and get your money back, but what do you do about the five or six hours you spent trying to make the thing work? You don't get paid for that. On sequencing programs, you know, we've easily personally lost 20 to 50 hours of sequencing time. Obviously there's operator error, but often it's in software.

Wyatt (1987b) agrees that manufacturers do not always release the equipment they promise.

> You can get a lot of information from the manufacturers themselves but then you are left with the question of what does it *really* do and how good is it . . . specifications for the piece that was designed are not necessarily the specifications for the piece that was built. [There can be] differences between models and differences between units of the same models. And I think there's differences in what you hear.

A reputation for reliability can go a long way toward generating sales, and the more people use a company's equipment the more people will see it in use, hence the large logos on the back of most synthesizers and other gear. Endorsements are a common marketing tool for equipment makers.

Manufacturers will go to great lengths to achieve a good reputation and to foster an air of progress and improvement with each release of a piece of new equipment. For instance, before Scotch/3M introduced a new tape formulation, Scotch 250, they changed the formulation of their old tape. The old tape became more prone to wear. Users noticed a change, but did not know of 3M's reformulation of the tape. To them, it appeared as if there was a need for a new, improved tape. And the new tape certainly did perform better than (what they thought was) the old (Wyatt, 1987a).

Competition in the recording equipment industry is intense, and research and development costs approach those of the computer industry. The similarity between the two industries is not surprising, given that most new musical equipment technology relies on microprocessors and vast amounts of computer memory. As Ensoniq's Senior (1987) said,

> [We try] to keep the cost to an absolute minimum, for a number of reasons. One is that we would like to supply as high quality a technology as possible to as broad of a market, for altruistic and for business reasons. Since we do a lot of custom chip designs for our products, to amortize the cost of that you want to expect to sell tens of thousands of units. That's a conscious plan. Business people and the engineers try to live within those constraints and make a system do as much as it possibly can, substituting intelligent software for hardware wherever possible. Trying to bring our experience and intelligence as musicians to the process, streamline machines so they're quick and don't get in your way . . . it enables us to stay in business, to compete with the Japanese companies.

Competition with Japanese equipment makers is difficult for U.S.-based Ensoniq, ART, Alesis, and other U.S. manufacturers. Trade restrictions and "chip wars" affect U.S. musical equipment manufacturers as they do the computer industry. The idea Senior mentions of reaching as broad a market as possible is one that Yamaha adopted in the early 1980s when it designed the DX series of synthesizers. Yamaha's goal was to create a synthesizer that served a vast array of purposes, from studio recording to weddings. Yamaha equipment and the FM method of synthesis it employs were an industry standard throughout the 1980s, until increased computer memory enabled designers to use sound samples as starting points for synthesized sounds. FM synthesis is still the most common method of sound programming currently in use.

Equipment makers favor the kind of music that is most popular. In the broadest terms, this means that most recording and sound equipment is designed for popular music generally, rock and roll specifically. When asked about the irony of a musically non-Western country such as Japan's producing equipment for Western music, Tascam Corporation's Oren (1987) pointed out that

> It's damn difficult to reproduce [non-Western] music electronically. And look at where Yamaha is coming from. The heart of the DX-7 came from Stanford. That was their technology license. Really, what do you sell more of, traditional Japanese music played on the koto, or rock and roll? Rock and roll is common throughout the world, and they're really building instruments to create rock and roll. Or contemporary music, let me say it that way.

Wyatt (1987b), however, is critical of the manufacturers' design of equipment for the rock music market, because it does not allow creation of non-Western or even avant garde music. The following exchange illustrates the point.

> **Wyatt:** [A lot of equipment is] specifically geared for pop music. It's designed for a specific market. They're not designing it for music advancement, they're designing it to make money. It's a business.
>
> **Q:** Will that constrict music?
>
> **Wyatt:** I think it already does. The equipment is designed for that particular medium, for that kind of music. The restrictions in the equipment are based upon the desires and uses and performance practices for pop music. Though I must say the DX7II surprised me. [The DX7II has microtonal capability to reproduce non-Western scales.]
>
> **Q:** Was the DX7 an afterthought? Did they have people like you in mind when they redesigned it?
>
> **Wyatt:** Having had numerous conversations with Yamaha executives, I don't think they had us in mind at all. They're unaware of most microtonal work. I believe their concern and interest in adding multiple tuning capabilities came from some of the experimenters in the pop field. Laurie Anderson, Bo Tomlyn, Adrian Belew, Philip Glass. Yamaha and others will listen to those people.
>
> **Q:** Why?
>
> **Wyatt:** Based upon money. In this country the decisions are based upon how much money can be made from those people who

are going to purchase. It's unfortunate because to my knowledge Yamaha did not ask anyone in education who worked in this area of music. They did not talk to Ussachevsky, or Appleton, or Morton Subotnick. They got feedback from the dealers, but most people who go in [to stores] are from the pop world.

Ironically, during the recording of the soundtrack for *Powaqaatsi*, Philip Glass used digital samplers to tune non-Western South American and African instruments to Western scales to incorporate them into his music.

Regardless of design philosophy and financial constraints, then, the perception of rock and roll as the largest market for musical equipment means that equipment will be designed for rock music. It also means that the range of available sounds will be limited to those that designers and programmers envision to be popular in that market. Though this may not prove problematic to some musicians and composers, to those who create non-Western music it makes it extremely difficult to find useful gear. Synthesist Wendy Carlos went so far as to learn computer assembly language to reprogram synthesizers for microtonal capability on one of her recordings. Moreover, in that rock music is by nature loud and unsubtle, most equipment made for rock music does not have to meet very strict standards for dynamic range, frequency response and lack of noise.

Moog (1987) said that equipment designers may have a specific type of music in mind when developing a product.

If you walk down the hall and talk to our software engineers at Kurzweil and you ask them what kind of music should be played on the instruments we design here, you'll get a different answer for every person you talk to. . . . There are two different thought processes: how you put music together and how you put electronic instruments together. It's very unusual that a person has a lot of insight into musical innovation and into instrument design. . . . I've always collaborated . . . the first modules I built with Herb Deutsch, who was a composer, teacher [and] musician at Hofstra University.

Moog's comment encompasses several points. First, though an engineer may have an idea of what kind of music should be played on an instrument, other engineers who collaborate on a piece of equipment often have different ideas. Thus, just as in the production of music, film, television, and so on, it is rarely possible to pinpoint the "author" of an instrument. Second, and more important, Moog separates *musical innovation* and *instrument design*. Two possibilities arise. It could be that instruments are designed for rock music because designers are not innovators and therefore follow a path of least resistance when creating an instrument. Or, and I believe this is more likely, they truly do design equipment with as few restrictions as possible. It is, as Jungleib (1987) said, the board of directors that places economic constraints on design and, even more importantly, thinks of the equipment as tailored for the rock music market and *markets* it for rock and roll.

Again, the search for new sounds and the concept of authenticity become issues. Manufacturers are in some ways caught in a bind, because though designers want to create equipment that is flexible and does not restrict music making, they must also meet the demands of the market. Thus, if there is a particularly popular sound that many people will want to emulate, manufacturers will include it in their products. However, most equipment makers have trouble pinpointing their market. Beyond describing it as a rock music audience, few can narrow it further. Certain instruments have become standard equipment in a given genre of music (for instance, the Roland TR-808 drum machine is found in most all 1980s rap music).

It is difficult to establish marketing demographics in terms of music and musical genres. Those who do try to design instruments for particular forms of music point not to music, or even sound, but to "the kids" or "nightclub" and "bar" bands. Some see their market as the people who purchase home recording equipment, and others perceive their market to be large recording studios.

Regardless of their perception, though, most agree that popular sounds sell equipment. ART's Gambacurta (1987) said, referring to Phil Collins's drum sounds,

> We call those cliche sounds. The vast majority of the market is duplicating the sounds that they hear on records. They have to do

that, a nightclub band, whatever. Unfortunately, often products end up being designed that have the ability to do that. Sometimes it may take away from their ability to be a truly creative tool. I've always wanted to develop products that were truly creative tools, designed without any cliches in mind. But in terms of market demand cliche sounds are important. So we do think about those. If you make a reverb these days it has to be able to do a gated snare reverb that sounds like a Phil Collins snare sound. You can't do that, you won't sell it. A studio engineer can usually do it with the tools he's got. The guy on the street wants to get that sound and not take two hours to do it. He wants to be able to hit a button and get it.

The market the manufacturers identify is often termed the *push-and-play* or *plug-and-play* market. It consists of people who do not want to get very involved in the technical aspect of recording and music making, but who do want to perform or create music. As mentioned in Chapter 3, an industry has sprung up around the selling of sounds for this market, as has a further twist on the debate concerning authenticity. As synthesizer programmers create sounds-du-jour for those who want to play and not program their synthesizers, the equipment industry as a whole designs many of its products with push-and-play people in mind.

Regardless of their economic value to the industry, the push-and-play people are usually derided by professionals in the music industry. Steven Cox (1987) described the difference between the push-and-play people and others this way:

> I think there's always going to be the push-and-play people, the folks who want it to actually make a sound they like when they turn it on because they do not want to go too much further with it. But there's going to be the upper whatever percent that is, ten percent, that really take the time and trouble to learn what the limits of an instrument are.

Cox's remark, that it is the "upper . . . ten percent" that will "learn what the limits of an instrument are," acknowledges that the vast majority of those making music are push-and-play people. The idea that someone who programs one's own equipment, or creates one's own sounds, is somehow more honest, authentic and sincere than someone who buys sounds has become common.

Push-and-play people are not synonymous with amateurs. Jimmy Jam and Terry Lewis, producers of Janet Jackson, the Human League, and other popular acts, claim that they do not have time to experiment with equipment (Doerschuk, 1987). Jam said,

> When I look at a synthesizer, I go for the presets. If the presets aren't happening, I don't want it. I don't have time to be fooling around. I just want to punch through some stuff, hit a sound, and say, "Oh yeah. This is it." I mean, people get paid at the factory to put programs in it . . . I'm not getting paid to get sounds out of a machine. I'm getting paid to make a record. (p. 80)

Cox (1987) went on to describe the effect those people have on equipment design:

> The marketplace has to toe the line. The operating system for the [Akai] S900 [sampler] for example, could have been much more elaborate than it is in actuality. But the cost would not be justified by the number of people ever using the features. You reach a point to where you offer what you can but then, yes you are playing to the plug-and-play people. Emulator sales are still doing very well even though there's three or four other brands on the market with a superior sound, because of their library and their support group.

An editorial in *Music Technology* magazine succinctly identified the problem:

> once an instrument has been successfully launched . . . it seems all rival manufacturers want to do is imitate its success by offering something very similar. . . . The manufacturers aren't entirely to blame for this . . . it isn't the manufacturers that decide which application of technology will be the most popular.
>
> The sets of disks that musicians, engineers and producers ask for as soon as a new sampler is announced (piano, strings, brass—all sounds which have been around for hundreds of years) give some clue to the kind of new ground most people are planning to break when they invest in new technology.
>
> But this isn't entirely the fault of the end users, either. Because like everybody else, even top players and producers need to stay in touch with musical fashion to keep the checks coming in. (New Horizons, 1986, p. 2; © Music Makers Publications)

Cox's opinion (1987) is that manufacturers do not do a good job of designing the user interface and therefore aggravate both the push-and-play people and the advanced user. When asked if equipment is designed for push-and-play use, he replied that

> the user interface is an area that is not even being covered. . . . I don't think [push-and-play use] excludes [advanced use] necessarily. User interface is I think where we're lacking in musical equipment. The equipment itself has capabilities far beyond the average user. But is that the user's fault or the designer's fault in that he didn't make it easier to get to? A Macintosh has many of its features easier to find than an IBM, even though they both have many features. The fact is Macintosh took the trouble to draw you a picture. And it gave you a place to point and shoot. So your natural curiosity leads you down a lane. MS-DOS is a language you have to learn. One is going to lead itself to childlike play much more than the other.

Everything from the placement of knobs and other controls to the writing of a manual contributes to the user interface. Jungleib (1987), who writes manuals for Sequential Circuits, said, "When you're doing a user interface you have to work backwards . . . you have to go from the top down." In other words, the purpose of an instrument or one of its function must be discerned, then all the steps leading to fulfillment of that function described. The increased use of computers for music production has had an effect on the user manual in that computers regularly offer help screens that are, in effect, on-line manuals. Jungleib (1987) believes most manuals will be available as help screens before long.

Cost can determine which features may or may not be included in a tape recorder, sequencer or other piece of equipment, and hardware and software design may also limit an instrument's flexibility. These limitations can also significantly affect the user interface, and thereby affect the process of recording and music making. Lehrman (1987) pointed out the effect such limitations have on music making with the Total Music sequencer.

> We're like any manufacturer of equipment that has a user interface, whether it's a car, or a recording console, or a synthesizer. Ideally what you have is an environment in which you can do anything.

That's what we were trying to do. We wanted to make it really flexible so that people could essentially do anything they wanted with it, but we recognized that at a certain level we had to make choices. There's just so much you can put on a computer screen at a time. We had to decide what's the way most people are going to want to use this. [A reviewer] criticized it for excessive modality, meaning that you had to use it in a certain way. And he was right. But we were hoping that that way would be the most common way to use it, and there would be other ways of using it that would be less visible.

Ultimately design considerations affect not only the usefulness and quality of musical equipment but also the process of music making. The design of a sequencer, for example, affects the way it is used. For the musician and composer the difficulty lies in not only learning to use a sequencer or other equipment but also in deciding what to purchase.

The Market and the Marketplace

The manufacturers and consumers of musical equipment agree that versatility, reliability, and cost are the most important considerations for evaluating a piece of equipment. Manufacturers design equipment with those points taken into account. Consumers (generally musicians, studio engineers, studio owners, and producers) go about evaluating that equipment in several ways.

Some are able to evaluate equipment professionally, as beta-testers. If they are not given the equipment they are testing outright, then they can usually purchase it at a substantially reduced price. Some consumers are able to attend the North American Music Merchants (NAMM), Audio Engineering Society (AES) and Consumer Electronics Show (CES) conventions, and to preview equipment before it is on the market.

However, most musicians rely on reports of these conventions in magazines such as *Mix*, *Electronic Musician* and *Music Technology*. The magazines also review equipment, and run advertisements that contain information about equipment specifications. Wyatt (1987b) explained that he determines what equipment is available and what is being released by "reading the trade journals, talking with people all over the country, and talking with enthusiasts who work with equipment and have access to the information. That's basically it."

Without actually using the equipment it is difficult to know what it can do, and perhaps more important, what it will sound like. Wyatt (1987b) described the process as "flipping quarters." He echoed the concerns of most consumers when he said, "I am trying to make a selection of equipment that can be versatile in its own right and constructed in such a manner that it will last for more than 2 or 3 years."

Not only are equipment purchasers concerned with physical longevity—that is, with how long the equipment will work—they are also concerned with determining how long the equipment will *sound* contemporary before it and its sounds become obsolete. In the headlong rush of new product introduction, equipment makers will make instruments obsolete within weeks of their availability to consumers (creating an enormous used equipment marketplace that, in its turn, has been a blessing for low-budget and home recording studio setups).

When selecting equipment for Glass's Living Room studio, according to Dan Dryden (1987), "descriptions, mostly from technical journals, and knowledge of the basic types of equipment groups" helped determine what piece to get. "If before we've had good results with a manufacturer in terms of the device doing what they say it will, reliably, then we would tend to go to them first. . . . We usually know what we need, then it's a matter of doing a little investigative work by talking to dealers, manufacturers, maybe a technician."

Price often determines an equipment purchase. Dryden (1987) said that the Living Room will often rent a piece of equipment for a specific session. For instance, though he prefers the recording quality of the Mitsubishi 32-track digital recorder, the high price prevents the Living Room from purchasing it. That does not stop them from renting it for an occasional session, especially when it is one for a record or film score that will bring enough money in to cover the cost of the recorder. Also, in that the studio is not used

solely for recording, buying a digital recorder is not a good idea.
Dryden explained that

> a lot of things we can do without the thing sitting here, like program-
> ming sequencers. You don't need a machine to develop voices, pro-
> gram synthesizers. When a machine costs $180,000 you don't want it
> sitting around not doing anything. We've got the analog machine and
> we can do most of our work on that, and then projects with budgets
> that allow [it], and the aesthetic need is demanded, dynamics, lack of
> noise, and number of tracks, we bring in the (32-track) machine. If the
> scope of the project requires that piece of equipment to realize it to its
> best sound, you bring in the piece of machinery that will best suit
> your need.

Wyatt (1987b) believes that price is the most important consideration when purchasing equipment.

> I believe the consumer makes decisions based upon purchase power,
> and what it comes down to is monthly payments or what they're
> shelling out at that moment. I don't know too many people who make
> decisions based on anything else. You try to get the best equipment
> for the amount of money you have.

Cost certainly seems to be of paramount importance for people
with home recording studios, judging by its emphasis in the reviews of equipment found in magazines and trade journals.

The Living Room is in an odd position relative to other studios,
but illustrates cost-cutting by way of equipment rental. It is not
quite a commercial studio, yet neither is it a home studio. In that
its principal owners are Glass, his producer Kurt Munkacsi, and
Glass's keyboard player Michael Reisman, the studio can be kept
quite busy with Glass's material. "We're primarily a service for the
individuals who own the studio," Rory Johnston (1987), the Living
Room's manager, said, and little commercial work is taken in.
Though that is changing, especially as Munkacsi becomes involved
producing other artists, it means that the Living Room does not
have the big budget that a large studio, such as New York's Unique
or Power Station. On the other hand, neither is it constrained by

the small music-related income of most home studios. A smaller studio could not even afford to rent a 32-track digital recorder. A larger studio can afford to buy one, because digital is "the way the industry [is] going to go" (Jacobson, 1987, p. 61).

Most larger studios, however, feel that client demand does not yet justify the expense of a multitrack digital recorder. One Nashville studio has not recouped its money three years after purchasing a Mitsubishi 32-track (Jacobson, 1987). Still, to stay competitive, most larger studios are buying digital recorders.

Johnston (1987) emphasized the economic aspect when deciding on equipment purchases.

> There [is] a desire always to get better equipment, but it's predicated on what you can really afford and what's absolutely necessary. As you get more and more into refining your system you want to make it better and better and as you use it you discover things about it that you're not totally satisfied with. A lot of this stuff does become obsolete. There is a lot of equipment in studios these days that is rented rather than bought because the investment to buy it is so huge and it does become outdated quickly. It's more economical, makes more sense, to be on a rental basis.

For musicians or groups not signed to a record label, equipment purchases are few and far between. Stories of equipment stealing abound, too; perhaps the most notorious has the Sex Pistols stealing some of David Bowie's equipment before a Bowie performance in London. Equipment ownership confers a kind of status, regardless of whether the equipment is a vintage guitar or a just-made-public synthesizer. As Sara Cohen (1991) pointed out in her study of Liverpool rock culture, most musicians are skilled at wheeling, dealing, and otherwise managing to scrounge equipment.

> Some saw the acquisition and accumulation of such gear as a means of achieving status or success. . . . Most band members showed great determination in acquiring their gear [and] employed considerable ingenuity in raising money to acquire what they wanted. [One] spent two weeks in hospital as a volunteer for drug experiments to raise money for his band. (p. 50)

Though price is often the determining factor, equipment performance is evaluated by producers and engineers as well as musicians. Although magazines from *Musician* to *Music Technology* contain equipment reviews, there are few ways an equipment buyer can compare different products, especially because dealers and other retail outlets tend to stock products by only a handful of companies, much as automobile dealers sell only one or two brands of autos. It is, of course, possible to go to an equipment retailer and try out *some* different models. However, a retail store is not an ideal location for trying out equipment. It can be noisy, and it rarely approximates a studio situation. Much information about equipment is passed on by word of mouth.

Few people find a piece of equipment that does everything they would like, and musicians, producers, and engineers often modify or build their own equipment. Bob Bielecki (1987), an engineer at the Living Room, custom builds equipment for Laurie Anderson and LaMonte Young, among others. Bernard Sumner, of the group New Order, said, "There isn't a sequencer on the market that can do what we want. I'm going to try and learn (about them) so we can build our own" (*Joy Division/New Order*, p. 118).

But the big problem for equipment buyers is obsolescence, especially considering the rapid pace with which manufacturers upgrade or delete their products. And, as new products are released, the price of old equipment falls dramatically. For instance, the Tascam Portastudio four-track cassette recorder retailed for around $1,000 when it was released. Since then the price has fallen by over half, and Tascam has issued new Portastudios with better specifications and more features. Likewise, the ART 01a digital reverb was approximately $1,100 when it was released in 1985, but it has since been deleted by ART. And, given the large number of inexpensive digital reverbs, its resale price has fallen to around $200 or less. Audio engineer Tom Curley (1987) said, "I have a Mirage, I mean I have an antique, one of the originals, I don't even have one of the new ones. I paid $1800 for a brand new Mirage and they bring out this new one in stereo with a better signal to noise ratio and it costs $1200."

Not only is it the equipment that can become old and outdated but the sounds it is used to create may also go out of favor. People may tire of them, or new sounds may come into use that cannot be made with old equipment. The use value of a piece of equipment is directly related to its flexibility. As Jonathan Pines (1987), producer, engineer and co-owner of Private Audio, a 24-track recording studio, said, "If a new . . . microphone, effects box, or new way of recording only has one or two applications . . . then I'm only interested in it if I can get it on a record quickly . . . then forget about it."

Despite the threat of obsolescence, old equipment does not necessarily lose value. With fluctuations in the Japanese yen, not all equipment has fallen in price. For instance, in the Spring of 1987 the yen rose dramatically against the dollar, and U.S. trade sanctions against Japan were put in place. The Fostex Model 80 8-track recorder went up in price, and its resale value followed. Equipment prices, it must be remembered, are also connected to the price of microprocessors and computer memory, and it is the decreasing cost of memory that has brought the price of much equipment within reach of most home studio owners.

Old equipment is still used by many musicians, producers and engineers for reasons that parallel rock music's concern for authenticity. In much the same way that guitarists, pianists or violinists prefer older instruments, those involved in recording often prefer old recording equipment. For instance, Mark Rubel (1984), owner of a 16-track recording studio, keeps a mixing board from the 1960s because it has a "nice, warm 60s tube sound." Recording engineer Bruce Swedien (1987) (known for his work with jazz and rock artists from Quincy Jones to Michael Jackson) said about purchasing new microphones that

> my suggestion would be to try and find a used A.K.G. 414eb, or better yet a pair. That's one of the better all-around mikes available. The new version of the 414 sounds like doo-doo to me, so a used one would be a great investment in sound. I don't know how much they go for used these days. I have six of them of my own. I hand-picked them myself, they are in perfect condition.

In other words, equipment is still useful even if a new or improved model is released. Certain equipment will have a characteristic sound that may be valuable to one person and not another. And equipment that has several applications usually retains its value for a longer time.

Regardless of the pace of technology, musicians, producers, and engineers are resigned to dealing with the equipment marketplace. As Wyatt (1987d) said, "the trick is to get something, use it, and sell it while you can." Curley (1987) agreed, and correctly associated the problem of obsolescence with the problem of user interfacing and push-and-play design.

> Don't ever sit and wait for something better because you're never going to buy something, it doesn't matter. You go out and buy the top of the line of whatever you want today and three months from now it's going to be an antique. But by the same token, I could spend the rest of my life playing with that Mirage [sampler] and I could never begin to plumb its potential. This is true of any synthesizer. As a matter of fact, that is a big danger of this big revolution, that a lot of people don't give a crap about what this thing can do, they just plug it in and dial it and if they like the sounds they go with it. They never really get to know the instrument because [in] a few months something better comes along and that's what they want to play with. It's a fact of nature. The same thing happens in the computer industry. I finally got around to picking up an IBM PC, a clone and now everyone is saying, "oh, the new IBMs are coming out." In 10 years the computers we own now are going to look like dinosaurs. That's a fact of life in the electronic industry. It's going to constantly improve and everything you buy is going to be constantly out of date. There is no reason why you still can't produce stuff on it.

One of the most significant problems musicians, producers, and engineers face today is equating creativity with the latest technology as Stanley Jungleib (1987) said, "You can always hold off buying something, but at what point do you really jump in? You have a 12-bit sampler as opposed to a 16-bit sampler doesn't mean you're a failure." Perhaps the bottom line is this: Owning the latest equipment is no guarantee of good music—or of success, financial or artistic.

5

Technology, Music, and Copyright

Copyright

Authorship, uniqueness, reproducibility, and a host of other issues occupy the business and legal transactions in the American music industry. Within that framework, copyright has traditionally been an author's protection against the copying and pirating of music. It has also been used by record companies for the same purpose, as they, and music publishers, often own the copyrights to songs. Copyright ownership has been a means for record companies to ensure income during periods of low sales. Copyrights are bought, sold, and exploited via licensing fees and royalties. But new technologies that enable a diffusion of authorship and ready reproduction are wreaking havoc with traditional copyright protection. Music is by no means the only creative field struggling with copyright problems. The U.S. film industry is still engaged in negotiation over videotape copying of films, and the computer software industry has been plagued by copyright difficulties since its beginnings.

The U.S. government has provided a means of copyrighting music since passage of the Copyright Act of 1909. In 1972, an amendment to the Copyright Act provided for copyrighting of "sound recordings." Four years later, the 1976 Copyright Act

provided copyright protection for both published and unpublished sound recordings.

The 1976 Copyright Act defines sound recordings as

> works that result from the fixation of a series of musical, spoken, or
> other sounds, but not including the sounds accompanying a motion
> picture or other audiovisual work, regardless of the nature of the
> material objects, such as disks, tapes, or other phonorecords, in which
> they are embodied. (Copyright Act, 1976)

The biggest and most recent controversy over copyright concerns home taping of records and compact discs. Though beginning in the mid- and late 1970s, when the recording industry's sales
slumped, it has taken on altogether new meanings with the development of digital recording.

The late 1970s found U.S. record companies no longer enjoying
steady, predictable sales. Home taping shared the blame with a
depressed economy and a stagnant musical climate. The cassette
had become a widespread high-fidelity means of taping records,
radio shows—music from all sources. Concerned that home taping
was cutting into record sales, the recording industry began advertising home taping as theft, and pursued the U.S. Congress to
amend copyright laws. Home taping, the industry reasoned, is
copyright infringement.

Little came of these lobbying efforts, however. In the early 1980s,
several home electronics manufacturers began marketing dubbing
cassette decks, essentially double cassette decks that enable duplication from just the one machine. The recording industry (in the
form of the Recording Industry Association of America, Inc., the
RIAA) again unsuccessfully lobbied Congress, this time for a tax
on dubbing decks. The reasoning was the same as with home
taping, but the industry went slightly further in their demands.
They originally called for a tax on both single and dubbing cassette
decks, with money collected to be distributed to recording artists.
The pay scale the industry suggested virtually mirrored the top
record charts, in that presumably those artists with the highest
record sales would also have their recordings copied most.

A bill was presented before the U.S. House of Representatives in 1985 (H.R. 2911, 1985) that proposed a tax on blank tape and tape recorders. Known as the Home Audio Recording Act, the bill included a penny per minute tax on blank tape, a tax of 10% of the retail cost on tape recorders, and a tax of 25% of the retail cost on dubbing tape decks. Money collected was to be divided among record companies and distributed to copyright owners, but no mechanism of distribution was established.

Although the law was to exempt individuals taping their own records, amateur musicians, and others who were purchasing tape recorders for their own musical use, there was no mention of how subsequent use would be determined at the time of purchase. The bill, though at one time tenuously connected to the Parents' Music Resource Center record rating issue, did not pass Congress. The *Washington Post* reported (Harrington, 1986) that the RIAA was moving its headquarters to Washington, D.C., to better lobby Congress for home taping bills and to pursue another legislative avenue, source licensing for film and television music. Source licensing is primarily concerned with residual payments for composers whose music is broadcast on television. Broadcast Music, Inc. (BMI) and the American Society of Composers and Publishers (ASCAP) are currently involved in litigation over source licensing in an effort to increase such income.

The recording industry's next lobbying effort came in the wake of the development of Digital Audio Tape (DAT). Regarded as the ultimate in home taping, DAT works on the same principles as the compact disc. Sound is sampled and reproduced digitally, with no distortion from copy to copy. In other words, dubbing a record or compact disc onto DAT does not produce a copy, it produces a clone, an exact replica. The threat to the recording industry is thus greater with DAT, as little or no copy degradation occurs. Presumably some home tapers were discouraged by the noise and hiss added to each copy generation, and DAT produces little to no noise and hiss. And, because compact discs are digitally recorded to begin with, DAT would be the perfect medium for copying CDs.

The problem was one the computer software industry faced from the start—protecting a product that is simultaneously creative and unique yet by definition copyable. Ultimately, some computer software began including copy protection devices that would cause a program to self-destruct or prevent copying. The recording industry opted for a similar solution for DAT by lobbying Congress for a trade bill that would force DAT manufacturers to include anticopying devices in their machines. The anticopying mechanism would read information from a compact disc and respond to a message to lock a DAT deck out of record mode.

Though successfully demonstrated in prototypes, the mechanism is expensive and produces a noticeable difference in sound when compared to machines without the anticopying mechanism. DAT manufacturers are (at best) reluctant to raise the cost of an already expensive device, and feel that the record companies should take the initiative in preventing copying; after all, they are the ones providing the software.

By 1991 DAT decks were available in the United States for around $600, with digital codes embedded in prerecorded DAT tapes (of which there are few on the market—due, in part, to the small size of DAT tapes and difficulties packaging insert material with the tape) that enable only one digital-to-digital copy from a tape. However, this code does not prevent multiple analog-digital or analog-analog copying. The development of digital radio is not overlooking inclusion of a similar copy-protection mechanism that will render copyrighted programs noncopyable.

It seems likely, then, that the record industry is less interested in home taping (for most home tapers would not be unhappy with the quality of a DAT-to-DAT analog-analog copy) and wishes to prevent digital copying that could lead to digital mastering and mass production and piracy. The dilemma faced by the recording industry is based primarily on the copying and piracy of compact discs (CDs), perhaps the industry's savior from its mid-1970s doldrums, and not records, because CDs are virtually perfect copies of the master tape.

The industry was slow to switch over to compact disc, but since the mid-1980s CD sales are booming and record companies are quickly capitalizing on the CD market. Part of the reason for their initial sluggishness in releasing CDs lay in the large capital cost of manufacturing CDs. However, the tremendous sums made by record companies reissuing albums on CD (albums for which recording costs have already been paid) brought in the necessary cash (Kagan, 1990). And, now that manufacturing costs are falling, the industry is immediately faced with pirating problems as it becomes affordable for pirates to press compact discs.

Record companies are also concerned that consumers will prefer DAT over CD because they can record on DAT. Technology to record sound on blank CDs is currently available, though very expensive and within reach only of the largest audio mastering facilities. The cost of CD-R (Compact Disc Recording) technology will, however, most likely fall as other such technology has, and Philips and Sony are both at work creating consumer versions of the equipment available to mastering labs. It is also likely that consumers will prefer a format that fits existing hardware, and Philips's DCC (Digital Compact Cassette) will probably be more popular than DAT, as its playback equipment will be compatible with analog cassettes.

DAT is currently becoming a pro-audio technology in the United States. To succeed in the consumer market it will have to address U.S. consumer tastes that are accustomed to purchasing products that include extensive graphics and artwork—the CD's biggest struggle was overcoming lack of space for artwork, posters, lyric sheets, and the like, a major incentive for many purchasers. DAT tapes are too small to provide adequate space for all but the minutest graphics.

In a landmark compromise achieved during the summer of 1991, record companies (represented by the RIAA) and DAT manufacturers (represented by the Electronic Industries Association, the EIA) agreed to jointly call for the introduction and support of legislation for a tax on blank digital tape and digital tape recorders. A fund will be established with collections from that tax, under the agreement, which will be administered and distributed by the U.S. Copyright Office. It is currently planned that

the fund will consist of two parts. One-third of the payments will
go toward the music composition fund which will be split 50/50
between music publishers and songwriters. The other, the sound
recording fund, represents the other two-thirds of the royalty. That's
where record labels, artists and backup singers are paid from. (Block,
1991, p. SR14)

The implications of this agreement are startling, and not only
because it represents the first time that hardware and software
manufacturers have reached a compromise. The agreement sets up
a framework for other compromises in other media spheres (computers and software, for instance). And, its wording, which is not
specific to DAT, makes it applicable to new digital recording technologies, such as optical disk formats, when they become available
to the public.

Though such tax legislation was introduced in the U.S. House
and Senate in the fall of 1991, it faces lengthy hearings and revi-
sions. It is also encountering opposition from consumer groups,
who claim, among other things, that most consumers copy recordings for their own use (for playback in their car, for instance). The
legislation will also encounter opposition from musicians who
claim that if they are not signed to a major record label they are
being unfairly taxed, in that their tape and tape recorder purchases
may be for professional use (i.e., not for dubbing of prerecorded
tapes).

These arguments are upheld by a 1989 U.S. congressional study
that showed "that a large majority of people who copied from
prerecorded music in their last taping session copied their own
recording for their own use" (U.S. Congress, 1989, p. 11). Moreover,
opposition will come from those who believe that it is the major
record labels who will profit from the royalty, unless an ironclad
payment structure is created that includes a mechanism of payment to independent record labels and unsigned artists.

Given the sheer lobbying power of the RIAA and EIA, it is likely
that such legislation will pass. Yet the consumer seems content to
continue purchasing analog cassettes. And as long as a digital tape
costs $15 and a CD costs $12, few people will be purchasing digital
tape on which to copy CDs.

Sound and Copyright

Despite the publicity surrounding home taping and copyright legislation, little has been made public about a pending U.S. (and, indeed, international) copyright problem—the ownership of sound. Modern synthesizers have enabled creation of unique sounds, and some of the programmers and musicians who create the sounds are keeping close watch on copyright matters. The issues can be roughly divided into two categories and are currently the scene of great debate in the United States. First, there is the issue of digital sampling of sound. Musicians involved in the recording of popular music have a habit of referring to sounds created by other musicians. For instance, during a recording session, a drummer may ask the engineer if he could get a "Phil Collins" type of drum sound. As one engineer said,

> For me the most pressure comes when an artist or producer says "I want this sort of sound" and I have to give it to them or else they'll get someone else who will. It's especially tough if it's something another artist has done because then there's no excuse. He got it so why can't you? Like one time I got a call from this guy the day before his session and he said, "I want the drums to sound like the drums on the Elton John album." That night I got hold of the album and listened to it at home and figured out ways to do it. (Kealy, 1974, p. 136)

Equipment manufacturers design effects units with the thought that they should make it easy to reproduce hit sounds. But an even easier method of reproducing many hit sounds is to sample them. Synthesizers such as the Ensoniq Mirage, Kurzweil 250, Fairlight, Akai S900, and many others, permit recording of sound events and subsequent manipulation and playback via a keyboard. Thus a musician can sample the drum sounds from a Led Zeppelin record, for instance, assign the bass drum to one key of the keyboard, the snare drum to another, cymbals to another, and so on. This of course does not mean that the musician can then *play* drums like John Bonham of Led Zeppelin, but he can *sound* like John Bonham—that is of crucial importance.

The second category that U.S. copyright legislators are struggling over is the copying of synthesized sounds by means other than sampling. Much of the problem revolves around the programming industry's selling of sounds. As with the computer software industry, there is little to prevent someone from purchasing a set of sounds and copying them at will. And, there is little to prevent someone from hearing a sound on a recording and programming that sound themselves with their own synthesizer.

The point is almost moot in fact, in that many of the most popular recordings use sounds that are created by the manufacturer, and consumers find them built into the synthesizer. They are, in computer software terms, public domain sounds. That is, they are free to be copied. A problem arises, however, because once they are used on a recording, it could be argued that the copyright notice on the record covers the sounds. Two forms of copyright can be filed for a published (i.e., publicly released) recording in the United States: a "circle C" which denotes a musical copyright, and a "circle P" which denotes copyright of the sound recording. As synthesist and programmer Bryan Bell said, "The circle P copyright is for the whole record album. The musical copyright is 8 bars or whatever it is. The circle P is for anything that's on there for any amount of time. Sounds included" (Bell, 1987).

The solution to these problems is by no means simple. For one thing, sampling and synthesis are intimately connected to concepts of authorship and authenticity. Public reaction to the introduction of the RCA Electronic Music Synthesizer, in 1955, set the terms of the debate between synthesis and acoustic instruments:

> Although crude-sounding, the results nevertheless came near to the actual qualities of the instruments, near enough to make them almost credible. As for the "new" sounds, that will have to be left to the creative musician rather than to the engineer to exploit . . . the synthesizer . . . could be made to reproduce the sound characteristics not only of an orchestra, but of its concert hall as well. There would be no need for the recording director to tour churches, auditoriums and theaters in quest of the "perfect" acoustical setup. . . . More important, the primary function of such a mechanism should not be to *imitate* the quality of existing sounds, but to create and experiment

with new sound . . . the synthesizer may some day offer remarkable opportunities to the composer—provided he has the patience and skill to manoeuvre his way around the complicated [electronics]. (Lawrence, 1955, p. 10)

The author was being quite open-minded. Musicians' unions had quite a different reaction, stemming from the fear that eventually there would be no need for the performer. Frederick Dorian (1942) foresaw the problem and wrote, "We have only to think of the possibility of an apparatus that will permit the composer to transmit his music directly into a recording medium without the help of the middleman interpreter" (p. 342). The debate centers on whether there is a need for live performers or not. In popular music, the synthesizer quickly gained acceptance in progressive rock, but in traditional rock forms it is still frowned upon. The synthesizer is inherently dishonest, the argument goes, because it imitates acoustic instruments and therefore presumably does not require the skill necessary to play an acoustic instrument. Brian Blain (Frith, 1986), British Musicians' Union publicity and promotion officer, gave the typical unionist perspective, saying that

the Union does seek to limit the use of synthesizers where they would be used to deprive orchestras of work. . . . However, I think it is to the Union's credit that we see the essential difference between that use of the synthesizer where it is clearly taking work away from "conventional" musicians and its use in a self-contained band where there would not normally be any question of another conventional musician being used. . . . It is hopeless to look for a totally consistent view but I must say that I see a big difference between a synthesizer in a band, which at least requires a musician to play it, and a machine which takes the place of a musician. (p. 264)

The drum synthesizer is particularly frowned on by rock and roll fans because it not only produces drum sounds but can also play rhythm patterns on its own. Sequencers also occupy a similarly less-privileged place.

The debate has shifted somewhat since about 1985 from duplication of acoustic instrument sounds to duplication of sounds in general. This may be due to the widespread use of synthesizers for electronic sounds and the public's quick acceptance of those sounds.

To couch the debate in terms of performance, however, is inappropriate. A performer of some kind or other is needed no matter the instrument. Even a sequencer or recorder needs someone to operate it. A more appropriate site for the debate is within the terms of the value of sound, for as recording technology has made the concept of "playing" music slippery, all one has left to use to determine authenticity is sound.

Bryan Bell has worked with many musicians, from Herbie Hancock to Neil Young. He founded a service called Synthbank that exists to publish sounds. It is "a consortium of professional programmers provid[ing] consulting services . . . a publisher of commercial sounds that can actually be bought and sold" (Bell, 1987). Synthbank, according to Bell, was "started to protect the authorship of the intellectual property and programming of sound." By regarding sound as intellectual property, the question of musical copyright takes on different dimensions. In effect, sound itself can be regarded as a creative work, apart from music.

Though Bell began it several years ago, Synthbank has not become a prominent player in the music industry. Part of it is located in the Performing Artists Network (PAN). Via PAN, Synthbank users can upload and download sounds by calling the data base from their computer.

The reason it will take Synthbank some time to get off the ground, if it ever fully does, is that copyright laws prevent its operation. The U.S. Copyright Office simply does not provide a means for copyrighting sound *apart from music*. The copyright office does make a provision for copyrighting sounds on their Form SR. One paragraph states:

> Use Form SR for copyright registration of published or unpublished sound recordings. . . . [B]riefly describe the type of sounds fixed in the recording. For example: "Sound Effects"; "Bird Calls"; "Crowd Noises." (Form SR, 1976)

The form defines sound recordings as "works that result from the fixation of a series of musical, spoken, or other sounds" (Form

SR, 1976). But the main problem is one of notation—how to submit a sound for copyright. Bell related his brush with copyright law.

> The copyright [for Synthbank's sounds] has taken us over two years to get. . . . Because they just went through a whole bunch of rewording in the law, in the grey area of the law, at considerable expense to try to get this more clearly identified in terms of commercial property . . . it's been a major hassle . . . I've been back and forth with the copyright office and my lawyer's office, about 15 times. We just sent in a final application but we have not received confirmation of its acceptance yet, but as far as the dialogue between my attorneys and the senior examiner, we've gotten everything in that we were supposed to . . . it'll be an acceptance of how to copyright. It'll be what format they have decided on as satisfactory, from that standpoint, it'll be a precedent. . . . It's just a matter of whether they classify it as a sound recording or a computer program. It's a clarification of what kind of intellectual property it is. It's a matter of whether it's backed up by source code or what kind of file. . . . Once it's done that will give us the ability to copyright sound. . . . We've been holding back on sounds because we've been working on this thing. (Bell, 1987)

As a sound publisher, Bell must place financial value on synthesizer programs and samples. His solution is pragmatic.

> Placing a value on the sound is, whether or not it's saleable, if it's unique or not unique. As far as the actual commercial value of a sound, I pretty much affix that to the instrument. You know, something like a Casio sound or a DX7 sound is about a dollar, say. A Chroma sound or an Oberheim is about two dollars. But when you get into the high end samplers like a piano for a Fairlight, that would be $200 . . . it's more in terms of what the user is going to get out of it. If the user can get 32 DX7 sounds for 32 dollars, that is a fair market value. Someone who has a Fairlight [and] is making a professional recording can pay $200 for the sample. So we are trying to attach the service to the value it has to the user. When it gets down to samples, it's the amount of time it took to make the samples. (Bell, 1987)

According to Bell, response to Synthbank from musicians has been excellent. And Synthbank provides a payment structure for programmers, without discriminating between professional programmers and amateurs.

The legal problems remain, however, regardless of the change in copyright law that Bell foresees. Just as nothing stops the consumer from copying a record onto cassette, nothing prevents someone buying a sound from Synthbank and copying it for a friend. Though a useful distinction can be made between someone who copies a sound and then uses it for a published recording (as the distinction is made between home taping and pirating) the difficulty of determining copyright infringement is tremendous. One would expect an enormous amount of litigation. Bell said,

> The point is that if a sound is made unrecognizable to an expert witness, [there will be] no case. If they play the record and play the sample and a jury can't tell the difference [there will be] no case . . . [there will be much litigation] but Columbia [Records] has 250 lawyers on call at all times, so some joker ripping off sounds to do McDonald's commercials will get sued. Synthbank was actually the devil's advocate for the consumer, saying let's protect the artist before the record companies do, and pay a royalty on sounds and distribute them to everybody and fairly, but pay the author. As far as I know I pay the highest rate. (Bell, 1987)

One can expect record companies to become involved immediately. In general, the circle P copyright is owned by the record company; will record companies claim ownership of sounds and samples?

The solution of having a jury decide whether copyright infringement of a sound has occurred is not as simple as it seems. First, in the case of infringement of a piece of music, court cases can take days and weeks. Second, it is hard to imagine that sound could be the only determinant of infringement. For instance, if an infringement of the sound of a car crash was claimed, and the sound of the two car crashes in question did sound alike but were taken from different accidents, would there be infringement? If Led Zeppelin's drum sound were sampled, and the frequencies between 700 Hz and 1kHz removed by equalization, would that be infringement? And one has to wonder about implications of precedent in other areas: what might happen to impersonators such as Rich Little? What of intent to infringe? What of prior access? And with the difficulty in determining authorship on modern pop records, how would one determine who is responsible for an infringement?

Sampling has created resentment among some musicians, which the following, excerpted from a *Wall Street Journal* article (Miller, 1987), illustrates.

> Frank Doyle, a New York engineer, recently plugged into his sampler the sound of Madonna screaming "hey!" on her song "Like a Virgin," raised it an octave and dropped the new sound into a few parts of a coming song by Jamie Bernstein. He took a horn blast from a James Brown song and turned it into a lush, mellow tone for a Japanese singer's love ballad. "I didn't feel at all like I was ripping James Brown off," he says.
>
> That's not the way James Brown sees it. "Anything they take off my record is mine," says the soul-music pioneer. . . . "Is it all right if I take some paint off your house and put it on mine? Can I take a button off your shirt and put it on mine? Can I take a toenail off your foot—is that all right with you?" (p. 1)

Frank Zappa, who features sampled sounds prominently on his recent recordings, included the following statement on his *Jazz From Hell* LP: "Unauthorized reproduction/sampling is a violation of applicable laws and subject to criminal prosecution." Most musicians alter beyond recognition the sounds that they sample. Sampling is a means of easily acquiring raw sound material, and shaping it is part of the creative process. A description of a recent concert performance using a sophisticated sampler illustrates sampling's potential:

> I recently attended a concert . . . and I was fairly skeptical . . . and it totally floored me, it was beautiful. Very wonderful music. A couple of days later [the composer] revealed that the entire piece was constructed from twelve samples, such as a ship's mast creaking, a breaking twig, water running, you get the idea. All these sort of bizarre mundane sounds, [he] put these sounds on hard disk and wrote a program to select which ones you want. (Jungleib, 1987)

Sampling technology is far from perfect, and creating samples requires a great deal of effort. It is not as simple as recording a sound, because samplers are not of sufficient quality to perfectly reproduce a sound that is fed into them. Instead, several sound parameters (frequency, equalization, etc.) must be altered so that what one puts in is the same as what one gets out. Jungleib (1987) described it best by saying that

> sampling is pretty easy, but it has its inherent problems. It's pretty easy to plug in a mic or a guitar. The hard part comes in deciding what to do about control of sound. That has been discouraging to a lot of people. You shouldn't have to think about mapping, about envelope shape.

Visual editing systems which allow the user to see the wave-shape and amplitude envelope help one sample, but are still quite costly and time-consuming.

Tom Curley (1987), who operates a small studio in New York and considers himself a sampling freak, concurred.

> How do you put a value on [samples]? Because I don't know if you've ever tried to make a sample, but making one is a real pain in the ass. Everybody thinks, oh, sample, oh, I just play a note and that's it. It's a lot harder than that, because of the vagaries of the machine once you get in and once you get out. Before the sample goes in you have to screw it all up and do all sorts of crazy equalization things to it in order for it to come out right. Then you've got to go in and set all your parameters and your envelopes so that it is appropriate to that instrument. In the case of the [Ensoniq] Mirage, you have to take multisamples. If you want to get a piano, you can't just hit a note and that's the sample, you have to take several samples because the sound is only good for an octave or so, so for every note you have to take 5-7 samples. In the case of the Mirage, you have to take two samples for every note, you have to take a sample when you hit it soft and a sample when you hit it hard. And then you have to get the synthesizer to adjust the mix of those samples so that the velocity is like when you hit a piano and the envelope has to be like when you hit a piano. And that goes for all the other instruments.

A further difficulty with sampling is the relationship of the keyboard to the sampled instrument or sound, especially when the sample is of an acoustic instrument. It is one thing to play a sampled piano—the piano itself is a keyboard instrument—but to play a sampled guitar on a keyboard is very difficult. The guitar, for one thing, is set up quite differently from a keyboard. Its strings are tuned in fifths, whereas a keyboard is a linear scale. Though a sound can be sampled, the performance characteristics of a particular instrument must be attended to by the performer if the sample is to resemble the acoustic instrument. Curley (1987) explained that

> (sampling) is definitely opening up a new world for coming up with new sounds. But initially most people will buy a sampler because they think they're going to have any instrument that they want. And you do. It's just not as easy as it sounds. The next thing that I find very interesting is as a keyboard player, I can play different instruments, because you can put up a saxophone sound and it sounds like a saxophone only if you play it like a saxophone. A keyboard tends to play everything like a piano. And it comes out sounding totally strange; like I've learned when to take a breath when I play the trumpet, could a trumpeter hold a note that long? Would a trumpeter do that kind of a trill? Well, obviously he couldn't play a block chord. Like with a violin, you can have a wonderful violin sample, but then you begin to think with a violin player, sometimes he plays it short with a pizzicato, sometimes he plays it long with a slow attack time with a nice long release time, sometimes they play with a quick release time. You have to change your instrument so that you have immediate control over all those parameters, so that you can then play like a violinist.

Performance characteristics are therefore vital to sampling, and it is doubtful that copyright legislation could cope with them. It would be absurd to believe a performance style could be copyrighted, but it is not inconceivable that litigation based on style infringement could come to trial.

What is most interesting about the issue of sampling and copyright is its insertion into questions of labor, income, and control. Copyright in the music industry has traditionally been associated with income, in that royalties are paid on the basis of copyright ownership. It has also been a means of control, because copyright owners can determine the uses to which a song is put. The administration of copyright, royalty, and control is performed by a music publisher. Until the advent of Synthbank, however, there was no such thing as a sound publisher. Copyright of sound was not an issue until sound could be marketed. And now that there may be an administrator of sound copyright, an entirely new branch of the music industry may grow.

Notation

In 1959, *Billboard* magazine reported the introduction of a congressional bill to modify copyright law to cover electronic sounds (Bill to Copyright, 1955). The bill was requested by "a composer of the new-type sounds who has contributed to a movie soundtrack, but has no way of copyrighting his music, since it has no conventional notation to deposit with the Copyright Office" (p. 1). The bill did not pass, though the Copyright Office now requires at least a recording of a piece of music if a notated lead sheet is not available.

What the bill points out is the change in musical notation following the evolution of recording. Prior to written notation, music was memorized by musicians, the same way that epic poems were memorized and recited. It is no coincidence that epic poems and oral history were sung, set to music. Folk music, popular music, is based on memory.[1]

Notation externalized musical memory, as writing is a form of external memory. However, written notation is not a medium of hearing, but of sight. As composer Andre Kostelanetz once remarked, "Music is not what you play but what people hear" (Eisenberg, 1987, p. 57). The notes on a page represent music, not sound. Chris Cutler (1985) argues that the development of notation brought about the division between composer and performer. Eisenberg (1987) writes that

> Perfect preservation is a matter not simply of technology, but of ontology as well. A defect of preservation is a defect of reification, and this is the trouble with clefs and quavers. They aren't music; they just represent it. The music itself is sound. (p. 13)

Recording presented a means of notating sound. Cutler (1985) writes that recording

> "remembered" actual performances; more importantly, it could equally well "remember" any sound that could be made, whatever its source. Thus, through the medium of recording, all sound became capable of musical organization and therefore the proper matter of music creation. (p. 95)

He goes on to say that recording enables the "reunification of composer and performer." In brief, that often accounts for the desire to record, in that one is able to perform one's own composition. Eisenberg (1987) writes:

> What are the causes of this impulse to create records? . . . Marks on paper can be misinterpreted. . . . When the composer is the performer, what the recording records is nothing less than the composer's intentions. (p. 129)

Recording enables those who cannot read music to nonetheless make music. The popular music artist can often be counted among those who do not have formal musical training, cannot read notes, but can play. This use of recording was highlighted early on (Lowe, 1955).

> Gordon Parks [composes] with a couple of tape recorders and a grand piano. Parks cannot write a note of music . . . [he] composes directly on tape, using two or even three recorders to develop counter themes, harmony and orchestral structure. Tape also serves as note-taker for his musical ideas. He files these work tapes, and refers to them when he needs ideas. "Otherwise, I'd never be able to remember or use many of the themes that occur to me," says the composer. . . . After he completes the composition, it is scored by a professional musician. (p. 21)

Written notation, then, is removed from sound—it is music transferred into the realm of sight. Analog recording returns music to its base in sound, but denies sight. Although one can see the grooves on a record or the iron oxide particles on magnetic tape, one can interpret them visually only with the greatest difficulty.

Digital recording combines sound and sight. By breaking music down into computer bits, it makes it possible to represent the music in either of two ways: by analyzing the notes or the sound, as reconstructed from the bits. Computer programs exist that allow a digital recording to be created in several ways, by writing notes or by performing a piece. They can then switch between playing the piece or printing it out as a score. Composer Steve Reich (1987) uses an Apple Macintosh computer for scoring.

> A Macintosh . . . is now my way of notating music. I am finished with writing out my scores. A copyist would send me to the cleaners for thousands of dollars. I am now liberated thank you, and the next piece I am writing for the San Francisco Symphony will pay for this Macintosh plus about ten times over it. . . . The pencil and paper has been replaced by the mouse and keyboard.

Although Reich does not use them, programs exist that create a score from a piece composed on a sequencer.

Digital recording also allows detailed analysis of sound waveforms. Computer programs like SoundDesigner let the user portray the waveform of a sampled sound on a computer screen, then modify it visually and hear the results. Sequencers contain menus and work areas that represent sound in terms of computer [hexadecimal] code, binary code, standard musical notation, or the software's proprietary format—and the user can switch between all formats in an instant.

But probably the single most striking feature of digital recording is its ability to interpolate bits. If a bit is missing, a microprocessor can substitute another bit by interpolating between the ones before and after the missing bit. In other words, sound, a continuous phenomenon, is converted into discrete steps. The steps can then be modified aurally or visually, by man or machine, and converted back into a continuous sound wave.

It is precisely such aural and visual control over sound that is creating copyright problems. Not only has the representation of music changed, but the representation of sound has been altered too. Is sound a wave created by differences in air pressure, or is it a series of bits, or a series of instructions for a synthesizer? Copyright lawyers will have to decide, as Bell said, because if sound is to be copyrighted the means of representing sound must be made uniform.

Copyright and Contradictions

The inherent problem with copyrighting music and sound lies in the nature of recording. The moment of musical production is extended beyond its origin by recording, and therefore control over the music and sound is surrendered. Copyright law, as Simon Frith points out, was conceived within the "terms of nineteenth century Western conventions," and is not well suited to coping with twentieth-century technology (Frith, 1987a, p. 12). The definition of "fixing" music has changed dramatically. Frith writes that

> In the days before recording, "fixing" music could only mean scoring it. The author of a song was the author of its sheet music, which frequently meant that the first person to transcribe a folk song or blues became its author and that a ragtime improvisation was credited to the first listener who could write it down. (p. 13)

Dick Hebdige (1987) wrote about reggae and hip hop cultures that pursue a folk-oral tradition but use modern technology to do so.

> At the centre of the hip hop culture was audio tape and raw vinyl. The radio was only important as a source of sounds to be taped. . . . The hip hoppers "stole" music off air and cut it up. Then they broke it down into its component parts and remixed it on tape. By doing this they were breaking the law of copyright. But the cut 'n' mix attitude was that no one owns a rhythm or a sound. You just borrow it, use it and give it back to the people in a slightly different form. To use the language of Jamaican reggae and dub, you just version it. And anyone can do a *version*. All you need is a cassette tape recorder, a

cassette, a pair of hands and ears and some imagination. The heart of hip hop is in the cassette recorder, the drum machine, the Walkman and the . . . ghetto blasters. These are the machines that can be used to take the sounds out on to the streets and the vacant lots, and into the parks. . . . By taping bits off air and recycling it, [they] were setting up a direct line to their culture heroes. . . . And anyway, who *invented* music in the first place? Who ever *owned* sound and speech? (p. 141)

The mix of technology and folk culture causes problems when viewed from within the music industry, but as Hebdige correctly asks, who owns sound, music, and rhythm?

In that sampling allows easy recombination of sounds, authorship becomes much more confusing. American rap groups, for instance, or the British group Art of Noise, use snatches of sound from various sources. Reggae groups use backing tracks dozens of times for different songs. These forms of "versioning" are widespread. How should copyright be established in these cases? This is not a new problem. Wallis and Malm (1984) note that in many Third World countries musicians record backing tracks that are used by producers for overdubbing singers and other instrumentalists. David Toop (1984) suggests that part of the reason for use of backing tracks is economic. "Versions are obviously a convenient way of making records," Toop writes, "as most of the ideas have already been worked out in the original" (p. 111).

The following description by music critic Nelson George (1985) of a song by New York rap group Grandmaster Flash and the Furious Five illustrates the confusion surrounding copyright and authorship.

[Grandmaster] Flash's concept was to turn the turntable on itself, making it a musical instrument in its own right. He did this by rubbing the needle against the groove, instead of allowing the needle to play the record normally. . . . The result was Jimi Hendrix's alien sound with a basic James Brown beat. . . . Study Grandmaster's "The Adventures of Grandmaster Flash on the Wheels of Steel" to understand how the masters do it. It begins with "You say one for the trouble," the opening phrase of Spoonie Gee's "Monster Jam," broken down to "You say" repeated seven times, setting the tone for a record that uses the music and vocals of Queen's "Another One Bites the

Dust," the Sugar Hill Gang's "8th Wonder," Grandmaster Flash and the Furious Five's "Birthday Party," and Chic's "Good Times" as musical pawns that Flash manipulates at whim. He repeats "Flash is bad" from Blondie's "Rapture" three times, turning singer Deborah Harry's dispassion into total adoration. (pp. 6-7)

It is interesting that digital sampling evolved at around the same time that kids growing up in cities, as Grandmaster Flash and Afrika Bambaataa did, were creating sampled effects with turntables. Multitracking, overdubbing, and versioning confuse copyright issues as much as sampling.

Currently, artists who sample employ a "four-second" rule, and ask questions such as, "Is the sample melodically essential to both the original and new work? Is it readily recognizable in its new context? Is it crucial to the financial success of both the original and the new work?" (Aaron, 1989, p. 23)

Such questions will no doubt become a kind of test should litigants ever come to trial for a case of copyright infringement via sampling. However, the emphasis has been on *melodic* infringment, and one must wonder what may happen when cases of *rhythmic* infringement come up.

At present most artists will print a credit for a sample on a recording's accompanying insert or jacket, or will negotiate for a license (as was the case with MC Hammer and Rick James for Hammer's "Can't Touch This"). At present, though, the U.S. recording industry is generally unprepared for such negotiations. In that licensing has been traditionally granted for full cover versions of songs, for which full mechanical royalties are paid, there does not exist a mechanism for payment of a percentage of mechanical royalties to pay for a sample. However, negotiation for licenses for samples has become rather commonplace in that most record companies now distribute records that include sampled material.

Sampling should be understood as evolutionary, not revolutionary. Musicians have quoted each other's work in all styles of music, from the Serbo-Croation epic poetry that was set to music to jazz and R & B. It is best to think of it in the terms Simon Reynolds (1990) sets forth.

Sampling can only be welcomed. What's the point in resisting? But what's yet to be welcomed is a concomitant breakdown of entrenched attitudes. The sampler is not a kidney-machine to give new life to the punk values of groundswell, breakthrough, subversion, a merry street dance of egalitarianism. (So often, the cry goes up that "everybody" is "out there" fooling around with their cheap samplers, thus somehow constituting a "groundswell." But even if they are, so what? Are the pavements cracking? Is a state of collapse imminent?) Samplers will certainly not be suppressed by the [music] industry. The "raging debate" about copyright laws will simply drag on at its current level for years and years, a bit like home-taping. . . . The real "crisis," or challenge to rock and pop posed by sampling concerns aesthetic possibilities and the fearsome prospect of the future and the infinity of sounds imagined by precursors such as Varese and Schaeffer. (p. 171)

It will undoubtedly take years for attorneys to sort out the legal issues involving sampling and copyright. The contradictions in copyright law must be worked out before it can cope with new technology. A recent decision by the U.S. copyright office to treat "colorized" versions of black-and-white films as "derivative works" if they show "a minimum amount of individual, creative, human authorship" (A.P. Wire Service, 1987) may set a precedent for music copyrighting. Probably the best illustration of the difficulties that will be encountered during litigation over sound and/or music infringement comes from the "Stars on 45" recording, as described by Frith (1987a).

The earliest great mastermix, a series of Beatles songs segued with fine imagination over a shifting disco beat could not be released in its original form because it breached copyright. A cover [version] of the mix was released though—for his Stars on 45 version Jaap Eggermont hired studio musicians to *reproduce* the sound of the Beatles. The latter duly got their mechanical royalties as composers; the deejay whose idea/beat/sequence was exactly copied was entitled to nothing at all. (p. 18)

And nothing illustrates the evolution of recording better than the current copyright struggle. When first invented, recording was thought of as a means of sound transmission, primarily via telephone lines. It was in essence an adjunct to the telephone and telegraph, meant to enable later decoding of very rapid messages. An auxiliary use was for storing sound. Since the late nineteenth century, the emphasis has shifted to retrieving of sound, and development has focused on facilitating retrieval. In an analysis of the history of copyright, Bettig (1990) noted that,

> The dominant trends in the development of U.S. copyright law and judicial interpretations were the extension of the duration of copyright protection, the application to new forms of artistic and literary creativity and expression, and the concentration of intellectual property in the hands of increasingly larger corporate entities. . . .
> With . . . technological developments, authors and artists found new outlets for their creativity, while publishers and other owners of the means of communication and dissemination found new ways to make a profit.

Such trends continue to this day. Even though it appears that sampling allows artists to reclaim or recontextualize sound, it must be remembered that sampling is a *production* method and not a means of distribution. So long as the structure of the U.S. music industry, the U.S. legal system, and U.S. copyright law, which support corporate ownership of copyright, remains intact, dissemination of sampled material will remain problematic. The use of digital recorders, compact discs, DAT, hard disk drives, DCC, and the forthcoming recordable CD is based not only on fidelity and mass storage but also on rapid recovery of sound as well. Recording without playback is, for all intents and purposes, senseless, and it is *playback* that is, in the final analysis, problematic for copyright owners.

It is difficult to imagine, despite the efforts of some musicians and computer programmers, that all sounds may someday be shared and copyright will no longer be an issue. As Branscomb (1990) points out,

> there has never been a time in history when covetousness was not apparent, theft used as a strategy for improving one's economic well-being, hoarding practiced by many to increase their security, and secrecy used as a fallback for protecting assets. (p. 88)

If it is unlikely that the material which is copyrighted will be of less value to copyright owners than it is now, then it is necessary to change the manner of thinking about that which is copyrighted. It is instructive to look back to the roots of property law, and even the roots of the word *property* itself.[2] Derived from the Latin *proprius,* meaning "one's own," the word *property* was a doublet of *propriety* in More's *Utopia.* In current usage the former is used to make reference to ownership, the latter refers to a standard of behavior or use. Copyright law intertwines the two, harkening back to the Latin *proprius* and its derivative *proprietas,* meaning proper signification with words. What is negotiated when one enters into a licensing agreement based on coyright is, in essence, proper signification, as determined by the copyright holder (hence the "Fair Use" doctrine, which allows use of copyright material for purposes that have been, ostensibly, socially sanctioned).

Digital recording and playback allow for, essentially, infinite signification, insofar as sound material may be limitlessly recontextualized. Consequently, it is necessary for copyright law to address not only ownership but use, and to do so in a more meaningful way for technologically mediated communication like digital sampling and digital recording.

Notes

1. For an analysis of popular music, memory, and censorship, see Jones, S. (1991). Ban(ne)d in the USA. *Journal of Communication Inquiry, 15,* 1, pp. 73-88.

2. Etymological information from Skeat, W. W. (1982). *An Etymological Dictionary of the English Language.* Oxford: Clarendon Press.

6

The Process of Sound Recording

Recording

The way a recording is produced depends on the recording medium. The phonograph, tape recorder, and digital recorder or sequencer require different recording methods based on their technical and aural qualities. As recording methods change, so do the relations of production. The musician, producer, and engineer assume roles based on the method(s) used. As editing, multitrack recording, and other technological developments took place, the producer's and engineer's roles were consolidated. Most musicians did not have the knowledge to operate tape decks and other sound processing equipment, though there are notable exceptions. As a result, the roles played by the producer and engineer in popular music creation became even more important. However, as music technology became more affordable, many amateur and professional musicians were able to acquire recording equipment and learn more about the recording process. To fully understand the significance of technology to the production and consumption of popular music, it is necessary to examine the process of recording sound, changes in that process, and changes in the relation of producer and engineer to musician.

Phonograph Recording

Even though called a *talking* machine, the musical uses of the phonograph were demonstrated early in its development (Hubert, 1889). It was reported that "the phonograph will reproduce any kind of music—singing, the piano, violin, cornet, oboe, etc.— with a beauty of tone and accuracy which will astonish the musician" (p. 258). Edison himself exploited its potential for recording music, and the Edison Phonograph Works in New Jersey contained rooms for recording music, duplicating records, and manufacturing phonographs.

In the late 1800s and early 1900s, recording was, simply, the mechanical opposite of reproduction. A performer would play or sing into the phonograph's horn, and the sound would be etched onto the disc or cylinder. An article in *Scientific American* (The Manufacture of Edison, 1900) provides a description of the Edison Phonograph Works and the recording method used.

> One of the upper floors of a large building in the record department is divided into a number of rooms, in which the specialists who are employed by the Edison Phonograph Works are kept steadily at work speaking, playing or singing into the recording machines . . . the violinist stands with his instrument immediately and closely in front of three converging horns, each of which connects with a recording phonograph. The only difference between a recording and a reproducing phonograph is in the nature of the little sapphire tool by which the diaphragm rests upon the wax record . . . the stylus is cup-shaped and ground to a fine cutting edge. . . . One of the first things that strikes a visitor to the record room is the rapidity with which the artists sing, the speed being much greater than that to which one is accustomed in a music hall or opera house. Moreover, the songs are sung with the full power which would be used before a public audience.
>
> Among the most popular records are those of band music, and for making these the company maintains a full instrumental band . . . the musicians are so grouped around the phonographs that the volume of sound from each instrument strikes full upon the horns, the front row of the performers being seated on ordinary chairs and those behind on raised seats. On the occasion of our visit there were no less than sixteen phonographs on the racks in front of the band, each with

its horn pointing toward the musicians. In this case, as in the case of solos, the music is performed at full power. (p. 390)

Opera singer Maria Jeritza described her first recording experience in America in an issue of the *Literary Digest* (How It Feels to Sing, 1924).

I already knew one thing . . . that I must try to sing just as naturally as I would on the stage. But when I arrived, I knew that the only way I could do so would be to forget my surroundings completely, for my setting was anything but a stage-setting.

First of all, the records were made in a small room, a room so small that the members of the little orchestra of ten or fourteen men which accompanied me had to sit close together, knee to knee. Then came the actual singing itself. With the orchestra so close to the singer the sound of the instruments is so overpowering that it drowns the voice, and I could not hear myself sing . . . but I found myself able to overcome this difficulty by holding my hands over my ears. . . .

Then there is the matter of adjusting your position, as you stand and sing, so that you are at exactly the right distance from the receiver. For deep register tones one comes closer, for high register tones one moves farther away.

The first record made is always an experimental one. It enables the singer to hear herself as she should *not* be . . . [and then come] as many more recordings as may be necessary to secure perfect results. . . . And in spite of the sound-proof walls of the recording-room, certain noises, if they are high and shrill enough, manage to get in. I know that all recording came to an end when we neared twelve o'clock, since otherwise whatever opera air I was singing would have been punctuated by the sound of the factory whistles which everywhere announced the noon hour. (p. 28)

Though Jeritza acknowledges the difference between stage and studio, she goes on to judge the recording by comparing it to the way she sounds on stage:

I forgot all about how hard I had been obliged to work to make some of my records what they are when I heard them in their final, definite form, and could feel that they were really representative, and that they sounded as I might have sung them at the Opera, on the opening night of the work from which they had been taken. (p. 29)

Her use of the word *representative* is interesting because jazz and rock performers, and critics, have often made aesthetic judgments of recordings based on how representative they are of a live performance. Jeritza's description shows that not only was the quest for an ideal sound a goal of early sound recording, but the search for an authentic sound based on the aesthetics of live performance was very important. Arthur Haddy, studio manager for Decca Records in the 1940s, admitted to attempting to achieve a live sound in the studio (Culshaw, 1981). One of his favorite sayings was that "it's the *sound* we're after" (p. 65).

However, the unique recording capabilities of the phonograph were also being discovered around this time. *Scientific American*, in an article headlined "Fun With the Phonograph" (Allis, 1905), describes recordings made using properties that are still used today for the manipulation of sound. "Speech by Tom Thumb," for instance, was made by slowing down the phonograph during recording, then speeding it up for playback; "A Whistling Duet by John Smith," in essence was created by a form of overdubbing, playing a cylinder backwards, and cutting two cylinders in half and editing them together (p. 415). It was becoming apparent that the recording studio was a place where sound did not have to be recorded and reproduced exactly as it was during a live performance.

The distinction between a live performance and a recording presents an interesting parallel to Walter Benjamin's (1969) writing on film:

> The artistic performance of a stage actor is definitely presented to the public by the actor in person; that of the screen actor, however, is presented by a camera, with a twofold consequence. The camera that presents the performance of the film actor to the public need not respect the performance as an integral whole. . . . Also, the film actor lacks the opportunity of the stage actor to adjust to the audience during his performance, since he does not present his performance to the audience in person.
>
> For the film, what matters primarily is that the actor represents himself to the public before the camera. (pp. 230-231)

Change the word *actor* to *singer, camera* to *recorder,* and so forth, and it becomes apparent that the consequences for the musician are similar to an actor's. Benjamin (1969) addresses an important issue regarding recorded music. "Even the most perfect reproduction of a work of art is lacking in one element," he writes, "its unique existence at the place where it happens to be" (p. 222). By recording music, the moment of musical production is extended beyond its origin. It is no longer only the performer who has power over the performance, but those who record and reproduce the sound (including the consumer) can also control it.

Manipulation of sound for phonograph recording became commonplace once electrical recording was invented. The microphone and the amplifier permitted precise control of loudness and tone, and wrought another change in studio recording. It was no longer necessary to perform into a recording horn at full volume—an amplifier could increase the loudness of a voice or an instrument.

The change in sound resulted in a change in recorded music. A comparison of acoustic recording to electrical recording by producer and musician F. W. Gaisberg (1942) reveals the differences.

> In some ways acoustic recording flattered the voice. . . . The inadequacy of the accompaniments to the lovely vocal records made in the Acoustic Age was their great weakness. There was no pretense of using the composer's score; we had to arrange it for wind instruments entirely. The articulated tuba tone was altogether too insistent. Though marked advances were made in the technique of manufacture which reduced the surface noise on the disc, nevertheless the artist and the selection had invariably to be selected with care so as to cover up all the instrumental deficiencies. Only full, even voices of sustained power could be utilized, and all nuances, such as *pianissimo* effects, were omitted. (p. 85)

Describing a recording session with an Italian opera singer, Gaisberg notes a further difficulty presented by acoustic recording. "It was an ordeal for her to sing into this small funnel," he writes, "while standing still in one position. With her natural Italian temperament she was given to flashing movements and to acting her parts. It was my job to pull her back when she made those beautiful attacks on the high notes" (p. 91).

In his memoirs, record producer and musician Joe Batten (1956) tells the story of a singer's discomfort at being too close to the recording horn and other musicians.

> In those days the singer never knew what might happen to him. Peter Dawson told me that when recording a descriptive scene, "The Departure of a Troopship," one of the effects . . . was thunder, this being suggested by the blows of a hammer upon an iron sheet. When his cue came, the man missed the sheet and struck Dawson on the head with the hammer with such force as to render him unconscious. (p. 81)

Gaisberg (1942) writes that acoustic recordings could not reproduce frequencies above triple high C (2088 Hz) or below E (164 Hz). Electrical recording permitted a frequency range fully four times greater. The difference was immediately noticeable.

> What [can be] heard coming from the [electrically recorded] records took [people] completely by surprise. For the first time they heard sibilants emerge from the trumpet, loud and hissing! . . . I saw that from now on any talking machine company which did not have this electric recording system would be unable to compete with it. (pp. 86-87)

Electrical recording became the record industry standard. Microphones replaced the phonograph horns, and record companies jumped at the chance to show off the new improved sound. A record by blues singer Ma Rainey was advertised as being electrically recorded, when in fact it had been acoustically recorded. When the deception was discovered by the public, the record company justified its ad by claiming that, while Rainey sang into the horn, an electric light had been on in the studio (Batten, 1956, p. 67).

To say that electrical recording revolutionized the industry is an understatement. For Joe Batten, "The advent of electrical recording had as much significance to us in our small world as the atom bomb ha[d] to a world still profoundly concerned with its influence on the future" (p. 132). Electrical recording also affected popular music style. Bing Crosby's style of crooning, for example, was "made possible by the development of the electrical microphone," according to Simon Frith (1986, p. 263). Crooning "suggest[s] an intimate, personal relationship with fans" (p. 19). Ironically, crooning relied on the introduction of an intermediary step between the singer and the phonograph, a step that allowed the singer to move *away* from the recording source.

Not only did electrical recording alter the quality of sound recordings but because the microphone could record sound at some distance, it also became possible to record on location. Several location recordings are recalled by Batten (1956), but problems with audience noise prevented a number of recordings from reaching the public. One occasion in 1927, during the recording of a symphony in a cathedral, defined the problem. Microphones were hung from the cathedral's ceiling. During a pause between movements, "a whisper travelled from the Cathedral via the microphones to the recording van. 'Tell me, my dear,' lisped an insinuating female voice, 'where did you buy your stockings?'" (p. 68). The cost of location recordings was enormous, as it involved negotiations with both artists and the owner(s) of the location, and considerable equipment expense. Sales of location recordings were not high enough to sustain record company interest, and the method was rarely used for phonograph recording after the late 1920s (Gaisberg, 1942, p. 177).

It did, however, find use as a means of preserving performances by blues singers and folk artists in the 1920s and 1930s. At that time most blues and country recording was done in the field. Its move to studios was partially due to economics. It was less expensive to bring the musician to the recorder than vice versa, and having the equipment already set up in the studio meant that attention could be focused on recording as many songs as possible. A description of sessions in the 1920s and 1930s (Dixon & Godrich, 1970) illustrates the result of this change.

Sixteen or more titles were recorded in a day. On 8/22/33, 35 titles
were recorded at Victor Records' studio in Chicago by a dozen
artists. . . . Whereas in the 'twenties Victor had normally recorded
eight titles a day in the field (while the competition would do fifteen
to twenty), they now aimed at twenty-five or more (the competition
still stuck to between fifteen and twenty). (pp. 77, 86)

Electrical recording also brought changes to the recording process and to the quality of sound, but other parts of the process
remained the same as for acoustic recording. A producer at Decca
Records' London studios (Culshaw, 1981) recalled in 1947 (about
twenty years after the introduction of electrical recording) that

> Despite the advances Decca had made in sound technology, the
> actual recording process had scarcely changed at all. To put it simply,
> the groove cut into the master disc could now accommodate a more
> accurate sound than ever before. . . . But at the studio end one was
> still recording directly on to a thick wax disc revolving at 78 rpm . . .
> it could accommodate music lasting between four and five minutes.
> There was no possibility of correcting either a musical or a technical
> mishap: if the artist played a handful of wrong notes, or if a micro-
> phone started making noises . . . there was nothing to do except to
> get a fresh wax out of the oven and start all over again. Worse still,
> the fatality rate for wax discs once they reached the factory for
> processing was high, which meant that it was pointless to make a
> four-minute piece . . . just once. The artist had therefore to record it
> several times over, and it was then up to the producer to decide
> [which] . . . versions . . . should be sent for processing; neither he nor
> the artist would know the result, either musically or technically, until
> weeks later. (p. 67)

Overdubbing was, at best, a difficult matter with phonograph
recording. Though Batten (1956) mentions using it in 1927 (he calls
it the "montage" method), the procedure required more luck than
skill. Two or more phonographs were played and their sound
combined onto another phonograph. Problems with timing, speed,
and so forth were numerous. For example, when Decca Records
began releasing Long-Playing records in 1948, the method was
essentially the same as for overdubbing. The LPs were assembled
from 78 rpm records by dubbing one four-minute record after

another onto an LP. Culshaw's (1981) recollection is of a frustrating process in which they had

> to join the end of one side [of a 78 rpm record] to the start of the next, while the result was simultaneously recorded (or "cut") on a lacquer, revolving at 33 1/3 rpm. It was a nightmare. . . . I stood there with a score and began a countdown during the last thirty seconds of a side and then shouted "Drop!", at which point one engineer would fade out the side that had just ended while another, with luck, would lower the pick-up on the beginning of the next side. If anything went even slightly wrong there was nothing to do but go back to the beginning, and . . . every LP had to be cut at least twice in case of an accident. (p. 83)

The solution to the problem of creating LPs was tape recording. With the capacity for 45 (or more) minutes of recording, tape recorders were well suited for LP recording. The widespread use of tape recorders coincided with the advent of the LP, and they also allowed easier overdubbing and editing. Tape, however, was not without its problems for phonograph recording studios, according to Culshaw. Referring again to creating LPs, he writes that

> eventually, respite came in the form of a tape-machine, which enabled us to copy the 78 rpm sides on tape without attempting to join them; the tape was then edited to give a continuous performance of the music and the result was then dubbed at 33 1/3 rpm . . . but as nobody knew much about tape splicing in those days there were several disasters. (pp. 83-84)

Tape recording proved very useful and economical in the studio, and by the early 1950s tape recordings could be made in stereo, while stereo phonograph records were not available until the late 1950s. Phonograph recording continued into the 1950s, although tape recording edged it out of most commercial and consumer applications. Roland Gelatt (1954) writes:

> Tape's invasion of the recording studio, begun in early 1949, proceeded so implacably that within a year the old method of direct recording on wax or acetate blanks was completely superseded. . . .

Eventually, of course, the recording on tape had to be transferred to a microgroove master disc, but at that point it would have been meticulously edited and approved by the performer. (pp. 298-299)

In the late 1970s phonograph recording was reintroduced under the name *direct-to-disc*, and marketed for audiophiles. Referred to by some as "superdisc," the process was essentially the same as electrical phonograph recording in the 1950s and earlier. It was often cited as a return to a more natural, musical form of recording, one that eliminated tape from the recording process and recorded sound directly onto a disc that would be used for pressing records. The issue was, again, one of authenticity. John Eargle (1979) of the JBL Laboratories audio firm argued that it was a "hands-off approach" (p. 58), acknowledging the attempt to remove whatever stands between the listener and the performance.

Direct-to-disc was an expensive proposition, however, as few studios were equipped to provide a disc cutting lathe, and, as was true before tape was invented, several discs had to be cut. Either several lathes would have to be employed, or several error-free takes recorded. The reintroduction of phonograph recording was ill-timed as well. Digital recording became feasible in the late 1970s, and led to direct-to-disc's (and thus phonograph recording's) ultimate demise.

Tape Recording

Because extraneous noises might interfere with a recording, even the earliest phonograph recording necessitated a barrier between the performer and the phonograph. A wall or some form of baffle usually separated the artist in a performance studio and the producer, engineer, and others in a control room. The partition had a hole in it to allow the phonograph's horn to protrude into the studio, otherwise the rooms were acoustically separate. The divided performance studio-control room arrangement continues to be used in most recording studios.

Tape recording brought about many changes in sound recording, but most were concentrated in the control room and not the studio. Splicing, editing, and tape manipulation are almost always accomplished by the engineer or producer in the control room. Rarely does an artist perform these functions. As Simon Frith (1981) has pointed out, tape recording allowed producers and engineers to manipulate performances as much as it allowed artists to manipulate sound. The aesthetic division is clearly illustrated in the language; spontaneous performance occurs in the artist's environment, the studio, while direction takes place in the *control* room.

Tape recording essentially replaced phonograph recording as the primary recording medium, both professionally and in the home. Much of the recording process remained essentially the same as it was for phonograph recording until the mid-1960s, however. As noted before, Elvis Presley, Carl Perkins, and other early rock performers were recorded live in the studio. There was no over-dubbing and the musicians performed in the same room. During this period the most noticeable changes in popular music recording were those brought about by the editing capabilities of tape, and by increased recording time.

Regarding the latter, it was no longer necessary to find convenient endings in the middle of a piece. Now, at first, classical music recording was most affected by editing, especially considering the length of many classical pieces, ones too lengthy to fit on one side of a disc. Yet tape also enabled popular songs to become longer. Other uses for editing were quickly found. For the musician, editing meant that a piece did not necessarily have to be performed all the way through. Instead, parts of it could be performed and then spliced together later. Moreover, editing ability meant that the "perfect" take could be assembled from several imperfect ones. The best parts of each take would be chosen and carefully joined into one seamless piece. The Beatles' classic song "A Day in the Life," for example, was edited together from two takes. "Strawberry Fields Forever" joins two separate takes, one sped up and one slowed down until they were in the same key. The aesthetic separation of live performance and recording was thus completed.

That separation became most apparent in 1966, when the Beatles ceased performing before audiences and declared themselves a studio band. Commenting on the decision to quit touring (Schaffner, 1978), Paul McCartney said the Beatles were not only working on new songs, but new sounds. "They are sounds that nobody else has done yet—I mean nobody . . . ever" (p. 60).

Concert pianist Glenn Gould had some interesting things to say about recording and public performance. Like the Beatles, Gould retired from public performance and opted for the recording studio. He became well-known not only for his performance but also for the sterling production and engineering of his recordings. Gould articulates what many musicians, classical and popular, believe about the two directions they are pulled in, public performance and recording.

> The true-blue concert artist will tell you that they . . . have achieved a special mood or communication between the stage and the first row of seats or the last row of seats—whatever! I don't believe that is what they do at all. . . . I know that what one really does in concert is concentrate on an individual collection of moments and string them together to create a superficial impression of a coherent result.
>
> In any case, I personally never felt that kind of rapport with an audience. I felt quite the opposite—that the audience was getting in the way of what I wanted to do, and what I really wanted to do was say, "I think I'll do another take of this work because I didn't like the first one." (Colgrass, 1988, p. 77)

The Beatles similarly voiced much frustration after public performances during which they could not hear themselves and performed sloppily. Recording, with the advent of tape, allowed for the achievement of perfection that a concert performance could not claim.

It is often claimed that the Beatles were the first rock band to fully utilize the studio as a compositional tool. Though this is true inasmuch as they were the first *rock* band to do so, they were hardly innovators when it came to studio technique. The backward tapes, splicing and effects used on their *Revolver* album and subsequent albums had their roots in electroacoustic music and musique concrete. And no discussion of sound recording is complete without some mention of Pierre Schaeffer and Pierre Henry, pioneers of those styles of music. The two men, working for French radio in Paris in the 1940s, presented a *Concert of Noises* in 1948 that consisted of mechanical sounds, trains, street noise, and conversation. Schaeffer, credited by avant garde composer Jean-Michel Jarre as "the first man to consider music in terms of sound and not notes, harmonies, and chords" (Diliberto, 1986b, p. 54), initially used phonographs to record and play his compositions. He quickly switched to tape, however, and used the tape recorder to edit sounds, create echo effects, and alter the pitch of found sounds. His work in Paris, along with that of others in Cologne and at Columbia University in New York, represents the first use of sound recording as more than a documentary device. No longer was tape recording confined to reproduction of sound as it occurs in nature; it was a means of going beyond the limits of natural sound. As Schaeffer himself wrote (Appleton & Perera, 1975), "traditional music not denied; any more than the theatre is supplanted by the cinema. Something new is added; a new art of sound. Am I wrong in still calling it music?" (p. 11).

The Cologne studio made perhaps the biggest impression on contemporary composers. It, in turn, was inspired by Werner Meyer-Eppler, a German physicist influenced by Shannon and Weaver's 1949 book *The Mathematical Theory of Communication* (p. 12). Through the 1950s and 1960s, the Cologne studio counted among its members Pierre Boulez, Herbert Eimert, Herbert Brun, and Karlheinz Stockhausen. Their influence on popular music is undoubtable and significant, and others such as Edgar Varese, Harry Partch, and Arnold Schoenberg had an impact as well. Between recording *Revolver* and *Sgt. Pepper's Lonely Hearts Club Band*, Paul McCartney took time off to, among other things, listen to Stockhausen's music (Schaffner, 1978, p. 74).

An example of this influence is evident in "For the Benefit of Mr. Kite" on the *Sgt. Pepper* album. John Lennon, who described his songwriting style during the mid-1960s by saying "I shoved a lot of words together then shoved some noise on" (Davies, 1978, p. 284), wanted to create the sound of a circus organ going crazy.

Along with producer George Martin, Lennon randomly cut up tapes of organs and calliopes, flung them into the air, picked them up off the ground and spliced them back together.

Jazz columnist Nat Hentoff predicted in the 1950s that electro-acoustic music and musique concrete would makes its way into popular music (Appleton, 1975, p. 17). That prediction proved remarkably correct in the 1960s, but its accuracy is even more startling when one considers the use of digital sampling technology in current popular music. As Schaeffer identified, "The concept of capturing any sound from the world around us, then bending and shaping it into something totally new, is the foundation of modern digital sampling . . . but that foundation dates back to 1948" (Diliberto, 1986b, p. 54).

Digital sampling makes the process easier still. As Herbert Brun often said to music classes at the University of Illinois, Urbana-Champaign, in the Cologne studio "500 [tape] splices a day was not unusual." Sampling eliminates tape splicing entirely, replacing it with digital editing of random access memory with software. Importantly, digital editing is a nondestructive process; that is, unlike tape splicing, one can return the recording to its unedited state with the push of a button, without concern for any signal degradation.

As shown by the Beatles and other groups' recordings,[1] popular music incorporated the recording techniques of electroacoustic music and musique concrete well before rap and funk music made it mainstream.

Prior to 1966, recording was usually done on monophonic tape decks, or occasionally on two-track stereo decks. From 1955 until 1957, England's Decca Records (which the Beatles approached for a recording contract in 1962 only to be turned away) recorded performances in both mono and stereo, but without the knowledge of recording artists. Every recording was made in mono, while a second was made secretly in stereo. Decca, fearing that artists would ask for more money if they knew about the two recordings, did not reveal the stereo tapes (Culshaw, 1981, pp. 132-133).

But besides the obvious changes brought about by tape editing, tape loops, echo, and so forth, the process of recording changed little. In the mid-1960s, multitrack tape recording brought about the most significant change of all.

The Beatles' *Sgt. Pepper's Lonely Hearts Club Band*, though it used many electroacoustic and musique concrete techniques, could not have been accomplished without a four-track tape recorder. Not only did multitrack recording incorporate previously used tape techniques; it added several more that were crucial to the development of popular music recordings.

First, it allowed overdubbing, a technique the use of which is first ascribed to guitarist Les Paul. On one of the tape's tracks a piano could be recorded, then later a guitar could be recorded on another track, and so on. A form of overdubbing could be achieved with sound-on-sound recording (taping one sound on one deck, then sending it to another deck while simultaneously adding another performance), with which Paul also experimented, but after several transfers between decks the tape would become quite noisy, with a very audible level of tape hiss.

Overdubbing had two immediate consequences. One, an artist could now perform all instruments without the help of a group. Two, band members did not have to perform their parts at the same time. The drummer and bass guitarist could record their parts one night, the keyboard player and lead guitarist could come in and record their parts the next night, the vocalist the next, and so on. This method of recording is standard practice, and is perhaps best described in Bob Greene's (1974) book about Alice Cooper, *Billion Dollar Baby*.

However, it was not until the early 1960s that overdubbing became standard practice even though it was possible to overdub via the sound-on-sound method at a much earlier date. Music industry economics dictated, as producer Phil Ramone (Fox, 1986) recalls:

> you were never allowed to overdub . . . you were supposed to record the singer and everything was to go down exactly as it went. You weren't supposed to replace the vocal. . . . [b]ecause the union said any time you replaced the vocal, all the musicians had to be paid. (p. 244)

Second, multitrack recording allowed for easy punch-ins. Recording engineer John Woram (1981) explains that

> in conventional recording, a series of takes are made until a satisfactory recording is achieved. Or, via editing, the definitive performance may be assembled by splicing together sections from two or more takes. However, when recording tracks on a tape that already contains previously recorded material, the manner of doing re-takes is quite different.
>
> To illustrate, assume that the instrumental background has been recorded and a chorus is now being added to the master tape. The chorus sings the first verse properly, but a mistake is made within the second verse. A new take of the second verse cannot be started on a fresh piece of tape, since the chorus must, of course, fit in with the previously recorded material on the master tape. So, the master tape is rewound to some point before the second verse. The tape is played and just before the point at which the second verse begins, the chorus track is placed in the record mode, while the chorus sings the second verse again. The new performance takes the place of the old, while the previously satisfactory first verse remains as is. The process may be repeated again and again until a complete performance has been recorded, perhaps phrase by phrase. (pp. 377-378)

With multitrack recording, not only could parts of different takes be edited together but individual parts also could be altered without changing other parts.

Third, multitrack recording enabled composers to create music by layering sounds, track by track, until they achieved a desired sound. Many contemporary classical composers, Philip Glass, Steve Reich, Brian Eno, Glenn Branca, and others, have used layering techniques in their recordings. Similarly, if one began to run out of tracks, they could be "bounced" down to an empty track. For instance, if tracks one, two and three were recorded on, they could be mixed together and recorded onto track four, thus freeing the other three tracks for more recording.

Fourth, multitrack recording put the producer and recording engineer firmly in charge of studio recording. In that sounds could be recorded on discrete tracks, they could easily be manipulated after recording. This manipulation and balancing of sound is known as mixing, and is the foundation of contemporary popular music.

Prior to multitrack recording, Woram (1981) points out, "song[s] . . . would be recorded . . . until the engineer and producer were satisfied with the balance, the performance, the room acoustics . . . and so on" (p. 371). Interestingly, Woram does not mention that the musician must be satisfied. After multitrack recording's introduction, songs would be recorded until the performance was satisfactory. The balance and room acoustics would be adjusted during the mixing sessions. Musician and producer Todd Rundgren creates mixes for each part of a song:

> The way I do mixes, I don't do automated mix-down. I tend to mix in pieces—a lot of pieces. I may be mixing a verse at a time. Because the way I have the board set up I may have three different types of ambiences and EQs set up for different parts of the song, and I have to go through and mix them—mix one part, and adjust, mix another part and adjust, then go back and splice them all together. (Davies, 1987b, p. 46)

Woram (1981) regards mixing as "a form of recording. However, in places of microphones, a previously-recorded multitrack tape is routed through the [mixing] console, mixed down to a stereo (or perhaps mono or quad) program, and recorded onto another tape recorder" (p. 370).[2] Woram does not mention the changes that could be made to the individual tracks' sounds. A vast array of sound processing equipment developed after the advent of multitrack recording. Some of it had been available earlier, but most studios rarely used it.

Sound processing equipment, or effects, can be divided into roughly three categories: reverberation-related effects, equalizers, and compressors/limiters.

Reverbation-related effects include those which can add echo or time delay, or simulate room acoustics. They were prominently used in electroacoustic music, by means of tape loops, tape delays and pitch-shifting by speeding up or slowing down a tape deck. Current effects, however, rarely, if ever, use tape. Most of the processing is done digitally.

Delay lines and reverb units are usually used to add ambience to a sound. In that it had become quite easy to add ambience after a recording has been made, acoustic isolation became even more important in the studio room. The "drier" (less reverberant) a sound was on tape, the better an artificial reverberation effect could create ambience. Moreover, if a sound were to leak through onto a track, it too would be processed along with the desired sound, and a muddy ambient sound could result. For this reason recording was often done piecemeal, with each band member recording his or her parts separately. Sometimes performers would be placed in different rooms, or large partitions and baffles would be used to minimize the sound coming from an amplifier or drum set. The goal is to have as primal a sound as possible, so that it could be developed later, in the control room, under the auspices of the producer and engineer.

Some odd effects can be achieved by using reverb units and delay lines, including flanging and phasing, chorusing and harmonizing. *Flanging*, a hollow, metallic sound, was first created by use of two tape decks running at slightly different speeds. The speed variation caused certain frequencies to cancel each other out periodically, creating the hollow sound. Similarly, *chorusing* uses a slight pitch shift between the original sound and the effected sound to create a thickness, or a swirling, organlike effect. *Harmonizing* takes pitch shifting further, enabling a sound to be altered more than an octave above or below its original pitch, effectively creating precisely controlled harmonies with the original sound.

Equalizers vary the amount of a specific frequency band and are used to alter the tone of a sound. Essentially precise tone controls, they are used to change the color of the sound, "according to the taste of the listening engineer or producer" (Woram, 1981, p. 207). A mixing board usually has some form of equalization for each channel.

Compressors and limiters restrict the level of a sound. Though engineers strive for a very wide dynamic range, some instruments can exceed a tape recorder's range. A limiter will ensure that a signal will not exceed a certain level, while a compressor will narrow the dynamic range. Noise gates are usually part of a compressor or limiter, and essentially shut off sound from a channel unless it reaches a certain threshold. They are often used to make certain that low-level, stray, unwanted sounds (tape hiss, shuffling feet, etc.) do not make their way into the final mix. They are also used to make rock recordings sound as loud as possible without exceeding broadcasting limits.

Though sound processing equipment does not record sound, its development is linked directly to the development of recording technology. Direct recording relied on microphone placement, equalization, room acoustics, and mixing *before* recording. Effects were rarely used because once recorded they could not be removed. And when they were used, they were usually applied to the mix as a whole. Only one or two equalizers were necessary.

Multitrack recording permits detailed and precise signal processing *after* recording. By the late 1960s, eight and 16-track recorders were common in most studios. In that each track could be processed individually, studios began accumulating effects to accommodate the proliferation of tracks. Engineers, producers, and musicians demanded more effects.

During the early 1970s 24-track recorders had been developed, and are still the recording industry standard. It is possible to slave together two 24-track decks for a total of 46 tracks, and 32- and 48-track recorders are available. However, standard recording tape width for professional recorders is two inches. The more tracks added to the tape, the narrower each track becomes, and the greater the difficulty of preventing tracks from "leaking" onto one another. 24-track tape recording has proven the most effective format with fewest technical compromises.

Home Recording

Though phonograph recording was cumbersome, it was possible to build a small home studio, provided one could afford it.

Tape recording, however, enabled home recording studios to flourish. The low price of tape coupled with its reusability made it the perfect medium for those who wanted to build a small studio in their basement. More importantly, multitrack recording's over-dubbing capabilities made it an ideal medium for the solo musician. Home recording equipment became to music what the single-lens reflex camera was to photography: a means for a mass audience to actively use a mass medium.

The home uses of tape recording had been recognized from the start. *Musical America* extolled its benefits (Lowe, 1955):

> While tape's inherent qualities recommend it highly as a playing medium, the tape recorder, as its name implies, allows the musician ... to ... make his own recordings. ... You do not need to be an expert to make a fine tape recording. ... One versatile instrumentalist who plays 14 different instruments used tape to make his dream of being a one-man band come true. (p. 21)

The same article mentioned composing with tape and recording practice sessions as additional benefits of home recording.

Electric guitar pioneer Les Paul was one of the first to build a home studio. His motives were less musical and more economic. According to Paul (1991), his "original goal was to get around all the nonsense of making records back in those days—unions, rules, regulations" (p. 39). Yet at the root of Paul's home studio efforts is the desire to retain control of the music-making process, a desire common among contemporary musicians. For some, like vocalist Tom Kelly, a home studio puts him directly in charge of the tape recorder.

> I stand in the middle of the studio with a microphone and do my own punches. I have my hands on the remote control which operates the tape machine and I stand in front of the microphone, so I work really fast. In the studio, you're out in another room behind a piece of glass, and then you have the engineer and producer who are stopping and starting the machine. (Gold, 1991, p. 21)

For decades after Les Paul built his home studio most musicians were unable to afford one, and those that could afford one could also afford to spend a lot of time and money at professional studios. Home recording got a boost in the 1970s when 4-track open-reel tape decks became affordable. Author Andy Bereza (1983) noted that one of the main reasons prices for 4-track open-reel recorders fell was because the market for quadrophonic never materialized. "As it turned out," Bereza wrote, "when the hyped-up quadrophonic market collapsed in the 1970s, redundant recorders were modified for multitrack" (p. 230). Home recording got its biggest boost in the late 1970s and early 1980s, though, when 4-track cassette decks with built in mixing boards were offered by Tascam and Fostex corporations.

The 4-track open reel deck became popular for home recording during the 1970s. Electronics dealers began offering mixing boards, microphones, and noise reduction units in addition to the more conventional products such as tuners, amplifiers, and cassette decks. In April 1977, the first Multi-Track Expo was held in Los Angeles. Home recording had become a recognizable industry, and the home recordist an identifiable market for the manufacturers. The exposition drew 4,500 registered participants, and featured workshops like "The Musician's Home Studio," and included exhibitors that had "formerly [been] regarded as 'for professionals only'" (Repka, 1977, p. 109).

The marketing of home recording equipment was aimed at the musician trying to achieve success in the recording industry. An advertisement typical of the marketing strategy is one in the December 1978 issue of *Stereo Review* magazine. Pioneer Electronics Corporation's advertisement for the RT-2044 4-track tape deck contains bold print stating, "For the price of a few hours in a recording studio, you can own one." The company's reasoning went as follows: because recording studio time (then) cost $165 an hour, and the RT-2044 cost $1,650 "just once," the Pioneer deck can be had for the equivalent of 10 hours in a studio. Of course, the advertisement does not mention that for $165 an hour one has access to considerably more than a 4-track deck, and that a 4-track deck alone does not make a studio. The appeal is nonetheless great, because "it's obvious that 'paying your dues in the studio' can be a prohibitively expensive proposition." Pioneer's appeal is twofold, and is typical of most all marketing of home recording equipment. First, they play on the musician's desire to learn more about "how to sound truly 'professional,'" intimating that professional recordings are the key to success. Second, and more important to the discussion at hand, they play on the traditional rock and blues notion of paying one's dues, of working hard for little or no reward and earning one's success, achieving it usually by being discovered in a bar or nightclub. The contradiction between having a home studio and being a struggling musician is obvious. An investment of at least $2,000 is required to purchase enough equipment for semipro 4-track recording. Presumably either one has paid some dues or payment to Pioneer is the equivalent of credit when the time comes to pay those dues. Moreover, "paying one's dues" traditionally meant sweating it out, night after night, in live performance at a small, smoky bar or nightclub. Suddenly it became equated with sitting in the basement, bedroom, or garage with a tape recorder and other equipment.

A Yamaha advertisement published in many music magazines during the late 1980s takes it one step further. "Go to your room and play," the headline reads. The text of the advertisement states that "using the MT2X Multitrack Recorder/Mixer, you can layer your recording just as you would in a real studio—one track at a time. . . . So if you've been wondering where you're going to get your first big break in music, now you know. At home."

During the early 1980s many records were released by rock "groups" of one or two people. Gary Numan, Soft Cell, The The, and others relied on multitrack recording to create their music. Some artists, such as Peter Brown, recorded hit singles and LPs in their bedrooms. Brown's account of his recording success is particularly interesting in regard to home recording. In a poignant reversal of the typical "I owe it all to my manager . . . wife . . . etc." dedication, Brown (1979) says

> I was an art student living outside of Chicago, and I supported my musical habit by working as an art store clerk and a garbageman— among other odds and ends. Today, I've had four hit singles and a gold album (*Fantasy Love Affair*) on TK Records, and I've performed for about a quarter of a million people, not including TV audiences. And I owe it all to my bedroom in my parents' suburban ranch house. (p. 107)

Rock producer Tony Visconti rightly recognizes home recording as an alternative to live performance (White, 1987).

> I'm amazed at the high quality of the tapes people are bringing me. What's more, a lot of the better material has come from home studios in England. . . . I believe that with the reduction in the number of live venues, people are creating some of the best music around in their own homes in the form of home demos. (p. 34)

The 4-track cassette decks introduced by Tascam and Fostex in 1980 created an unprecedented interest in home recording. The decks, priced at $1,300, were portable, built into their own small mixing console, could bounce tracks, used inexpensive cassette tape, and just needed a microphone or cable plugged into a channel to record. The editing capabilities were limited in that cassette tape is thin and difficult to splice, but low cost and portability more than made up for that drawback. In 1985 Fostex released an 8-track open-reel tape deck that recorded on 1/4-inch tape.[3] Several months later Tascam followed with its own 8-track complete with mixing board. A host of other manufacturers have joined in making cassette and open-reel decks for home recording, including Yamaha, Akai, Ross, and Audio-Technica.

It must be emphasized that the availability of 4-track and other decks for home recording was not in itself sufficient to create the tremendous demand for equipment. Several other factors were involved. First, electronic instruments such as organs and synthesizers had been developed to a point in which they, too, were both inexpensive and small enough to place in one's bedroom. Second, the integrated circuit enabled the reduction in size of most recording equipment. And, more important, it reduced the cost of the equipment while increasing its reliability. Third, in that most recording equipment is manufactured in Japan, fluctuations in the value of the Japanese yen and the American dollar meant that at certain times equipment would be priced very favorably.

Home recording's popularity is attested to by the number of books and magazines that have been published since the late 1970s. Periodicals such as *Music Technology, Electronic Musician, Cozmo,* and many others contain useful information for the home recordist. But perhaps better testimony to its impact is the number of home recordings released in the past several years. Underground music magazines like *OP*, *Sound Choice* and *OPtion* review dozens and sometimes hundreds of records and tapes created in basements, living rooms, and bedrooms. Jon Pareles (1987a), writing in the *New York Times*, identified a "cassette underground" brought about by "affordable music technology, especially the advent of inexpensive multitrack recorders" (p. C13). Pareles quotes Scott Becker, *OPtion*'s publisher, as saying "we get 50 to 75 [cassettes] every month [for review], from all over."

In 1982, a friend in a rock group in Champaign, Illinois, made the offhand comment that "in a few years kids will have more portastudios and synths in their bedroom than Barbie dolls and baseball gloves." He now lives in Denver and has a small 4-track studio in his basement. Home recording has changed the economics of production. As George Martin (Anderton, 1978) notes, "every third person I meet is either a record producer or trying to become one" (p. 3). Indeed, the opportunities for professional recording work are greater than they have ever been, thanks in large part to the proliferation of affordable recording technology. Prior to the late 1960s only record companies owned recording studios, as only they were able to recoup the capital outlay for recording equipment. Consequently, recording time itself was at a premium, and recording was generally only an option if one was signed to a record label. But the rise of independent recording studios (like AIR, the one started by Martin in the late 1960s) meant that recording was no longer controlled by record companies.

Still, the economics of distribution have changed little, and large record companies continue to operate their own studios. What has changed, as Larry Grossberg (1987) noticed, is the means by which record companies find new artists. They no longer look for bands that have paid their dues, sending A&R (Artists & Repertoire) executives to see bands perform live. Instead, they go fishing for artists. They listen to demo (demonstration) tapes bands send in, they pay attention to recordings released on independent record labels, and use those recordings as a kind of farm system, in a way similar to the scouting work done by professional sports organizations. The shift from Tin Pan Alley songwriting, to A&R scouting, to angling for new artists in the independent marketplace, is a response to the shift of the site of music production brought about by changes in recording technology generally, and home recording particularly.

Digital Recording

Digital Tape

The Audio Engineering Society's 1977 convention in New York marked the introduction of digital recording as a viable studio technology (Hodges, 1978b). Though digital recorders had been developed several years earlier, the 32-track digital recorder introduced by 3M was "the first of its kind likely to be purchased by the recording companies" (p. 15).

In some ways the 3M deck introduced at the convention physically resembled analog tape machines. It used one-inch tape moving at a slightly faster speed than on an analog deck. The description in trade journals and magazines following the convention, however, focused not on the physical aspects of the deck, but on its sound. Phrases like "stunningly good . . . utterly captivating" (p. 15) and "you won't believe how good it is . . . the best you've ever heard" (Miller, 1978, p. 112) were common in reviews of the deck.

In essence, the descriptions for digital recording were remarkably similar to those for tape when it was introduced in the late 1940s/early 1950s. Jeanne Lowe (1955), in March 1955, wrote of analog tape recording:

> Generally recognized as the most faithful and sensitive of all recording media, tape is also considered the ultimate in sound reproduction. As contrasted with disk, magnetic tape's reproduction is inherently free of surface noise, and remains noise-free through countless playings. There is no conversion of physical energy to an electric signal, no deteriorating contact of stylus with disk surface, no grooves to

collect dust. The clean, brilliant sound of a high-fidelity tape recording does not deteriorate with wear. It sounds just as good after the
tenth, hundredth, or even thousandth playing. (p. 21)

Twenty-three years later, after the AES convention (and almost exactly 100 years after Edison patented the phonograph) Len
Feldman (1978) wrote that

> the widespread use of digital master recording systems could well
> make (noise reduction) devices obsolete. . . . The lack of contact be-
> tween the disc and the pickup arms means that there should be no
> performance deterioration no matter how many times the disc is
> played. . . . Nor will there be any acoustic feedback (howling) and
> surface noise in a disc that requires no more delicate handling than
> present-day LPs. (p. 59)

Concomitant with the introduction of 3M's digital recorder was
the introduction of the digital compact disc (CD) and PCM recorder. Both were home stereo systems, and it is no coincidence
that their introduction corresponded to 3M's release of their deck.
Without suitable home playback equipment, digital recording
could very well have gone the way of direct-to-disc recording and
become an audiophile-only medium. As John Eargle (1979), vice-
president of JBL Laboratories said, "The analog disc is really being
strained by the kind of signals we can now put onto it. So are most
playback systems" (p. 57). Despite its advantages, digital recording's increased dynamic range and lack of noise are virtually
neutralized by conventional record pressing. The manufacture of
phonograph records from digital recordings renders most of the
advantages of the recording method inaudible.

It is likewise not a coincidence that direct-to-disc recording and
digital recording achieved prominence at about the same time.
Direct-to-disc provided high-fidelity appeal but digital provided
that and multitrack capability. As Feldman (1978) states,

> Anyone who has heard [direct-to-disc] can attest to [its] better sound
> quality. Making a direct-to-disc record, however, means bypassing all
> the sophisticated multitrack capabilities that have been developed
> over the years and are responsible for present-day high-quality

recordings, since later editing and mixing is not possible. By introducing digital master tape recordings as the initial studio recording technique, the advantages of multitrack recording can be combined with the sound quality of direct-to-disc techniques since the digital master tape system introduces no intermediate degradation of the music signals. (p. 59)

It is, therefore, not surprising that direct-to-disc recording was exhausted almost immediately after digital recording was introduced.

Recording studios were a little slow in acquiring digital recorders, not because their price was high but because of already heavy investments in analog tape equipment. In 1978 the price of the 3M deck was around $150,000. Though high, when viewed in relation to some of the more expensive analog 24-track decks which cost around $80,000, the price for recording studios was competitive. The increase in number of tracks was certainly attractive, but the savings in tape (24-track decks use 2-inch tape, digital decks use a smaller tape format) would quickly add up. Also, studios could advertise their acquisition of the latest in recording technology and perhaps draw in new clients—and raise prices. As Josef Nuyens, manager of Castle Studios in Nashville, said, the purchase of digital recorders "absolutely affected the kind of business coming in. We have as many outside clients, from New York, L.A., and England, as we have from Nashville" (Jacobson, 1987, p. 61).

Nevertheless, digital recording, though in demand, still has not penetrated beyond the larger professional recording studios such as Universal in Chicago, the Record Plant in Los Angeles and the Power Station in New York. Smaller studios, such as the Living Room, occasionally rent digital recorders for specific projects, but few have the investment capital to acquire digital recorders. At the 1990 and 1991 manufacturer's trade conventions, however, smaller versions of professional digital recorders were exhibited by Alesis and Akai. The price tag for these recorders, which are eight-track units (but can be chained together for up to 24-track recording) is under $10,000, and foreshadows the penetration of digital multitrack recording into the home recording market.

As with the introduction of tape recording, the recording process itself initially changed little as studios began acquiring digital recorders. Henry Pleasants (1978), after attending a digital recording session, wrote:

> How, one wonders immediately, does the fact of digital recording affect a recording session? The answer is not at all, except in relieving the performers, and especially the percussionists, of certain dynamic inhibitions inherent in conventional analog recording. . . . Even the control room is unchanged. (p. 44)

The point about "relieving . . . dynamic inhibitions" is interesting when it comes to rock music. Despite being an inherently loud form of music, rock has not utilized digital recording's wide dynamic range to its fullest. Perhaps this is because rock has traditionally had a narrow dynamic range (musicians often joke about playing at one volume level—loud) and it may take some time for rock music producers, performers, and listeners to adjust to the sound of digital recording. It is also likely that broadcast restrictions for radio are closely adhered to by recording engineers who know that, should their recording exceed radio station standards, their recording will not be played on the air, or its sound will be compromised by signal processing at the station.

Just as tape's editing capabilities revolutionized recording, the first prominent change brought about by digital recording also involved editing. Digital recording does away with razor blade splicing. Instead, electronic editing is performed with the aid of a microprocessor. The degree of precision that electronic editing offers is far beyond that of analog recording.

The musical consequences are enormous, as Eargle (1979) explains:

> Digital editing is incredibly precise. When you splice an analog recording, you usually try to do it in a spot where there is a musical transition—and you can get away with a lot because there *is* a transition. But let's say you want to edit right in the middle of a French horn note. A splice in a sustained note is almost impossible to conceal. (pp. 58-60)

In most rock music, splices are made on snare drum beats since they can be easily matched up from splice to splice. With a digital recording, however, splicing by hand is impossible. There can be thousands of bits of information on a fraction of an inch of tape, and locating the proper edit points is out of the question.

Instead, one can observe the sound waveforms of a specific track on a computer monitor, and locate points at which the waveforms match. The points are stored in a microprocessor's memory and, when they come up during playback, the microprocessor switches from one point to the next imperceptibly. Each track can be previewed in that fashion so that edit points do not have to be the same throughout the recording. The best edit points for each track can be selected. Edit points within ten microseconds of absolute accuracy can be attained. Eargle (1979) continues:

> You can edit just [one] track alone, without touching the others if you don't want to. The next track can be edited in the same general time frame, but at a point that is best for its waveforms. When the editing decisions have been made, the two tapes that you're joining are played on two separate machines, and you make your edited copy on a third. And, since this is a digital process, there is no degradation of signal in the copying process. (p. 60)

Just as older home playback equipment was changing, so studio equipment changed. The noise-free qualities of digital recording revealed noise coming from other sources: microphones, mixing boards, effects units, and so on. Their noise had gone undetected because the noise inherent in tape recording covered it up. As Eargle said (1979), "The output of noise from all the microphones through a console can virtually wipe out the signal-to-noise improvement that we're getting from systems of wider dynamic range" (p. 59).

Home recording has, so far, been unaffected by digital multitrack recording. However, DAT recording has had a tremendous impact as a form of home tape mastering, and PCM recording has been in use in home recording studios also. Pulse Code Modulators (PCMs) were introduced in 1978 as a means of storing digital signals on videocassette recorders. They have not caught on, however, because they are expensive and the tape cannot be edited without thousands of dollars of additional equipment. They too, have found use in some smaller recording studios and home studios as mastering decks. Recordings are taken from the PCM and transferred to analog as needed for editing, record pressing, and so forth. Some field recording uses of PCMs are common as well. To capture native sounds for Philip Glass's soundtrack to *Powaqaatsi*, the sequel to *Koyaanisqaatsi*, an engineer from the Living Room spent several weeks in South America and Africa with a Sony PCM recorder.

Digital Audio Tape (DAT) is more amenable to home recording use, especially as a stereo master tape deck. DATs provide the recording quality of compact discs, though in a cassette format. Again, few editing provisions are available, but its cost is less than that of PCM machines, and as it becomes a format used by professional studios, home studio users will adopt it to a greater degree as well.

The impact of digital audio on home recording is most felt in the area of digital sampling. As described in an earlier chapter, sampling involves the recording of short samples of sound that can be played back via a musical keyboard. The sounds that were recorded in the jungles of South America and Africa are being sampled for use with Glass's score. Sampling has enabled importation of sounds from virtually any source into the controlled environment of the studio—or the home.

In the near future, depending on its introduction in the United States, DAT may prove more amenable to home recording use, especially as a stereo master tape deck. DATs provide the recording quality of compact discs, though in a cassette format. Again, few editing provisions are available, but if DAT catches on as a consumer home audio device, its cost could fall to within that of analog cassette decks.

Sequencing

The most widespread use of digital recording technology is not digital tape recording, but sequencing. Though arguably not a method of recording[4] sequencing is being used by more and more musicians as both a means of sketching out musical ideas and producing master tapes.

Sequencing is, in essence, a method of recording control signals that are fed to synthesizers (or any other equipment capable of responding to the signals) that can cause the synthesizers to perform a given task, be it playing a note, changing volume, or changing a waveform. Prior to 1982, sequencing was accomplished by means of sending control voltage signals to synthesizers. The problems with this method of sequencing ranged from difficulty storing the control signals[5] to lack of a standardized signal code that would allow synthesizers made by different manufacturers to operate together.

In 1982 all that changed. MIDI (Musical Instrument Digital Interface) was introduced, and it allowed several electronic instruments to receive data from a sequencer. Since MIDI was a standard code, virtually all the instruments incorporating it could work together. Essentially a string of data bits, MIDI data could be easily stored in a computer (or on a floppy disk) and MIDI sequencers soon flooded the market. Many MIDI sequencers are simply software designed for existing personal computers such as the IBM PC, Macintosh, Atari ST, or Commodore 64. They use the computer's microprocessor for sequencing.

The impact on composition and creation was immediate. MIDI sequencing was a means of capitalizing on the availability and sound-generating potential of digital synthesizers and samplers. The design of most software-based sequencers is such that they simulate tape recorders, and sequencers are, functionally, tapeless tape recorders. Many sequencers can pay for themselves in terms of savings in tape. Instead of having to use several reels of tape working on an idea, a sequencer can store work on a cheap floppy disk. And the sound quality is excellent, primarily because one does not deal with any sound recording medium at all. Every recording made from a sequencer is a master, in that it is the direct output of the synthesizers that is being recorded. Though a sequencer does not store sound, a user can get around that limitation by using it to trigger a device that can, such as a sampler.

Unlike the introduction of tape and digital recording, MIDI changed much of the recording process almost overnight. As noted in a *Forbes* (Benoit, 1984) article, "With a personal computer or synthesizer and the right software, a composer can now write songs (or program them, actually) on a cartridge and pop it into the synthesizer or computer when he gets to the studio" (p. 102). What makes MIDI sequencing an attractive device for saving studio time (and money) is its flexibility in editing not only notes but *sounds.* The degree of precision when editing is remarkable, because by using a personal computer individual notes can be edited. However, in that it is not sound that is being recorded, the synthesizers can be programmed and reprogrammed for different sounds as the composer desires. Moreover, MIDI can send data to change a synthesizer's sound (in mid-playback, if so desired), and thus extremely precise control of sound can be attained easily and inexpensively.

More than any other technology, MIDI is enabling musical creation by virtually anyone. As The (1986) points out,

> Equipped with a MIDI interface, a computer becomes the digital heart of a musical system that can support synthesizer keyboard input at one end, and a speaker system or recording gear at the output end. With such a setup, you don't even have to be able to read and write music in order to make music . . . revisions and what-if explorations are easy. (pp. 89-90)

The primary use of sequencers is as a musical word processor. Along with the tape recorder-style features already mentioned, most sequencing software comes with word processor-style cut-and-paste features, enabling quick and easy songwriting. Such a feature is especially useful in popular music styles that rely on repetition, as repetitive phrases can be cut and pasted together. The following, from *Keyboard* magazine, concisely explains MIDI's impression on music making.

> Using a sequencer changes, and radically, the way music is made. The product (good-sounding music) is no longer linked to the muscular process. This linkage started to break down in the late 60s when

multi-track taping made it possible for musicians who had never even met to "play together" by laying down overdubs, punching in phrases and even single notes so as to perfect their product.... When MIDI appeared in 1983, it became relatively simple for the first time to treat a musical performance as a stream of digital data, much like the words in a word processor ... MIDI made it possible to build a device that would record and play back any electronic keyboard performance. And that blew the lid off. Once a performance has been recorded as a stream of digital events, hitting the playback button is one of the least interesting things you can do with it. . . . The nice thing about digital data is that it is inherently plastic. (MIDI & Music, 1987, p. 32)

Sequencing has quickly become a standard procedure among a majority of musicians. Frank Zappa has given up recording on tape altogether, preferring to store his compositions in his Synclavier synthesizer's sequencer. As jazz guitarist Jeff Lorber pointed out, "Sequencers have ... made it that much easier to control the overall sound and arrange my music . . . sequencers are great tools for working out the form and a lot of the parts of a song before you go to tape. . . . Using sequencers can end up saving you thousands of dollars" (MIDI & Music, 1987, p. 56).

Many manufacturers are now providing sequencers built into synthesizers and samplers, creating a form of digital workstation. The most elaborate of these (the AudioFile, Synclavier and Lexicon Opus, for example) combine all the features of mixing consoles, sequencers, editors, digital recorders, samplers, effects units, and even synthesizers, in one machine. Particularly attractive to recording engineers, producers, and musicians is that, when using these machines, at no time does a sound have to leave the digital domain (that is, it is converted to analog only for playback through the speakers, *not* for any sort of recording or processing). Workstations are very expensive (most begin at around $100,000, though ones that utilize personal computers for processing power are less expensive), but are finding frequent use in film and video scoring and postproduction, where their ability to synchronize with visual media is very valuable.

Lorber (MIDI & Music, 1987) identified the main reasons for sequencing's popularity: ease of use, control, and economy. With various methods of synchronization that allow sequencers to be locked up with tape decks for vocal and acoustic instrument recording, sequencers and workstations are providing the recording industry with powerful new methods of creating music. And, perhaps more importantly, they are fitting directly into the home recording market (especially by way of personal computers), providing inexpensive yet extremely powerful recording capabilities for anyone inclined to using synthesizers and/or computers.

Summary

The recording process has come far since the days of phonograph recording. Today's trend in recording, toward combinations of digital recorders and sequencers, makes sound an entirely malleable medium. And home recording has not only become a reality, but a commonplace.

A bias toward editing is clearly evident in the development and use of recording equipment. As it has evolved, recording equipment has enabled more precise editing of music. Currently, extremely fine editing is available via digital recording and sequencing. Editing is often used to correct mistakes. However, because it has become easier to edit and edits are less likely to be detected, creative editing is routinely done to enhance a song's impact. Several versions of a song may now be released, each differing only in the way they are edited, but each having a different overall impression, each targeted to a different audience, and each exploiting the mechanism of earning royalties via the exploitation of publishing and copyright.[6] The traditional roles of producers and recording engineers, though remaining intact in large, professional studios, have fallen away in other spheres of music production. Preproduction can now be accomplished at home or elsewhere, and the willing musician can operate sequencers and synthesizers without much difficulty. In such cases, learning about studio procedures is almost inevitable.

With preproduction occurring largely outside the studio and, if desired, exclusively by the musician, once in the studio the producer is faced with music that is almost completely realized. However, owing to the malleable nature of sequencing, it becomes possible for radical alteration of song structure and arrangements even in the late stages of production. The producer and musician are thus faced with more decision making throughout the recording process, thereby lengthening the time it takes to make a recording.

Modern digital recording and sequencing offer much more than any previous recording medium. But when faced with a stunning array of possibilities, it becomes difficult to determine exactly what decision to make, what choice is the right one. Recording was once fettered by the medium—phonograph recording allowed for short recordings of a certain volume, for example, and performances had to be live, in the studio. Sound, performance, and music can now be entirely flexible, and creativity unbound by the physical restrictions of a recording medium—there is a new-found freedom in popular music recording that could enable creativity to flourish, not only among professional musicians but among amateurs as well.

Notes

1. Examples of the incorporation of these techniques in popular music can be found in the following recordings (among others). The Beatles, *Revolver* and *Sgt. Pepper's Lonely Hearts Club Band*; Pink Floyd, *Dark Side of the Moon*; Jimi Hendrix, *Electric Ladyland*; Roxy Music, *Stranded*; George Harrison, *Electronic Sound*. Most of these records fit into the "art rock" category, though they are noticeably different from traditional art rock performed by groups such as Yes, Electric Light Orchestra, and King Crimson. The latter were more concerned with incorporating classical music styles into a popular music form. The former were concerned with incorporating experiments with sound into popular music.

2. A mixing console, or mixing board, contains separate channels for each track of a tape recorder and channels for adding processed signals. Each channel's volume and position in the stereo field can be individually adjusted to achieve a balance between the tracks.

3. Though the smaller tape format meant lower fidelity, the cost of one reel of 1/4-inch tape is $12, versus $32 for 1/2-inch tape, a very significant difference to home recording enthusiasts.

4. It is a method of recording control signals for synthesizers and other instruments and effects, not a method of recording *sound*. For more discussion of sequencing's relation to recording, refer to chapter two.

5. Until the early 1980s, computer memory was expensive and in short supply. The first inexpensive home computer, the Altair 400, was advertised as having a (then) phenomenal 4K (kilobyte) memory. Taking into account the length of most pieces of music and the number of notes involved, a sequencer would quickly run out of memory for even a short piece.

6. For a discussion of the impact of editing and remixing on popular music, see, Tankel, J. D. (1990). The Practice of Recording Music: Remixing as Recoding. *Journal of Communication, 40*, 3, 34-46. Also see Fikentscher (1991).

7

Technology and the Musician

As stated at the outset of this book, without technology, popular music would not exist in its present form. Without electronics and without the accompanying technical supports and technical experimentation, there could not be the mass production of music, and therefore there would not be mass-mediated popular music. Of equal importance, without technology there could not be the creation of sounds that are today intimately associated with popular music.

As the printing press enabled production of mass-circulation newspapers, which consequently affected newspaper content (for example, the inverted pyramid news story, the objective account, etc.), music technology affects the content of music during its creation as well as its consumption. Newspaper writing and editing are collaborative processes (between writers and nonwriters such as editors, designers, and so on). So, now, is the production of music wed to compromise and collaboration. Though it could be argued that the making of music has, to an extent, always been collaborative, modern popular music, and especially recording, has a different texture. In this case the collaboration is between musicians and nonmusicians, engineers, producers, and the like. The decision-making process during recording has been permanently altered by the use of technology. That process is affected not only by technology but also by the culture within which technology is produced and consumed.

To compose on any instrument one must know a certain technique. It certainly takes some time to master an instrument—acoustic or electric, ancient or modern—and to master a musical language. But now the representation of music is changing through technology (from standard music notation to visual representation by digital means). Technological language becomes increasingly important to the creation of music.

Musicians have consistently been interested in the sonic capabilities of technological objects. Recent technology has enabled musicians to create sounds they had previously not been able to create, with a clarity not previously possible. However, as music technology has become more complex, the mastery of it has become as important to the composition and realization of music as is musical knowledge. Although one need not know the operating system of a synthesizer to be able to make music with it, one must understand it to create timbres with it. Currently, a class system with three categories is developing: performer, programmer, and performer-programmer. Performers play synthesizers, programmers create sounds with them, and performer-programmers do both. Stratification has come with this class system, and the ideas and ideals that permeate popular music permeate its technology too. The concepts of authenticity, honesty, and sincerity, long used by pop fans and critics, become woven into the mesh of music and technology, and into the fabric of recording itself.

The Studio—Composition, Compromise, and Creation

The separation of the control room and recording studio illustrates the traditional separation between *musical* activity and *production* activity in popular music. Musicians occupy the studio; the producer and engineer remain in the *control* room, and presumably remain in control. As rock producer Tony Visconti (White, 1987) recalled, bands were never allowed to go into the control room. . . . The producer might know one of the band, but generally he kept himself separate from the musicians. This man behind the glass would tell everyone what to do and everything was very formal. (p. 31)

Changes in recording technology primarily affect control room procedure first, performance in the studio second. The aesthetic decisions made during recording, though usually involving musicians, producer, engineer, and others, are typically made after everyone has been brought into the control room to listen to a playback. Changes then are discussed and implemented.

In that the producer and engineer are responsible for activity in the control room, it is usually they who decide what those changes should be. As an engineer at Pacific Recording Studios pointed out, "Today, the recording room is no longer the heart of a recording studio. The control room is where the action is. . . . The control room is the 'creation room.'" (Wickersham, 1969, p. 38). Producer and musician Brian Eno (Bacon, 1981) remarked, "The synthesizers I use are very, very simple indeed. What I really use is the control room. . . . The whole control room is my synthesizer" (p. 20).

Traditional studio design is intended to give musicians and groups space to play in and to provide for a variety of acoustic set-ups (using variably sound-reflective materials for walls, baffles, and the like). Control room space is limited, in that little movement is required by engineers and producers, and equipment is designed as compactly as possible. Indeed, most recording studio control rooms greatly resemble airplane cockpits, and the association is carried further by equipment designers who seem to aesthetically plunder Boeing and Lockheed.

But some studios have moved the control room out into the recording area, giving musicians not only better access to recording equipment, but to the decision-making process as well. The Living Room, a New York recording studio operated by Philip Glass, Kurt Munkacsi, and Michael Reisman, was traditionally designed with a small control room and large recording area.

However, after several years using that setup, Glass and company decided they needed more space and switched the control and recording areas around. Because most of the music recorded at the Living Room is electronic and does not need to be recorded with a microphone, this posed few problems. The small recording area provides a small, acoustically isolated space for vocal and acoustic recording.

According to Living Room manager Rory Johnston (1987), the new set-up is much better suited to Glass's style.

> Originally, when the studio was built, it was conceived to [be] the opposite way around that it is. The main room, where the [mixing] board is now, was actually going to be the main recording room. For our purposes, because we're computer and keyboard/synthesizer oriented, that main function is switched around. That arrangement seems to be a way a lot of people favor, because everybody's recording in this fashion now. More and more recording is becoming synthesizer oriented, and people record by going direct and using headphones . . . rather than having a live sound going on in one room.

In some measure the control room is almost superfluous. According to rock producer Ron Nevsion:

> I don't need to spend $2,500 a day in a place like the Record Plant to do the leg work. I could do it in my living room if I wanted to. Recording vocals, guitars and synths doesn't even require a studio, just a control room. (Armington & Lofas, 1988, p. 65)

Popular music recording has come to rely less on microphones and more on direct electronic connections to a mixing board and tape deck, thereby making studio acoustics less critical. Likewise, when a microphone is used, it is for "close-miking"—that is, for placing the microphone as close to the source of sound as possible. This miking method will mask, or practically eliminate, any room acoustics. In combination with the addition of reverberation during mixdown, it seems unnecessary to consider the space within which recording takes place, so long as it is quiet.

To some musicians and producers the standard control room/ studio room arrangement is awkward. Country music producer Jack Clement said that the first thing I think you have to understand is that I decided that recording studios are the worst place in the world to make a record. I came to that realization about ten, twelve years ago, so I started recording here in my house. . . . That's when I realized that I didn't ever want a control room window. You see, when I set up [the control room] here, I didn't want to take the bathroom out that lies between here and the bedroom, so I didn't have a control room window. . . . I really like the fact that when people are in the studio cutting there's nobody looking at 'em. That was the whole thing about windows anyways. I mean, we ain't doing TV, we're only doing audio. . . . You'd have the artist out there singing and somebody's clowning around in the control room and he (the person singing) thinks they're laughing at him. (Gleason, 1988, p. 59)

The use of headphones in the studio contributes significantly to the sound of a recording and the musical performance, in that it is the primary means by which musicians hear themselves while recording. Yet the significance of headphones is overlooked.

Headphones often present a problem to musicians. It is virtually impossible to record without them, because sound from the control room is piped into them (a significant fact in itself, as it further establishes the power of those in the control room). It is possible to set up speakers in the studio that would amplify the sound, but if there were a microphone set up for vocal recording, the sound from the speakers would leak into the microphone.

Headphones are a fact of life in the recording studio. During the course of a recording session, a "rough mix" is made by the engineer so that the performers and those in the control room can get an idea of what is being recorded. The rough mix is sent to the performers via headphones. If they are overdubbing a track, they then can hear what they are recording along with what already has been recorded.

The experience of hearing music via headphones is entirely different from that of listening to speakers. With headphones, the feeling is one of immediate intimacy, of music coming from inside one's head. Evan Eisenberg's (1987) analysis of listening to music on headphones, though written from the point of view of record listening, is applicable to recording as well.

Headphones give this feeling [of stretching across space] instantly, but in a somewhat different form. While it is hard to say whether my self has expanded or the world imploded, the violent privacy of the experience makes the sense of implosion stronger. Because the music seems to be coming from inside me, it merges with my direct experience of the will. As a result, the music seems to express my feelings of the moment, even when by nature it ought to be at odds with them. Another result is one Nina noted: I do not seem to be listening to the music so much as playing it. (p. 249)

Pop producer Phil Ramone (1983) tries to sit in the studio with headphones on during most takes. "It's better to sit in with the musicians because in the control room you don't hear what's in the musician's headphones. You can use a monitor, but it's not exactly what they're hearing because of the vibration of the studio itself" (p. 279).

It is not surprising that a form of music called *headphone music* emerged in the 1960s, when exploring inner space was a western pastime. Headphone music's most notable creators were Pink Floyd, the Beatles, Jimi Hendrix, and scores of psychedelic rock bands. The creation of headphone music was facilitated by the recording studio, because the musicians initially experienced their music via headphones. Nine times out of ten it was subsequently mixed on speakers in the control room, but its origin lies with the headphone.

The sound quality of studio headphones varies, as does the mix that is sent through them. The headphone mix can be altered just as the final mix can be altered, with the addition of effects and changes in instrument balance. However, most engineers prefer to put the effects on only in the headphones, and not on tape. Their goal, as mentioned earlier, is to get as dry a signal as possible on the recording, so that it can be more easily changed during the final mixdown.

For the musician, however, this can cause trouble. A poor headphone mix can result in a waste of studio time and money. If the musician cannot hear properly, or does not like what is coming through the headphones, it can affect the performance. As guitarist Franco Fabbri (1987) said, "The sound engineer always said, 'The reverb comes later, we will hear it with the reverb later, now just lay down the sounds.' I always said I want to listen to it now as it will be at the end, because I will play in a different way if I have the reverb. I will think about adding other instruments in a different way." During a recording project in 1983, Fabbri (1987) said, drummer Chris Cutler had an argument over the use of headphones that illustrates most sound engineers' neglect.

> One of the biggest problems was headphones. Chris was concerned with that, and he had an argument with the sound engineer who didn't realize how important it was for Chris to hear what he was doing in the best way, because he would perform differently according to what he could hear. . . . If you have the right mix in the headphones you play differently. The expression, and everything. They had just one channel for headphones, so they couldn't give him a different mix. Every studio I have been in this is a problem. Whenever you go out from the studio to go and listen to what you've done, go back and put on your headphones, you hear a difference.

The addition of effects via the headphones can also greatly affect the performance. Reverberation, for instance, can add a long sustain to a note. If the musician hears reverb in the headphones, it is likely that his style of playing will change to accommodate the long sustain. But because the engineer is not putting the reverb on tape with the performance, the musician may later wish to redo his part. The reverb can, of course, be added later in the mix. However, it is unlikely that the exact same reverb setting can be used,[1] and it is likely that, with the subsequent addition of other tracks, the performance may fit the piece differently. The musician may like the effect in the headphones very much, yet it cannot be recreated during the final mixing session. Fabbri said, "For [the] record we did in 1981, I had a couple of impressions that what we were doing during recording didn't come out when we mixed. I remembered a wonderful effect the sound engineer got with my guitar with [a] compressor. But when we went to the final mix he wasn't able to do it again."

Sound engineers sometimes disregard musicians, and by doing so impose their own values upon a recording. Recording engineers occasionally take the attitude that the musician is technically un-sophisticated and should stay out of the way. This attitude may stem from good intentions, in that the engineer may feel that it would take too much time for the musician to add his technical input to the recording. Or, the engineer may feel the musician is unqualified to operate the studio's equipment.

Compromise and Communication

It is often difficult for musicians to communicate with engineers and producers. Not only are their occupations substantially differ-ent, but their individual languages can be a barrier to understand-ing. The following exchange (Kealy, 1974) illustrates the point.

Drummer:	Is that "popping" like it should?
Producer:	What do you mean "popping"?
Drummer:	It sounds "weak."
Producer:	What do you mean "weak"? We got terminology problems here.
Drummer:	It doesn't sound "thick" enough.
Producer:	Oh, thick (still not sure, turns to assistant producer). How does it sound to you?
Assistant Producer:	On the lean side of thick.
Producer:	(makes an adjustment . . .) How does it sound now?
Drummer:	Yeah! What'd ya do?
Producer:	We thickened it. What else? Once we know what you're talking about, we can fix it. (pp. 141-142)

The recording engineer's occupation requires a precise lan-guage, and it is common to find this sort of exchange (Jones, 1981):

Guitarist:	Can you make it sound a little warmer?
Engineer:	I can boost it around 1K (makes adjustment).
Guitarist:	It needs to be a little hotter.
Engineer:	Let me try about 3 db more around 2K.

Cohen (1991) observed the mixdown of a Liverpool group's demo tape, during which the guitarist asked that his guitar be made to sound "'chunky,' 'resonant,' 'upfront,' 'dead punchy,' and not 'too tinny,' 'wimpy,' or 'velvety'" (p. 168).

A recording can be affected by lack of communication between musician and engineers. For instance, if the engineer is unwilling to work for a sound the musician is after, it is more than likely that the engineer will get his way. It depends, of course, on the engineer. An article in *Newsweek* (On the Right Tracks, 1968) stated that

> the new studios . . . have their own engineers who understand both the new equipment and the new music. "The old-guard engineer sits and watches his noise meter to make sure there will be no distortion," says [Record Plant recording engineer Gary] Kellgren. "They don't realize that this music *is* distortion. If a group wants a certain kind of sound, those engineers will tell them it can't be done. Here we work out a way to do it." (p. 45)

Such situations are becoming less common, however, especially in that the affordability of home recording equipment is letting those musicians interested in recording gain experience. Nonetheless, an offhand comment by recording engineer and mixer Bob Clearmountain (Cioe, 1982) illustrates the almost unconscious separation between musician and engineer.

> When Bruce Springsteen came in to try cutting a song, he got his drum sounds in an hour, and reportedly quipped, "It took three months at the last place I worked at." He has recorded at the Power Station ever since. Clearmountain asserts that this kind of efficiency is no accident, the engineers have been trained, he says, "not to burden the musicians with things like getting the right sounds on their instruments" for recording. (p. 69)

For most musicians it is not a "burden [to get] the right sounds on their instruments." It is a process in which they are happy to become actively involved. Again, Attali's (1985) previously mentioned correlation of sound and political power comes into play. A recording engineer can impose an idea of what the "right sounds" are.

To an extent, the musician's involvement is determined by the amount of money available for recording. Perhaps the single most obvious compromise during a recording session occurs when an overdub cannot be done, or another mix attempted, because the record company, or the artist, runs out of money. Studios charge anywhere from $25 an hour (for a 16-track studio without an engineer) to $200 or more an hour (for a 32-track digital recording studio with an engineer). And, as Cohen (1991) notes, there is tremendous pressure even on unsigned groups to spend more time and money in the studio "to satisfy the record companies for whom most demos [are] produced" (p. 52). Apart from demonstration tapes, the costs build up tremendously, especially considering that most popular music is recorded for an LP or compact disc format, which means that anywhere from 35 to 65 minutes of music are recorded. There is little recording of 45 rpm singles, except at the small, independent record company level. And that too is fading away, because few radio stations play 7-inch records anymore; most singles are culled from full-length albums and not recorded on their own.

Experimenting

The multitrack studio, while enabling a different creative process, demands time, and therefore money. As an engineer at a Grateful Dead recording session said,

> You record a layer of sound—the rhythm on one track, the vocals on another, add instrument solos on another, and the chorus on still another. . . . After all the [tracks] are recorded, group members and technicians gather in the control room for the mix-down session. There the creative work begins. We vary the volume of different tracks to change the mood of the music. . . . We add to [the sound] by reverberating [echoing] selected tracks to give a certain feel. The distinctive sound associated with many of today's groups is actually created more by the engineer than by the musicians. This is known as "composing" with a machine. This has been made possible by the

availability of the 16-channel recorder which allows more time for experimentation and introspection. (Wickersham, 1969, p. 38)

The engineer's assertion that it is in the control room where the creative work begins is telling. The implication is that what goes on in the studio room is somehow not creative, or at least not *as* creative as the work in the control room.

Though multitracking "allows more time for experimentation and introspection," it must be remembered that someone is paying for that time at a rate of $100 or more an hour. Most artists save time by being well rehearsed before going into the studio. However, in that the studio permits a wide variety of creative options, there are few artists who know exactly what they want when they get in the studio. And given the interactions between artist, producer, and engineer, the recording process can take a very long time. Even in the 1960s, when four- and eight-track recordings were the standard, recording was a long process.

> For Simon and Garfunkel, a song that takes four minutes to perform on stage may easily take dozens of hours to perfect on a four-minute record. A standard 12-inch disc often represents a minimum of 125 studio hours . . . and though a portion of that time is spent by agile technicians adjusting multiple microphones and sound balances, most of it is consumed by Simon and Garfunkel, exercising their "artistic control" to achieve the effects they desire. . . . Today's new pop artists are not interested in setting speed records. "It's no good right now, Art," says Simon after the take. "I'm not into it. Let's work on the other parts and I'll come back to it." (Ames, 1967, pp. 63-66)

That particular session ended without much result.

Simon and Garfunkel and other well-known groups usually can afford to spend quite a bit of time in the studio. It is general recording industry practice that the record company pays for the recording, then deducts the expenses from the artists' royalty checks. The profit on a top 40 recording is large enough to allow a large studio budget. Still, even the biggest groups can run into trouble with record company accountants. The Beatles' *Sgt. Pepper's Lonely Hearts Club Band* album, which took four months to record, was reportedly intended as a double album. However, "time and finance (in the form of horrified EMI [record company] auditors) finally intervened and *Pepper* emerged in the form in which we know it" (Carr & Tyler, 1978, p. 68). For small, independent record companies, recording budgets are virtually nonexistent and the artist must often pay for the recording.

The Beatles most often recorded in linear fashion; that is, they began and ended one song at a time (Lewisohn, 1988). Currently, when recording albums, any number of songs may be in progress at the same time, each awaiting different overdubs, or perhaps awaiting a fresh burst of inspiration. It is most common to find artists recording backing tracks in one sitting (drums, bass, guitar), then, as the studio is set up for other instruments, such as saxophone for example, recording the sax on *all* songs that include it. This process saves time (it is unnecessary to keep changing the studio set-up for each song), and is aided by use of multitrack recording, because discrete tape tracks are available for individual instruments.

But multitracking was not the origin of studio experimentation. Early jazz recordings were molded by the studio's license to play around with music. Evan Eisenberg (1987) writes,

> records not only disseminated jazz, but inseminated it . . . in some ways they created what we now call jazz. It is important to remember, first of all, that numbers were often "composed" just before a recording session. . . . The Hot Five was almost exclusively a studio band. Armstrong played with and led various Chicago dance bands in those years, but it was only in the studio that he could experiment freely with the light-textured, daringly improvised music that was in his head. . . . In the recording studio Armstrong was insulated from both the danger of failure and the lure of easy applause. The atmosphere was casual . . . Jelly Roll Morton . . . composed in the studio. (pp. 145-148)

Given the current costs of recording in a professional studio, the atmosphere may be anything but casual. Home recording technology allows artists to try out ideas before they get in a professional studio, and where else can a musician be most "insulated . . . from . . . the danger of failure"? The recording studio is a licensed space away from the stage, away from the audience.

It is rare for home recordings to make it beyond a preliminary stage, and some work must therefore be duplicated. As a member of the British group Heaven 17 said:

> We used to get all our ideas together . . . with a little Casio [synthesizer]. But we found it very wasteful doing demos and then re-recording them in the studio; you do things on demos that for some reason you can't recreate when you get into the studio. It's a bit futile actually trying to re-create something you really like anyway. (Goodyer, 1987b, p. 69)

More than anything else, home recording technology has enabled artists to capture musical ideas on the spur of the moment, in the form of demo tapes. Tascam Corporation's David Oren (1987) noted,

> I worked with the Alessi Brothers in the past. They started out in four-track then quickly went into Portastudios. Their statement to me was "unless we had the Portastudios we would not be able to capture the dynamics of the moment, when a piece is created." Bobby said he's woken up a number of times in the morning and he found his Portastudio on. He woke up in the middle of the night, had an idea, turned it on and went for it, went back to sleep. I know it's a far-out example, but had it not been for something small, compact, easy and convenient to use as a Portastudio, Bobby would not have captured the sound he heard in his head and that's really what everyone wants to be able to do. Capture the sound you hear in your head with the dynamics of the moment.
>
> The boys always carried a Portastudio around with them for demos and a bag of cassette tapes, and a little book that told you on what tape at what counter number you could find a piece of music. . . . They went into a major 24-track studio here to do an album three years ago, after each take they'd play back their Portastudio tape and see if they could get the dynamics and realism of that tape, because that's what they're shooting for. Ultimately it wound up that the Portastudio tracks went on the album.

Terms like *dynamics* and *realism* that once were used to set aside live performance as something special now are used as readily in the recording industry to differentiate recording methods. The pop music industry is thus still very much attuned to live performance *standards* if not methods.

Part of the reason that some artists build their own studios is precisely for capturing the spontaneity Oren describes above. If the artist is particularly happy with the sound of a demo, it can be extremely difficult and time-consuming to recreate it in a professional studio. It is also convenient to be able to record whenever one pleases. A recording studio is something an artist can have at his disposal, tangible evidence of success. As a member of British pop group Orchestral Manouevres in the Dark said, "We thought: 'Right, we're never going to sell any records, so let's take the money and build a studio so we'll have something to show for it'" (Goodyer, 1987b, p. 33). The group took the record company's advance intended for recording and built their own studio, at the same time recording their first album. A number of artists have their own studios, among them Todd Rundgren, Jan Hammer, and Lindsey Buckingham; the Beatles had one built as part of their own Apple Records company. Musician Peter Gabriel put it well when he said, "The real pleasure of having a studio setup of my own is that I can experiment in a way that I could never afford to do in a commercial studio" (Goodyer, 1986, p. 20).

As some pop artists have demonstrated, it is possible to make high-quality recordings in semi-professional or home studios. Though the quality may not be as good as that of a professional studio, many commercially successful records have been recorded in semi-pro studios. It is at the noncommercial level that semi-pro recording has had the biggest impact, however. Jon Pareles (1987a) identified a "cassette underground" risen from

> affordable recording technology, especially the advent of inexpensive multitrack recorders, [which] has made it possible to turn a bedroom or a kitchen into a studio for less than $1,000 . . . many musicians have begun to treat the home recorded cassette as a finished product. (p. C13)

Bruce Springsteen's *Nebraska* LP was recorded on a cassette multitrack machine, ostensibly because Springsteen wanted to record a "pure" album (as did the punks). Again we find the presence of terms like *authenticity* and *purity*. Springsteen's record, however, had the benefit of a professional recording engineer operating the deck, along with high-quality microphones and other equipment.

What the home and semi-professional recording studios offer is the ability to experiment with recording without excessive drain on the recording budget. The avant garde electronic music composers realized this as soon as tape was introduced. Hugh Le Caine (1963) wrote that

> the manipulation of recorded sound, rather than live sound . . . is considered the most important technique. . . . Sound generators . . . are expected to provide, not finished compositions, but material which will be developed by the usual techniques based on the recording process. (pp. 83-84)

The studio became the site of experimentation and investigation into the possibilties of sound, a licensed space in which the unusual (and sometimes undesirable) could be used to advantage. Even the earliest recordings contained examples: "Prokofiev . . . had his eyes opened for him. . . . Even the imperfections of recording equipment might have their uses: for example, the crackle produced by overload" (Eisenberg, 1987, p. 115). Many dub reggae recordings from the early 1970s, recorded on low-quality equipment, contain examples of tape hiss boosted at rhythmic intervals to sound as if the hiss was part of the music.

As popular music encompassed aspects of the avant garde, it embraced this ideology of experimentation. Artists from Frank Zappa to Brian Eno to the Beatles used the studio as a laboratory. Ultimately, some knowledge of the studio became necessary. A commonly held, but mistaken, belief, though, is to think that musicians had to become technically proficient. This is not necessarily so, although technical proficiency does not hurt studio work. From the beginning some musicians had a natural curiosity about the recording studio, and this inclination led to their education in studio techniques. Other musicians could easily get by with virtually no knowledge of the technical means of recording. But *all* musicians must have knowledge of the *possibilities* offered in the studio.

The combination of popular music and avant garde recording techniques, though difficult to precisely locate,[2] meant that the studio became a musical tool. To use it, those working in the studio had to have a knowledge of what the tool could do, even if they could not operate the tool. As composer Vladimir Ussachevsky (1980) said,

> the available means of manipulating recorded sounds make it almost mandatory for a composer to run through a certain number of routine experiments before he can determine the full range of his raw material. Experience gradually teaches one what to expect. I now habitually imagine a sound as if it were changed by the following mutation techniques, among others; pitch transposition . . . snipping off the attack . . . playing it backwards . . . depriving it of some of its harmonics through filtering . . . reverberating it. An intricate interrelation exists between an abstract formal concept which a composer might have formed about his forthcoming composition and the manner of developing his raw sound material. There can be a decided interaction between the two which makes itself felt through all the early experimental stages. (pp. 205-206)

Writing from a position within experimental music, Ussachevsky nonetheless identifies the importance of the studio. The effect the studio has on the composer is on *thinking* about sound. Comments that the recording studio is a "compositional tool" are common and are usually first associated with the Beatles. Though in some sense the studio is indeed a compositional tool, it may more accurately be described as a realizational tool. It is the place where compositions are realized, and during the process of realization the composition not only takes shape but often changes. Ussachevsky goes on:

> The tape medium is particularly felicitous for giving the composer a chance to hear and to shape his sound material as he proceeds. His

decisions regarding the final form of a composition are not infrequently influenced by the results of his experimentation with the sound material. (p. 206)

Mixing

The single most important activity in popular music production, mixing, is also the site of greatest experimenting with sounds—and of greatest compromise. Mixing has become the point at which records are fully realized, and mixers are in great demand. Edward Kealy (1974), in a study of the social organization of recording engineers, divided them into several categories, but essentially they fit two: those who work for major record companies, and those who are independent. Mixers are in demand as much as producers, and there are those who play both roles.

Kealy argues that mixers have in fact lost control over sound recording, because technology has become widespread and many musicians are aware of the possibilities the recording studio offers. This is true to an extent, but few musicians are capable of mixing their own recordings and operating the equipment in a control room. Most need an intermediary, usually an engineer. Also, people without musical ability have been able to use mixing equipment to create sounds. Rap music thrives on the work of mixers such as Grandmaster Flash, Jam Master Jay, and others. These performers blend sounds from records and other sources by means of a mixing board, adding them rhythmically to a rap song. Some mixers, such as Arthur Baker, Jellybean Benitez, Shep Pettibone, and Bob Clearmountain are as much in demand as producers for their ability to create exciting mixes, and remixes, and hopefully, hits.[3]

Tankel (1990) identified the importance of mixing as a form of artistic, musical creation.

The remix is a unique artistic act whose artistry is produced through the technology, since the craft is in manipulating both the *sound* and the music . . . remixing *is* recoding, the reanimation of familiar

music by the creation of new sonic textures for different sonic con-
texts. (p. 44)

During a mixdown session, several mixes, or versions, of a song
can be made, and a decision on which to release can be postponed
for days, perhaps weeks. Often several mixes of a song will be
released, one for each format; a short mix for AM radio, a longer,
more elaborate mix for FM radio, a long mix with many effects and
edits added for dance clubs, and a version of the FM radio mix with
effects and "sweetening" added specifically for combining the
song with a video. Reggae music relies heavily on mixing techniques for what is called the "dub" style of reggae. Dub involves
dropping instruments in and out of the mix and adding reverberation and delay to instruments.[4] The producer will simply add an
effect to a track, or cut a track in and out of the mix manually.
Automated mixing consoles, which incorporate a microprocessor
and computer memory, are able to memorize moments during
mixdown, enabling an engineer and/or producer to work on one
element at a time, and not "run out of hands" with which to
manipulate the console. Without multitrack recording, dub, and
indeed any form of remixing, would be very difficult to create,
because both rely on the recording of instruments on individual
tracks.

For most musicians and composers, mixing represents the final
stage of work, a kind of postcomposition that wraps up a piece of
music. Philip Glass (1987), when asked about his role during
mixdown, replied, "It's fairly minor. I go mainly for accuracy that
the composer is ultimately responsible for. In the recording studio
the more essential role is for the mix. The actual balance of the piece
is decided at that moment and I'm always there for the mix." The
distinction between mixing, composition and realization of a piece
of music is often unclear. Mixing will often include a search for a
new sound or effect. The most common distinction is one which
Glass describes. "It's easier to develop the sounds at the recording
level," Glass said. "There's so much going on in the mix that we
find it better on the level of the basic track to make the definition
of the sound." During the mixdown an overall sound is estab-

lished, an aesthetic balance between each instrument, each track. During recording the sound of each instrument and each track is developed individually.

Mixing is what distinguishes popular music from classical music. Bruce Swedien has won Grammy Awards for engineering a recording by Quincy Jones and Michael Jackson, among others. He has been recording both classical and popular music for the past 30 years, and has this to say about mixing (1987):

> When I started recording classical music, in a big way (I worked for RCA in Chicago, my gig was recording the Chicago Orchestra) I soon began to feel as if I was taking dictation, or something. In other words, the most that I could do in recording classical music was to re-create the original sound-field. On the other hand, in pop music (all types, rock, R & B, etc.), the only thing that limits the sound image that we create is our own imagination. Mix up those reverb formats, get crazy, don't try to rationalize anything.

Mixing is the point in the recording process most affected by technology. Prior to the use of multitrack tape recorders, mixing was done before recording. That is, the sound from various microphones was treated with equalization, reverberation, or other effects, then sent to the tape recorder. Multitrack tape recorders allowed mixing after recording. In that practically every instrument has its own track, the sound can be manipulated separately from the performance. Each track can have an effect added to it, then can be recombined and balanced with the other tracks. This final mix is sent to another recorder.

During a mixing session virtually all of the decisions regarding a recording's aural quality are made. Editing decisions usually are made during the mix. But even more importantly, certain parts of a piece can be heightened or camouflaged in the mix. During a particularly good saxophone solo, for instance, the sax track can be brought up in level. Alternately, if, later, there is a mistake on the sax track, its level can be brought down or it can be muted altogether. Pre-editing can thus be accomplished—but more important, the dynamics of the music can be altered. The mixer will often listen to just one track over and over, adding effects and changing the sound until satisfied. The amount of experimentation varies, but can take much longer than the actual recording session. At one mixing session, Scott Wyatt took over an hour to mix a 45-second-long piece of music. Mixing allows producer Ron Nevison to make decisions later rather than having to make them on the spot: "I didn't [always] have the tracks to play with . . . now I'll have two or three different . . . feeds. . . . I'll dump them onto separate tracks so later on, I'll have choices to work with. . . . [I]t's not something I'm required to make a decision about right away. (Armington & Lofas, 1988, p. 67)

A studio's equipment is especially important when it comes to mixing. If there are four tracks that need different reverberation effects, and only three reverberation units available, a compromise must be made. Similarly, a lack of tracks may mean that some parts were doubled up on one track, and cannot be altered independently. For instance, a bass guitar and drum may be on the same track. If there is a decision to lower the level of the bass, or perhaps change the equalization on the drum, the other sound will be affected as well. There is virtually no way to treat one sound and not the other. Likewise, a lack of input channels on a mixing board may mean that only so many effects can be added.

Another determinant of the final mix is the recording medium for mass production. In the case of cassette, LP, and compact disc production, the final mix is recorded in stereo. Some few applications, such as television broadcasting, often require monophonic mixes, though stereo TV broadcasts are becoming common (MTV, too, transmits in stereo). The recording of the final mix is used to make the final product, be it record, tape or compact disc. The process, called *mastering*, often involves slightly altering the sound of the final mix. The alteration depends on the quality of the final mix in relation to the mastering medium. If a record is being mastered, and the dynamic range of the final mix is greater than a record will allow, the mastering engineer will limit the dynamic range. Slight changes in overall equalization can also be made during mastering.

Norman Mendenhall (1979) described the phonograph disc mastering process this way:

During disc mastering, the master tape is played on a special tape machine that provides the signal for the disc cutter, which in turn inscribes the signal as a complex mechanical undulation [the groove] on the master lacquer. . . . The intention in disc mastering is to put as high a sound level [volume] on the record without distortion *and* without cutting into the [disc] or causing the stylus to lift away from the lacquer surface. As straightforward as this sounds, it requires a few hundred thousand dollars worth of equipment, and someone who really knows what he is doing, to accomplish properly. (p. 78)

The master lacquer is then electroplated, and a stamper is made from which records are pressed.

The difficulty mastering poses for the recording process lies in the fact that the final mix is not the final product. In effect, the mix must be made with mass production in mind but no one in the studio can hear a record of the mix until after mixing. The result is that mixing is done with the final product in mind, with someone, usually the engineer, compensating for possible difference between the master tape and the final product.

Even in the early 1950s, there was a distinct compensation during recording for the mass medium. In 1952, *Newsweek* (Men Behind the Microphones, 1952) reported that

most records are . . . made with a slight but deliberate distortion: The volume of high-frequency tones is boosted. This step is taken to override needle hiss, which is a melange of high-frequency noise. Phonographs are supposed to be designed to compensate for this distortion by automatically suppressing high tones. The net result, ideally, is balanced tone with reduced needle noise. (p. 56)

Some recording engineers will add more high frequencies to a mix than sound good on tape. Their thought is that most of these high frequencies will not be reproduced on a record, so they overcompensate in the mix. Perhaps the biggest difficulty is that the master tape can be used for mass producing cassettes, records, and compact discs. Unless a different master tape is made for each medium, or the mastering process can compensate for problems with the master tape,[5] the final mix will not sound good in all media.

Skill, Technology, and Authenticity

Mixing is the result of the control afforded the producer and engineer by recording technology. It is made possible by multi-tracking and by the development of auxiliary recording equipment (reverberation units, equalizers, etc.). It is a process that is the absolute opposite of hearing sound in a natural environment. But the goal of most recording is to create a natural sound. Eisenberg (1987) notes the contradiction.

> There are two ways to make a record seem "alive." One is live recording, which sometimes conveys a real sense of occasion. . . . But sometimes a live recording sounds embalmed. . . . The other way to make a record seem alive is to step up the use of studio techniques. Aggressive mixing and overdubbing, especially in rock, can give a sense of conscious intelligence and so of life. (p. 113)

But mixing and overdubbing are *not* live events; they are the arrangement of events into an ideal event. Not surprisingly, mixing received its fair share of criticism for being unauthentic, dishonest, and so on. Such criticism illustrates the difficulty in determining who is responsible for a popular music recording. Simon Frith (1981) identifies the difficulty in his book *Sound Effects*.

> Rock music, like other works of art in an age of mechanical reproduction, is not made by individual creators communicating directly to an audience—record-making depends on a complex structure of people and machines. . . . The rock *auteur* (who may be writer, singer, instrumentalist, band, record producer, or even engineer) creates the music; everyone else engaged in record-making is simply part of the means of communication. For many fans it was this sense of individual creation that first distinguished rock from other forms of mass music. (pp. 52-53)

But it is only the *appearance* of an auteur that brings this "sense of individual creation." Musicians may appear to be in control of their sound, but they often choose engineers and producers for the sound they can bring to a recording, making authorship diffuse. Mick Jagger and Keith Richards, for example, are usually credited as the Rolling Stones' directors. Though undoubtedly true, in that they have the money and power to pick and choose whom they will work with and to make decisions about the final mix, it is also true that those they work with add their own style to the music, be it in production, engineering, or musicianship. With artists who have less control over recording, it becomes even more difficult to discern who is responsible for the sound and music.

Eisenberg (1987) considers Phil Spector to be

> the first auteur among producers . . . [whose] work was perhaps the first fully self-conscious phonography in the popular field . . . his influence on his musical betters was immense. Frank Zappa . . . and the Beatles . . . took up the construction of records where Spector left off, expanding from singles into albums and elevating kitsch into Dada. (pp. 126-127)

Zappa and the Beatles, however, were themselves interested in recording technology and assumed some (or occasionally all) production roles. The only clues as to authorship could be found in album liner notes and credits—but even these could be ambiguous, and as musicians, engineers, and producers became involved in all facets of recording, their titles became as problematic as their job descriptions.

It was recording technology's increased complexity in the control room that facilitated the diffusion of authorship and uncertainty in the relations of production. There was a critical reaction to this in the 1950s and 1960s, when electronic effects became noticeable in recordings. The backlash took place in the discourse of authenticity mentioned earlier, in a particularly vociferous manner, which producer John Hammond's remarks (Natural Sound, 1954) about using audio effects illustrate.

> Mitch Miller's a great guy . . . but ever since about 1948, when he started playing tricks with sound—making those horrible echo-chamber recordings, for one thing—all the record companies have been knocking themselves out to achieve phony effects. Fun for the sound engineers, maybe, but tough on the musicians. What's the good of having every instrument in a band sound as if it were being

played in the Holland Tunnel? Anyhow, we're fighting all that electronic fakery and we've got just the place to fight it in. Our hall has
marvelous natural acoustics, thanks to perfect proportions and a
wonderful wood floor. (p. 27)

Hammond's room with "perfect proportions" could now be reproduced in the studio. Quantec introduced a digital reverberation
unit called a "Room Simulator" in the mid-1980s. It allows precise
recreation of an acoustical environment, and was used in the film
The Cotton Club to recreate the acoustics of the club.

Some criticism came from a misunderstanding of the work of
producers and engineers. They were not all engaged in "playing
tricks with sound," though they were able to manipulate sound
more than ever. *Time* magazine's 1965 definition of the producer is
equally appropriate at summarizing most people's perceptions of
production work in the 1980s (Age of the Patchwork, 1965):

> The grand designer of [recordings] is no longer the conductor but the
> producer. . . . With a mountain of sophisticated machinery at his
> command, he has become a space-age sculptor of sound. His raw
> material is the performer, his workshop the glass-enclosed control
> room. (p. 90)

All suggestions of collaboration are swept aside in this description
of the producer. He is not the "grand designer" but the dictator, an
idea as misleading as the belief that the synthesizer would replace
the performer.

The question of authorship provided pop music's critics with
ammunition, as the following passage from the *New York Times
Magazine* (Wilson, 1959) demonstrates.

> Recording techniques have become so ingenious that almost anyone
> can seem to be a singer. A small, flat voice can be souped up by
> emphasizing the low frequencies and piping the result through an
> echo chamber. A slight speeding up of the recording tape can bring a
> brighter, happier sound to a naturally drab singer or clean the weari-
> ness out of a tired voice. Wrong notes can be snipped out of the tape
> and replaced by notes taken from other parts of the tape. . . . The
> gadgetry dam really burst after Elvis Presley's recorded voice was so

doctored up with echoes that he sounded as though he were going to shake apart. Since then "sounds" have often taken precedence over music. . . . When [an] actor (for a TV pop music show) reluctantly submitted to an audition, it was found that he . . . could not carry a tune (a failing so common among potential pop singers that it is almost taken for granted). (p. 16)

The same article mentions pop singer Fabian, stating that he cannot sing and his records are not hits, but he succeeds because of his looks. This is virtually in the same breath as the criticism of recording techniques and shows another side of the criticism of pop music as inauthentic.

The article goes on:

Almost every pop recording made today, even by well established talent, carries some evidence of the use of echo chambers, tape reverberation, over-dubbing or splicing . . . [tape reverb] is a common device on rock 'n' roll recordings because it is a simple method of covering up a paucity of instruments or poor voices. . . . Two hit recordings by the Coasters . . . "Charlie Brown" and "Yakety Yak" were created (after the performers have left the studio). . . . Tom Dowd, chief engineer for Atlantic Records, recorded the original performance . . . on . . . eight different tapes . . . mixed these tapes in whatever proportions or sequence he desired . . . slowly building and shaping the final record as though he were working with colors or clay instead of sounds. (p. 17)

The article never mentions that classical, jazz, and other recordings use the same effects, but perhaps not as prominently. One of the most outrageous illustrations of early pop criticism comes from the same article:

"Judy's Turn to Cry" by Lesley Gore . . . embodies what the trade calls "the dumb sound." "The dumb sound," explains one record company executive, "is the teen-age sound, the sound that lets a kid identify with a record because it sounds like himself." . . .
Some analysts in the business feel that the true dumb sound is attainable only by youth. . . . By getting on in years a singer simply outgrows the dumb sound and his audience. (pp. 17-18)

With time, understanding of the roles played by the producer and engineer brought a delicate harmony between the critics of pop music and the pop music producers. Bruce Staple, director of New York's Electric Lady studios, said, (Drukker, 1976)

> I don't think you can place the label "fair" or "unfair" on these electronic techniques. Making a record is a form of entertainment . . . people are buying disk or a tape to be entertained. They don't ask how it was made, or why. We are giving them the state of the art. This is the way it's done. People are buying it; they seem to like it. Is it fair or unfair? (p. 115)

Nonetheless questions persist about authenticity and authorship. In late 1987 a young singer by the name of Tiffany found herself in the same situation as Fabian and other teen idols of the 1950s and 1960s, as this newspaper story (Van De Voorde, 1988) attests.

> Tiffany may . . . wind up taking the fall in some circles for a questionable production gimmick [producer George] Tobin allegedly uses on "I Think We're Alone Now." Certain vocal phrases on the record, says one rock producer, sound suspiciously similar—a tip-off that Tobin may have sampled [Tiffany's] vocals and then literally "cut and pasted" a song together with the results. The practice is not unknown. But it could hammer a few dents in MCA [Record's] attempts to portray Tiffany as a singularly gifted young diva. (p. C1)

Staple is clearly wrong when he asserts that the listener does not ask how a recording was made. Not only do rock fans often want to know about recording sessions, but the pages of serious music magazines such as *High Fidelity, Musician* and *Stereo Review* are filled with reports of recording sessions and new recording techniques. Moreover, fans regularly pass judgment on musicians based on their perception of whether or not studio gimmicks were used.

Staple's double entendre, "[m]aking a record is a form of entertainment" is particularly interesting. It is entertaining to the fan, who likes to know what goes on behind the scenes. But it is also entertaining to those involved in the production. A sense of fun permeates many recording sessions, and much of the experimentation with new sounds is playful. Many producers, engineers and musicians call their effects units "toys." Producer Peter Asher once said (Sutherland, 1977), "There are a lot of effects [on those recordings]. . . . There's tons and tons of toys that I use all the time, but I think if they're used right, they can sound completely natural" (p. 110). Producer, engineer, and studio owner Jonathan Pines also calls his effects units toys. Recording sessions become a game, the studio is a playground, and devices for making and manipulating sound are toys.

The mixer and producer are stars in their own right, as inseparable from the recording as the songwriter and musician. Value is placed on those who can make a good mix, and a knowledge of mixing is prized. Mixing becomes the favored pastime in the playground/studio, a form of pleasure. It is the pinnacle of realization, the moment when sound and music come together to create the song. The control of technology during mixing is characteristic of what Grossberg (1986) identifies as "technologically based popular culture" (p. 63). His comments concern:

> the proliferation of personal computers and the increasing computer sophistication of youth. [Technologically based popular culture] not only provides them with a clear-cut space of their own (an apparatus which is defined technologically but which has empowering effects as well), it has become a form of pleasure. (p. 63)

Recording now involves many of the same thought processes as personal computer use, and it is clearly empowering. One only needs to think of the vast cassette underground Pareles (1987a) writes about to discover the liberating potential of modern recording. If "the sound that lets a kid identify with a record because it sounds like himself" (Wilson, 1959, p. 16) is both a measure of commercial and artistic success in popular music, recording is undoubtedly both empowering *and* pleasurable.

If young people cannot have a clear-cut physical space of their own, they can at least have a clear-cut aural space (Eisenberg, 1987, p. 251). And what could be more pleasurable than creating that space for oneself? A line from a Beatles' song, "It's All Too Much" is particularly interesting in light of such matters. George Harrison sings, "Show me that I'm everywhere/But get me home for tea." For many, music serves to take them everywhere, without travelling very far at all. One is reminded of Kosinski's archly titled *Being There*. Brian Eno mentions that "We can use recordings to insert a sense of place in the various locations that we end up in" (Korner, 1986, p. 78). It is quite possible that it is for these reasons that home recording technology seems to be popular among youth. Where a desk may once have only had a baseball glove, doll or model, there is now often a Casio synthesizer as well. As Eisenberg (1987) writes,

> if the music is worth its salt, it will assert itself as the true reality, and all the lovely furniture of one's room will seem (if one is aware of it at all) a mere picture. . . . Can any other "home entertainment" device pull off this trick—superimpose its own space on the space people live in? (p. 1)

Recording provides control of that space—it is a home away from home, even though the studio can be located in one's house. Eisenberg quotes Stockhausen:

> I listen to . . . music best and my imagination is most free when I am alone, just listening, preferably with closed eyes in order to shut out the things around me too. Then the inner eye opens to visions in time and space which overstep what the laws of the physical world around us permit. (p. 134)

Stockhausen identifies what youth discovers and desires in popular music—freedom and oneself. Perhaps this, too, accounts for the popularity of the Sony Walkman.

In 1963, a record company executive said that "outside of records there are no other Canaverals left in show business. A record is the last launching pad a kid has left if he wants to shoot for the stars" (Aronowitz, 1963, p. 91). But in 1963 few kids had access to recording equipment. In the 1990s, many do. And many, many more people than ever before are composing, realizing, and releasing music to the public.

Notes

1. The reverb sound may be reconstructed precisely, in that most digital effects allow for storage of all settings and parameters. However, once other tracks are recorded and reverberation added to them, it is probable that the reverb sound will have to change, as the overall ambience of the sound will have changed.

2. Did pop absorb avant garde techniques, or did the avant garde move into the mainstream? The question may not be very important, for what is important is that studio techniques from the avant garde became a staple of pop recording, due to the pop industry's search for new sounds.

3. Some notable examples of songs released with different mixes are M/A/R/R/S's "Pump Up The Volume," U2's "Desire," The The's "Uncertain Smile," Grandmaster Flash's "White Lines," Echo and the Bunnymen's "Lips Like Sugar," Madonna's "La Isla Bonita," EMF's "Unbelievable," The Happy Mondays' "Step On," and Julian Cope's "World Shut Your Mouth."

4. Among the finest examples of dub are Augustus Pablo's "East of the River Nile" and Burning Spear's "Garvey's Ghost." The Burning Spear record is a track-for-track dub version of their "Marcus Garvey" LP and a side-by-side listening, made easy in that Island Record's release of both LPs on one CD, is virtually a lesson in dub mixing.

5. Because only the final stereo mix can be altered during mastering, and not individual tracks from the multitrack, it is usually undesirable to make many changes upon mastering.

8

Rock, Roll, 'n' Record

Control

The theme running throughout this work has been the increase in control over sound during the evolution of recording technology and the effect of that control on music.

The development of recording technology is biased toward control, whether it be control of music, time, space, or any of several other facets of recorded music. The most obvious example of the desire for control over sound is the acceptance of recording media based on their editing capabilities. Tape recording was quickly adopted in recording studios not only because of its aural qualities and low cost but also because it enabled easy editing.

Popular music, a form of music that relies on concepts of spontaneity, inspiration and creativity, is in some sense directly opposed to control. Yet it is precise control over all parameters of sound—volume, rhythm, spatial location, timbre—that now enables recordings to sound animated. A recording made over the course of several months, musicians recording their parts individually and never in personal contact with each other, can sound as if the musicians had been rehearsing together for weeks—thanks in some part to technology, but mostly because of expert use of that technology.

Regardless of the importance of editing, the most important development for recording popular music was the multitrack recorder. Modern recording technology is founded on the ability to overdub and layer sound. What marks out music made with modern recording technology from music made in pre-multitrack days is the difference between design and creation.

In simplified terms, prior to the use of multitrack recorders, recordings were made by musicians who were well rehearsed and relied on their performance to inject life into their music. Producers and engineers made sure that the recording equipment functioned smoothly and captured the performance.

Multitrack recording also permits musicians to play spontaneously, to perform, and producers and engineers are forever looking for that spark of life that makes a recording vital. Multitrack recording, however, allows musicians to *work* on their spontaneity. A single part can be recorded over and over until it is, in effect, spontaneous enough. The contradiction is obvious; the result is that expert use of recording technology results in a recording that sounds natural.

Donald Hughes (1964) believed that recording was "removed from spontaneity." He wrote that

> the inevitable effects of mass reproduction of music, and particularly of folk music, are not all good. We have seen that one of the chief features of folk music is its spontaneity, its immediacy. . . . Now these conditions are the precise opposite to those of commercial recording . . . the technique of the recording studio itself is utterly removed from spontaneity. Takes and re-takes continue until a performance is passed as perfect; and the final issued version may be a synthetic construction from a number of performances joined together by tape and scissors as a film is cut and patched. (pp. 160-161)

But it is not that spontaneity has left popular music. It is the definition of spontaneity (and with it authenticity) that has changed.

Determining whether or not a price has been paid for increased control in popular music production thus depends on one's definitions of music and sound. In other words, the difficulty is not in determining the price but in establishing the currency. Without precise definitions of spontaneity, creativity, inspiration, and authenticity, the effect of technology on the aesthetic dimensions of popular music is difficult to surmise. As much as fans and critics of popular music rely on these concepts to judge artists and their music, it is impossible, given modern technology, to ground the concepts in any traditional way.

For instance, inspiration does not only come from the soul. Where people hear sounds and how they become aware of sounds are of critical importance to the sounds they will later create themselves. It is hard to subscribe to a notion of individual creativity any longer when in some sense people are stealing sounds (and music) from their own history. What exactly is inspiration? Popular music thrives on its revision. A familiar sound or melody helps identify a group or at least places it within an overdetermined structure of pop music styles.

Regardless of its precise definition, inspiration is by no means diminished by use of modern recording technology. Creation requires imagination, and a successful musician or producer will be able to, if not create "original" music, recombine music and sound in a unique way. Realization of a piece of music occurs via a creative process that has been compared to other arts, notably painting. Color is sound, brushes are instruments, and the canvas is the recorder. Modern recording, though, allows more than creation—it allows design. To further the painting-music analogy, the recorder is both sketchpad and canvas, model and painting.

Prior to multitrack recording, planning a recording session usually involved rehearsals and some discussion of how to begin and end a piece. With multitrack recording, preproduction planning often occurs, but just as often is altered (and even instigated) during the recording process. It is not just that the music can be altered, but that the process itself is completely malleable. Producer Todd Rundgren put it well:

> When I was working with XTC. . . . We did one song using a drum machine. . . . We spent an entire day, and at the end of the day we had the bass drum and the snare drum. It had this effect of causing

everybody just to listen to it too hard, almost every single beat. You know, we'd go through it and lay it down, and say "Fine," and someone would say, "No, let's go back and change this one beat." The reason why was because you *could* go back and change the one drum beat—so everybody insists on going back and changing the drum beat. If it had been a real player, none of that would ever come under consideration. (Davies, 1987b, p. 45)

The high cost of recording in a professional recording studio necessitates preproduction decisions and discourages such revision and attention to detail. Still, Rundgren's point is that the technology *encourages* such work. The opportunities for second-guessing grow exponentially as the opportunities for editing expand. Within popular music's marketing structure, particularly as it relates to radio play, second-guessing the public is elevated to an art. In the recording studio, second-guessing the public, the record company, the producer, and even the recording artist is made inevitable as more and more occasions are made available for editing. Many popular music artists now prefer to plan very little and create in the studio instead (and stories about groups spending months in the studio abound). To some degree, home recording now allows for an endless amount of experimentation. The production of popular music has become quite labor intensive, a craft unto itself separate from the performance of music.

Currently, modern recording combines design and creation. To return to the metaphor of recording as painting, imagine a painter whose palette would dry up within several minutes. The painter would have to be very well prepared to execute the painting, or else try to paint it several times, preparing new paints each time. This is roughly analogous to pre-multitrack recording. A recording had a definite beginning and end, dictated by the length of the cylinder, disc, or tape. The musician had to create within that time frame.

Multitrack recording dissolved that time limit. The musician could go back over a track (or only part of a track). In terms of our metaphor, the painter can now paint over parts of the canvas until satisfied with the overall picture, changing shapes, colors, and so forth. Similarly, the musician can record until satisfied with the overall piece, changing sounds, balances, spatial location, effects, and so on. The design process occurs continuously, from recording through to mixing.

Also, as paint affects the look of a painting, so recording technology has an effect on a piece of music. A thick brush may not allow for much detail. Similarly, an old, monophonic tape recorder does not allow for detailed layering of sound.

The painting-recording metaphor breaks down when the collaborative nature of sound recording is taken into consideration. The painter may not have someone mixing colors, adding shapes to the canvas. The musician, though, does have someone doing just that: the producer and engineer. The mediation of recorded music begins when the artist(s), producer, and engineer begin working. The compromises that occur between them constitute a large portion of the design of modern recordings. And, the artist's work is subject to modification by the producer, engineer, or anyone else having access to the master tape and recording facilities. Though a musician may gain control over sound by recording it, he also surrenders some control to the person who recorded it, the person who is responsible for the overall sound of the recording, the person paying for the recording, and so forth. Regaining such control is usually the motivating force for most musicians' construction of home recording studios.

As the production of popular music has become increasingly labor intensive, the time required to produce it has, literally, dilated. Multitrack recording extends the time of musical production from a mere instant to days, weeks, months, even years. To fully utilize modern recording technology demands a lot of time; to record a three-minute long pop song can take anywhere from three hours to three weeks or longer. For a medium known for its evanescence this is astounding.

The shift from performance to control is rooted in this extension of time by way of multitrack recording. It lets the musician, producer, and engineer endlessly second guess themselves. Though that may be conducive to achieving as nearly perfect a piece of music as possible, it can also result in frustration and wasted time. Modern recording offers so many possibilities in terms of sound creation and manipulation that it becomes difficult to assess the value of each possibility, and impossible to try each one. Composer Harold Budd, when asked if technology may offer too many options, replied, "The answer generally is yes. . . . I feel that if you can do anything, then you're liable to end up with everything . . . or indeed nothing" (Diliberto, 1986a, p. 76).

In reality equipment availability and time limits act to curtail experimentation, even in home recording studios. Budd said that where he records, equipment and time are limited, so he cannot try every possibility.

Technology and Music

The practice of recording not only affects the sound of music but also note-by-note composition. Budd remarked, "In many respects, the sort of treatment you hear on the piano influences exactly the note-to-note process; the length of time between musical gestures, and the kind of taking advantage of ringing timbres which I am very fond of" (Diliberto, 1986a, p. 76). A British group, the Cocteau Twins, claims that as

> soon as we start something, even before we've made up the rest of the track, we usually have a good idea of how it's going to end up soundwise. It's really recording it. That's the art. It's not just mixing it that is the production, it's recording it as well. I'd much rather spend three hours messing around with a guitar sound when it's getting recorded, than just sticking something down and then trying to tackle it [in the mix]. 'Cause the sound that we make, that's the sound that sort of inspires the notes that we play. (Dark, 1987, p. 32)

What a musician hears will affect what that musician plays.

Live performance in particular is haunted by troubles with stage monitors, loudspeakers that enable musicians to hear themselves, going awry. The resulting performance is usually mediocre at best, and at worst, grinds to a halt as each musician performs at a different tempo, in a different key, or plays a different song altogether.

What is surprising is that music technology has only recently begun to match the sound of live performance to the sound of recording, primarily, I believe, thanks to the development of consumer electronics equipment like the CD player and Surround-Sound. The audience has driven the sound reinforcement/public address industry to achieve new levels of fidelity as that audience has come to expect higher fidelity from their home audio equipment. But musicians have had an impact on sound reinforcement as well. They may not want to sound the same on stage as in the studio, but they want to be able to hear their playing as clearly during a concert as they can hear it in the studio.

For example, while mixing sound for a variety of groups in the Midwest between 1981 and 1985, I found group members often complaining to me that they could not hear themselves as well as they would like. Most groups not signed to record companies have poor stage monitoring systems because they have little money with which to purchase or rent such equipment. After a performance in 1982 by a group called the First Things, using an extensive monitor setup borrowed from another band, the group's bassist remarked that he could for once hear himself sing as well on stage as in the studio. He was extraordinarily happy, and for some time insisted the group purchase a better monitoring system. He was happiest on stage, where he could perform before an audience, but preferred the studio, where he could hear his voice clearly.

The popular music audience is also concerned with how well they can hear the performers. Popular music fans criticize technology, often within the terms of authenticity and performance. "Live bands sound better" versus "[I'd] rather listen to [the] record, [it's] more polished than live" (Australian Broadcasting Tribunal, 1985, pp. 97, 104). The point common to each side is sound quality, and the schism between live and recorded sound delineates one of the major breaks among the pop music audience. If popular music ideology is by necessity based on elitism (my group is better than your group) the difference between live performance and recording gives that elitism an added edge. Fans often criticize recordings by saying, "they [the group] are much better live." But live performances by any given group are few and far between for most fans, and recordings still form the basis of popular music appreciation.

Popular music's authenticity is most often judged by examination of the difference between live and studio performance, and musicians often state in interviews that the stage and studio must be kept distinct—it is difficult to *exactly* reproduce a studio recording on stage. In rock music, authenticity is most often measured by how "live" a recording is. Yet *liveness* is not something that can be measured in any meaningful way, as recording splinters the live musical performance into many facets.

Relative to live performance, recording has had its greatest impact when used for lip-syncing. Though singers mimed to their recordings from early on (the practice was common in Hollywood musicals from the start), popular music fans demand a level of trustworthiness from performers. Even though lip-syncing is regularly used during televised performances (Dick Clark's American Bandstand used it exclusively) in concert it is frowned upon. Even back-up tapes or samples, meant to supplement a group's sound, are criticized by fans. Yet to provide an elaborately choreographed stage show pop stars such as Madonna, New Kids on the Block, and Janet Jackson must, of necessity, lip-sync.

The most publicized case of lip-syncing involved the pop group Milli Vanilli. It was disclosed that the two group "members" who were featured in music video and live performance were in fact not the ones who recorded the Milli Vanilli album. What infuriated the National Academy of Recording Arts and Sciences (NARAS) (who awarded Milli Vanilli a Grammy in 1989) the most was that they were unable to distinguish between the identity of the live and studio performers, a fact that testifies to the sophistication of recording technology. Not only does it render questions of authenticity superfluous when it comes to recordings, it does so for live performances as well, so much so that NARAS insisted that the 1990 Grammy Awards telecast be as live as possible, using multiple, elaborate, stage setups.

Even with the use of sequencers during concert performances, musicians must at least look like they're performing. As Andrew

Goodwin (1990) has pointed out, "audiences need to *see* their pop musicians *doing* something" (p. 269). At a 1990 concert by the group New Order, fans were occasionally displeased when song introductions or breaks emanated from the PA speakers without the group's performance on an instrument. Such use of technology is what particularly troubles Chris Cutler (1985), for whom machines that play "perfect" sounds at the push of a button are (regardless of the ironic word choice) inimical to musicmaking.

Popular music is similarly criticised along the lines of "I don't like the synthesized stuff—it seems they're cheating somehow if they make hit records and they're not really playing music" versus "good beat, good sound" (Australian Broadcasting Tribunal, 1985, pp. 97, 104). Such comments illustrate the odd position of popular music in culture. On the one hand, it is taken very seriously—musicians are rated highly for sincerity, feeling, and authenticity. On the other hand, it is also valued for fun, enjoyment. The ideology of popular music forever totters between these two poles. As Sara Cohen (1991) points out in her study of fledgling Liverpool rock groups,

> Technology stood in the way of [these groups'] ideal of honest musicmaking. The problem . . . was how to maintain and project that honesty whilst recording: in other words, how to use advanced technology to produce music that sounded "raw" and expressed an aesthetic of simplicity opposed to technology. . . . [W]hilst technology . . . was seen as a constraint, its creative, beneficial potential was also recognized. (pp. 179-180)

Musicians, engineers and producers often criticize each other in terms similar to those used by critics and fans. But they work among a circle of people who value technical innovation, whose thinking about technology and music is based on production as well as consumption values. A musician may dislike the sound of a new record, but admire the engineer's skill in getting that sound. Musicians, engineers, and producers rarely criticize each other's work and are rarely critical of technology, except when a piece of equipment they desire costs too much. Indeed, they should be criticized for their unwillingness to take a critical position except when it comes to economics. Chris Cutler's (1986) point that the use of technology is based on consumption values is particularly appropriate in this regard.

> Choosing rather than making has come to mediate the creation of music: choosing from the expanding array of prefabricated musical units. . . . To be producers we now need only buy the units and lay them on top of one another, empirically: choose and judge by *listening, as consumers.* (p. 27)

A good sound is not necessarily an authentic one. A common criticism found in magazines like *Rolling Stone, Creem, Spin* and many others is that a recording sounds too slick or glossy, that is, overproduced—the sound may be good, but at the expense of feeling, of authenticity. The average musician is caught between wanting to sound good and wanting to sound authentic: in Cutler's terms, between choosing a sound and making a sound. As Tony Bacon (1981) pointed out:

> one camp says that it is not important which instrument you play, the feeling is what counts; the other that technique is all, and that the newest toys that technology can offer should be exploited to the hilt. Between these two exaggerated stances lies the average musician's attitude; a balance between technical knowledge and strong emotions. (p. 8)

As stated at the outset, the development of recording technology has run parallel to a reorientation in popular music production. The goal of getting a good sound is no different now than it was when the first recordings were made, but the idea of what a good sound is and how it should be achieved are radically different. The best example of this reorientation is illustrated by the phrase "fix it in the mix." But before that can be properly analyzed, a philosophical framework must be established, accounting for the interplay of technology and ideas.

Technology and Ideology

Simon Frith accurately placed the interplay of music and technology within Marx's concept of alienation. Frith (1987c) writes that

> It is because of our experience of the *immediacy* of music making that its industrial production has always been somehow suspect. . . . The contrast between music as expression and music as commodity defines twentieth century pop experience and means that however much we may use and enjoy its products, we retain a sense that the music industry is a bad thing—bad for music, bad for us. . . . What such arguments assume (and they're part of the common sense of every rock fan) is that there is some essential human activity, music making, which has been colonized by commerce. . . . In the language of rock criticism, what's at issue here is the *truth* of music. (pp. 53-54)

Frith properly places authenticity within the realm of common sense, or ideology. It should be added that these issues are part of the common sense of musicians, critics, producers, engineers (and scholars). Decisions are made during production as well as consumption and these decisions embody an ideology, a common sense view.

But ideology is one thing to an observer, and another to the ordinary person to whom it is a way of life. In broadest terms, ideology is a system of meanings that is created, constructed, reproduced, asserted, fought over, and lived within a culture. It is the language with which we make sense of the world. Ideology is situated within the very practice of constructing the symbol. It is thus a social formation related to political and economic practice, in the individual's acts of signification, representation, production, and articulation of and location within specific meanings.

Ideology functions, at least in part, to fix the individual in a certain place at a certain time by organizing the world. The individual constructs reality from a position already inside that reality. The trick is to discover how the construction occurs: what is the process and what are the mechanisms?

As discussed in the first chapter, in the realm of music, technology takes basically two forms. First, it is "an activity which immediately produces artifacts" (Mitcham & Mackey, 1972, p. 2). It includes the creation of music as well as the creation of musical instruments and equipment. The second form of technology to be considered is "know-how" (Jarvie, 1972, p. 54). In music, Jarvie writes, technology "contains within it both pure tools and all knowledge" (1972, p. 61). It both enables and restricts realization of ideas by providing knowledge of how to do things and tools with which to do some things and not do others.

This second form of technology is particularly important in relation to popular music, for it is the medium of exchange, the currency, bartered by producers, engineers, and musicians. Each is in some way involved in selling their *know-how*. Manfred Stanley (1978) says of this form of technology that it "appears to . . . be a method of legitimation reflecting a particular kind of world view. [It] . . . is alleged to be an ethos, a collective mentality" (p. 14). Stanley goes on to write that it is "a phenomenon comprising unconsciously taken for granted assumptions, not a set of principles consciously accepted" (p. 9). He formulates his criticism of technology around the intrusion of technical modes of thought into nontechnical areas of life such as culture, politics, and ethics.

Similarly, Jacques Ellul (1964), in *The Technological Society*, is concerned with what he calls *la technique*. La technique, Ellul writes, is the "totality of methods rationally arrived at and having absolute efficiency . . . in every field of human activity." It "does not mean machines, technology or this or that procedure for attaining an end," but rather the worldview that brings the machine into society. It is the ordering of society in such a manner as to organize thought around the technical (p. 19). Cutler's point that popular music production now often relies on choosing, rather than making, is actualized in the exchange of know-how. Namely, as Rimmer (1985) put it, "Very glibly: in a consumer society, you are what you buy. As you choose what you spend your money on—within the limits both of what's on offer and of what you can afford—you choose what you *are*" (p. 11).

To put a different twist on Rimmer's expression and examine it on another level requires only to add the word *into* at the end of the first sentence. By choosing instruments, studios, producers, musicians place themselves within an overdetermined structure, constituted by sound.

The determinations operating upon popular music production therefore determine the possible formations within which consumers explicate for themselves the function of music in their lives. This is thus a curiously circular structure, for, as Frith (1988) writes,

> What is possible for us as consumers—what is available to us, what we can do with it—is a result of decisions made in production, made by musicians, entrepreneurs and corporate bureaucrats, made according to governments' and lawyers' ruling, in response to technological opportunities. They key to "creative consumption" remains an understanding of those decisions, the constraints under which they are made, and the ideologies that account for them. (pp. 6-7)

Much of the reason for the circularity lies in the ability, by way of "creative consumption" (even during *production*) to insert the self into the structure, to personalize by way of choosing (regardless of the overdetermined nature of the choices at hand).

Ellul's and Stanley's ideas resonate with Frith's and Cutler's insofar as all are concerned with the interposition of personality, technology, music, and production/consumption. Ellul's and Stanley's ideas can be found realized in music technology, illustrated in that technology's development. Sound recording technology personalized mass production. Tony Bacon (1981) noted that "record sales are considered by some [musicians] to be much more important than live performances, and much time is consequently spent in the recording process" (p. 12).

Records are considered more important not only because they are the primary source of income within the pop music industry but also because they are the vehicle of expression for the musician, producer, and so on. Compared to the mass distribution of recordings, live performances are seen by a relatively small number of people. Those involved in making a recording want to include themselves in it, differentiate it from other recordings, and put themselves into it the same way they would in a live performance. The reason perspectives on rock and roll as folk music or as mass art fail to achieve full resonance with the experience of rock and roll is that the two are inextricably entwined. The combination of rock as folk music *and* rock as mass art is an outcome of the recording process.

Put another way, popular recordings bear the stamp of their creators. They bring an "immediacy of communication," as Frith (1981) calls it. He writes that "what a performer could sell . . . was his or her unique *approach* to songs" (pp. 16, 17). Frith locates the essence of the approach in the human voice, and I have previously mentioned that one may consider the voice in popular music in terms of Barthes' *signifiance*. Now I would like to broaden the scope of *signifiance* to include all identifiable individual musical style. The guitar sound of Jimi Hendrix, the drum sound of Phil Collins, the saxophone sound of Sonny Rollins, all identify the performer and give a sense of immediacy.

It is because of this that recordings, though a mass product, are not vilified as inauthentic. They are not necessarily documents of a live performance, but they are documents of expression. Frith quotes Joachim-Ernst Berendt's comment of the 1960s and 1970s: "We were hearing from electric bassists sounds with human, expressive, emotional and even narrative qualities" (p. 18). It is not that these instruments can sound as if they *are* the human voice, but that they can express the same range of feeling. As an aside, it will be interesting to see what effect new music technology, such as samplers, or the Korg DVP-1, and similar units, will have. This equipment lets the voice control synthesizers via conversion of voice sounds to MIDI signals, and control voice sounds via keyboards.

Such personal expression via recording ties directly into popular music marketing techniques that are geared toward selling personalities. The following passage by Frith and Horne (1987) concerning the Rolling Stones and their grasp of rhythm and blues in the early 1960s relates authenticity and personality.

[C]oupled with the commitment to musical truth was a belief in R & B as a means of individual expression. . . .

It was this individualism that explains why these musicians, for all their explicit anti-commercialism, became pop stars—they were marketable as personalities, and their music, whatever its "authentic" roots, could stand for the fantasies and desires of their own generation. (p. 89)

Recording enabled these personal, expressive and musical qualities to be mass mediated. And yet it is these same qualities that make authenticity such a difficult matter. As Lipsitz (1990) points out in his analysis of popular culture and memory:

To speak someone else's words or to wear someone else's clothes meant hiding one's own identity. . . . This contained the essence of egalitarian and utopian thought by challenging the legitimacy of static identities inherited from the past, but it also threatened a sense of authentic self-knowledge and created the psychic preconditions for the needy narcissism of consumer desire. (p. 7)

Though Lipsitz writes about the theater in this instance, in pop music terms the "challenging" of "static identities" is appealing to fans, to youth. And, simultaneously, by way of establishing personality (often by way of *signifiance*) in a recording the threat to "authentic self-knowledge" is reduced by, at least, acknowledging the authentic (often by way of quotation, be it musical, lyrical, or stylistic).

Sound recording also allowed the degree of control over sound necessary to achieve such expression in the first place. The vagaries of live performance made it difficult to achieve precisely the same sound at each show. The studio not only allowed control, it demanded it. Recording equipment operates best within certain limits of loudness, pitch, and timbre. To exceed those is to render a recording not reproducible, and therefore useless. And recording also made it worthwhile for musicians to work on their sound, in that mass production and distribution brought a large audience and the promise of profit.

With recording valued for its ability to create personal statements, time spent working in the studio increased. If one was going to put part of one's self in a record, it had better be done right. Jon Pareles (1987b) writes that

> By the time the need to answer "Sgt. Pepper" receded, studio craft had mutated into a virtue rather than a technique, and albums had become self-conscious statements to be labored over, layering track by track and agonizing over the final mix. Improvements in recording technology since 1967 haven't sped things up; from a 1980's perspective, the four months the Beatles spent making "Sgt. Pepper" are a comparatively short stint for a band at work. (p. 18)

Thus was born the clearest expression of the argument over spontaneity in popular music. An actor acts differently before an audience than he does before a camera, and a musician plays differently before an audience than he does in the studio. As mentioned before, the studio became a place isolated from a real audience—the only audience was in the control room, or in the mind. Producers and engineers are thus professional listeners, giving the artist audience feedback. Adding to the confusion created by the change in performance and recording practice brought about by technology is the difficulty of establishing "a distinct line between the tools of performance and those of recording" (Eargle, 1976, p. v).

Even the language used by musicians and fans to describe recording, in particular the phrase "going into the studio," conjures up visions of isolation and removal. The studio becomes a mythical place. "We're going into the studio," a group says, and thousands of questions come to a fan's mind. "What will you record, how will you do it?" Fans eagerly await the music that will come out of the studio, and few have much knowledge of the recording process. Music magazines' gossip pages are filled with tidbits of information about a group's work on a new album, and MTV's Music News occasionally broadcasts previews of music in the making. For pop music fans, it is as if some combination of performance and magic yields a record. Musicians do not go into the studio to "play" (as they might play music); they go there to "work" on music. But no one except those present at the recording sessions can be sure what the nature of that work is.

Recording technology mystifies music making, and music-makers have a stake in being vague about the processes they use. Why should those involved in recording be vague about it? Because in part recording is legitimized and perceived authentic because of its status as a craft, the same way that songwriting is thought of as a craft. If it were not, its value as a creative act would diminish. As Cohen (1991) states, the search for authenticity, and, ultimately, meaning, is "reflected in the mystification of musicmaking, involving an attitude of secrecy towards composition and performance . . . which heightened the sense of importance involved" (p. 199). Moreover, as musicmakers trade their know-how, their technical knowledge, any clear elucidation of that know-how strips the individual of their power over it.

Chris Cutler casts this argument in a different light, but I believe the result is the same. Cutler said,

> There is, for instance, in every copy of the magazine [Re Records Quarterly] at least one article by a group talking about the recording studio as a composing instrument—how it's actually done. This is because I think in order to appreciate or to get involved in any kind of musical activity, it's necessary not only for producers to know the nuts and bolts but for consumers to know them as well. (Chris Cutler, Pt. 1, 1987, p. 29)

Some punk groups attempted to deconstruct the recording process in the late 1970s by releasing records with instructions as to how they were made, or providing a track by track analysis of the recording as a bonus track on one side of a record. But music-making has traditionally been a mystical art—inspiration (or, colloquially among musicians, *feel*) is the key. The design of recording technology often perpetuates its mystical image. Only an adept person knows how to operate much of the equipment, and the words used by studio professionals (dB, RAM, headroom, bias, etc.) constitute a language of their own.

The concept of control is in large part contrary to inspiration, and it might seem that recording is therefore inimical to spontaneity. But the contradiction is bridged by those who maintain that they must have everything ready to capitalize on a flash of inspiration.

Thus the oft-repeated story of the fellow who wakes up in the middle of the night with a melody in his head, and thanks his muse for having a four-track recorder at his bedside so that he can capture the moment. Humming a few bars into the recorder is much easier than writing them on a staff, and it also captures the spirit of the moment—the root of inspiration. The desire to own a home recording studio is based on this eagerness to capture inspired moments. Many musicians are now in a constant state of readiness, eager to record their inspiration along with their music.

In fact, the recording studio requires spontaneity on demand, a difficult proposition for most musicians. Rock guitarist Frankie Sullivan's experience with making an album is typical.

> As the guitar player, you're playing rhythm guitar on a basic track, and you don't get to really play a whole lot for the first three weeks. Then, all of a sudden, they say, "Okay, let's do solos!" And you're supposed to burn. (Pollock, 1986, p. 44)

Record producers not only demand control, they call for control of ultimately uncontrollable variables like inspiration and performance. Editing allows for some degree of control over those variables.

But that alone, however, accounts only partially for the desire to control sound when making a recording. Opera Singer Leonard Warren remarked, "Recording is the worst job in music. You have to put over emotion in bits and pieces, and all the time you feel you're singing not for the evening but for always" (Recording in Italy, 1957, p. 68). It is this feeling that one is performing "for always" that fuels the need for control.

The current accessibility of recording equipment can lead to loneliness, and to the strongest criticisms of recording technology. Ivan Illich (1973) argues that technology should not expand beyond the limits of a natural scale. He writes that

> Society can be destroyed when further growth of mass production renders the milieu hostile, when it extinguishes the free use of the natural abilities of society's members, *when it isolates people from each other* . . . or when cancerous acceleration enforces social change at a

rate that rules out legal, cultural and political precedents as formal
guidelines to present behavior [italics added]. (p. xi)

Recording technology may have passed its limit in regard to the
social production of music. Musique concrete composer Pierre
Henry once described his life this way:

> I lead a monastic life. I go to work at 6 a.m., spend ten to twelve hours
> at a stretch with my tape recorders. By the time I get home I'm
> completely "dingue" (Parisian argot for "off my nut"). (The Loneli-
> ness, 1966, p. 50)

Recording studios are isolated, usually windowless places
where time evolves along with a piece of music and not with the
world outside. Producer Mickie Most likens most studios to "a bit
like being in prison . . . [you] feel this oppression, this confined
mental as well as physical inhibition" (Tobler & Grundy, 1982,
p. 140). Some artists work best in such an atmosphere, and others
crumble under the pressure. In either case recording has turned
musicmaking into a lonely pastime. Some musicians miss interact-
ing with other performers, but some, like Frank Zappa, enjoy being
able to work every part out themselves (Davies, 1987a).

Of course, nothing prevents one from working in the studio with
others. However, studio technology is evolving toward individual
production—MIDI and the increasing use of computers in particular are designed so that one person can perform all functions. The
image of what goes on in the studio, conjured in a *Newsweek* article
on producers, combines magic and technology in a bizarre mix of
art and electronics (Miller, 1984, pp. 67-68). Even the headline, "The
Wizards of Sound," invokes a kind of electronic mysticism.

One of the clearest paths popular music technology has directed
musicmaking toward is that of composition, with a concomitant
steering away from performance. One can understand these relationships by way of the following parallels. Tape recording technologized musicmaking in a way similar to that of printing's
technologizing of the word (Ong, 1982). Along the same evolutionary parallel, current music technology is akin to word processing.

It appears likely that in the near future, certainly by 1995, music-making will have its equivalent to desktop, or personal publishing. As digital recording formats fall in price, and Sony and Philips both work toward consumer digital formats, it is probable that anyone with a personal computer and Sony's mini-CD will be able to record, master, and manufacture CDs of their own music (or that of others) individually, or in large quantities. It would not be surprising if the software for CD mastering included some sort of drawing function, providing for creation of CD tray inserts and cards on a laser printer. The home studio will become the home pressing plant, and, indeed, the home record company.

Is It Live or Is It Authentic?

If something goes wrong during a recording session and a part cannot be perfectly recorded, the producer, engineer, or musician will frequently say, "we'll fix it in the mix." Ostensibly what this means is that the part can be somehow modified or even dropped out completely during mixdown. But more often than not, it means that the track can be electronically processed in a way that will cover up or correct something perceived as a problem. If it doesn't sound right—remix it.

Purists will argue that remixing alters the performance and therefore the authenticity of a recording. Regardless of one's recording philosophy, a problem does arise when one considers that the technical fix can become a crutch—not a replacement for performance, but a never-ending search for equipment that will solve any problem, whether there happens to be one or not. The very idea of what is or is not a problem depends in part on one's familiarity with possible solutions. Recording technology is forever solving problems—equipment is often marketed as the solution to something or other—and it is hard to resist the idea that unless you have the latest technology, you will have a problem. At the very worst, all your equipment will break down. At the very least, your equipment will be outdated.

There is a constant struggle among recording studios to stay abreast of the latest technology. Some have purchased digital recording equipment because their clients demand it—it's the latest recording medium. Studios often advertise the signal processing equipment available for mixdown, because they feel they attract customers who are looking for a state-of-the-art sound. That sound, the thinking goes, can be achieved only with the latest technology. Competition among professional studios requires that they stay on top of new technology. They must meet the demands of their clients, which are often based on the sound of other recordings and casual conversation with others in the recording industry. If musicians hear a sound they like, and are later told it was done with a Widget X-200, they may balk at recording at a studio that does not have one.

In the home recording market, the technical fix takes the form of the "I need more stuff" syndrome. Most home recordists begin with a 2- or 4-track recorder. Then they purchase an 8-track, 16-track, and so on. Creative decisions play a role in this, in that obviously one can have more control over sound with an 8-track deck as opposed to a 4-track one. But more often than not there is a belief that one cannot sound good without certain equipment, just as a tennis player may believe he cannot play without the right racket, or a computer user believes he always needs more memory and a faster machine. The difficulty is in discovering which is the problem; lack of equipment, or lack of belief in the equipment? And given "better" equipment, moving from an 8-track to a 24-track deck for example, changes one's thinking about musicmaking, without question. There are suddenly 16 more tracks to fill up, three times the space for sounds. Even if a song does not require more than eight tracks, there is a tendency to fill up the other 16 anyway. The common sense of recording technology is based on the tenet that "more is better."

To return to the parallels between the technologizing of the word and the technologizing of music, it is possible that modern music technology restructures consciousness in a fashion similar to the restructuring of consciousness brought about by writing. Ong (1982) wrote that

> with writing or script . . . encoded visible markings engage words
> fully so that the exquisitely intricate structures and references evolved
> in sound can be visibly recorded exactly in their specific complexity
> and, because visibly recorded, can implement production of still more
> exquisite structures and references, far surpassing the potentials of
> oral utterance. (pp. 84-85)

Computer-aided musicmaking moves music into a visual realm, especially during use of digital sampling and recording, and sequencing. Music is represented in a variety of visual forms, including, among others, binary code, hexadecimal code, MIDI code, and audio waveforms. Though music notation performed a similar function, it did *not* record specific performances, and allow for manipulation of those performances. As McLuhan and Carpenter (1970) noted, technology made explicit what writing (or, in this case, music notation) made implicit. What followed was a sensory shift. Work, such as editing, that was once performed by way of hearing, is now performed visually, bringing music into, in Ong's (1982) words, a "new sensory world" (p. 85).

Trends toward visual representation of music, of isolation during the recording process, and of an increased primacy of composition, parallel Harold Innis's (1950) ideas regarding the effects of technology on culture. Thus one finds in music, as Carey (1989) noted in a discussion of Innis's ideas on communication technology, that technology "alter[s] the structure of interests (the things thought about) by changing the character of symbols (the things thought with), and by changing the nature of community (the arena within which thought developed) (p. 160).

Interests, symbols and community have, as the preceding chapters have shown, changed signficantly as recording and music technology have evolved. Yet one must be aware, as Shepherd (1991) warns, "that there is [not] an inevitable relationship between media and certain modes of cognition, thought and social organization" (p. 17). Power groups within popular music, ranging from record companies to musical equipment makers, musicians to fans, permit or encourage (to paraphrase Shepherd) certain modes over certain other modes.

The relationships between sound recording and computer use are, I feel, particularly noteworthy. Sound recording practice increasingly involves use of computers or computer-like devices. But more importantly, the image of the sound recordist is becoming like that of the computer hacker. Recording is becoming an increasingly cybernetic art. Norbert Weiner (1948) coined the term *cybernetics* from the derivative word cybernate, which "came to mean 'to control automatically by computer, or to be so controlled'" (Leary, 1987, p. 90). In current usage, cybernetics means "the study of human mechanisms and their replacement by mechanical or electronic systems" (p. 90). There is evidence of this already in the use of computerized mixing consoles, and in the use of two recently marketed devices, the Southworth Jam Box and the Kahler Human Clock. The Jam Box provides a musician with someone (or thing) to "jam" with, to improvise and try new ideas. It is a fully automated system, which relies on musical input from the user, then in essence plays along. The Human Clock takes a drum input from a human drummer and converts it into electronic pulses that will synchronize a drum machine, sequencer, or synthesizers to a person's drumming. Software that improvises music within a set of parameters established by the computer user are available.

The mixture of technology and popular music is frought with contradictions, and none is as compelling as the one between rock and roll and high-tech. Leary (1987) quotes novelist Bruce Sterling:

> a new alliance is becoming evident; an integration of technology and the 80s counterculture. . . . The counterculture of the 1960s . . . was rural, romanticized, anti-science, anti-tech. But there was always a lurking contradiction at its heart, symbolized by the electric guitar. Rock tech has grown ever more accomplished, expanding into high-tech recording, satellite video, and computer graphics. Slowly it is turning rebel pop inside out, until the artists of pop's cutting edge are now, quite often, cutting-edge technicians in the bargain. They are special effects wizards, mixmasters, tape-effects techs, graphics hackers, emerging through new media to dazzle society. . . . And now that technology has reached a fever pitch, its influence has slipped control and reached street level. The hacker and the rocker are this decade's pop-culture idols. (p. 90)

I hope it is clear from my account of recording that I do not reject technology, but do challenge it. I agree with Simon Frith (1987c) when he writes that

> music "machines" have not, in short, been as dehumanizing as mass media critics from both left and right perspectives have suggested. For a start, it was technological developments that made our present understanding of musical "authenticity" possible. Recording devices enabled previously unreproducible aspects of performance—improvisation, spontaneity—to be reproduced exactly, and so enabled Afro-American music to replace European art and folk musics at the heart of Western popular culture. . . . This affected not just what sort of music people listened to but also how they listened to it, how they registered the emotional meanings of sounds and the musical shape of their own emotions. Recording . . . has extended the possibilities of expression in all pop genres. (p. 72)

With that extension of possiblities has come an opportunity for reexamining concepts such as authenticity. In that recording renders authenticity difficult to discern, at least, or meaningless, at most, music criticism should take a different approach, one that will enhance and broaden knowledge of the music industry. The goal of future study should be to discover what sources *outside* music the musician, fan, critic, and so on, goes in search of establishing authenticity and credibility. Though this may simply be further removing us from the issue at hand, or substituting one constructed text for another, it is important to recognize the whole range of influences working within popular music generally, and the music industry specifically, that are organized specifically for the creation and maintenance of credibility and authenticity. One example of this process may be a band's performance of "cover" versions of songs as close to the original as possible, or from an "accepted" canon of songs, to establish credibility before they themselves have any hits. Likewise, live performance in and of itself may be a means for a musical group to establish credibility as musicians and performers. Perhaps one of the functions of copyright law now is to determine authenticity in a medium where property boundaries are continually shifted by technology.

Iain Chambers (1988) writes that

> Dada's direct refusal of "art" . . . profoundly undermined the tradi-
> tional demand for artistic "authenticity." This had now become a false
> request, an irrelevancy; not, as Adorno was fond of repeating, because
> the world had grown "false," but because the conditions of percep-
> tion, reception, and artistic production had irreversibly changed.
> (p. 608)

Similarly, demand for authenticity in popular music is a false
request, because such a demand is made with the assumption that
music exists in some pure form. Ingarden (1986) views music as a
potentiality within an interpretive scheme, not as something objective. This leads the way to Frith's (1987c) suggestion that

> the flaw . . . is the suggestion that music is the starting point of the
> industrial process—the raw material over which everyone fights—
> when it is, in fact, the final product. The "industrialization of music"
> can't be understood as something that happens *to* music but describes
> a process in which music itself is made—a process, that is, which fuses
> (and confuses) capital, technical, and musical arguments. (pp. 53-54)

Music technology has opened new avenues of musical explora-
tion, and reinvigorated, or, as Tankel (1990) writes, "recoded,"
popular music styles. Rimmer's (1985) argument for technology is
a little simplistic, but sets the tone for what I believe is typical of
the effect of music technology.

> The idea of electronic pop is a bit of a red herring. Depeche Mode,
> Soft Cell and others all found fame and fortune by playing classically-
> structured pop songs with new-fangled instruments. But the tech-
> nology was important. By obviating technique, it allowed a lot of
> non-musicians to enter the fray. By providing new noises, it gave early
> New Pop a sound quite different from what had gone before. (p. 84)

Just like the CD prompted the reissuing of hundreds of previously released phonograph recordings, music technology is first
used to recombine sounds and forms that have gone before. Ultimately the "new noises" that are available are incorporated within
the process of recombinance, and, to borrow from Fred Gaisberg
(1942), the music goes round.

References

Aaron, C. (1989, Fall). Gettin' paid. *Village Voice Rock & Roll Quarterly*, pp. 22-26.
Age of the patchwork. (1965, September 24). *Time*, p. 90.
Allis, D. W. (1905). Fun with the phonograph. *Scientific American*, p. 415.
Allison, R. (1978, February). The future of audio technology. *Stereo Review*, p. 75.
Ames, M. (1967, September). Simon and Garfunkel in action. *High Fidelity*, pp. 63-66.
Anderton, C. (1978). *Home recording for musicians*. New York: Guitar Player Books.
Anderton, C. (1986a, June). Thomas Dolby. *Electronic Musicians*, pp. 56-60.
Anderton, C. (1986b, September). Editor's note. *Electronic Musician*, p. 6.
Angus, R., & Eisenberg, N. (1969, July). Are cassettes here to stay? *High Fidelity*, pp. 46-53.
A. P. Wire Service report, June 21, 1987.
Appleton, J. H., & Perera, R. C. (1975). *The development and practice of electronic music*. Englewood Cliffs, NJ: Prentice-Hall.
Armington, N., & Lofas, L. (1988, February). The Nevison touch. *Home and Studio Recording*, pp. 64-67.
Aronowitz, A. (1963, October 5). The dumb sound. *Saturday Evening Post*, pp. 91-95.
Attali, J. (1985). *Noise*. Minneapolis: University of Minnesota Press.
Australian Broadcasting Tribunal. (1985). *Young Australians and music*. Melbourne: Australian Broadcasting Tribunal Research Branch.
Bacon, T. (Ed.). (1981). *Rock hardware*. New York: Harmony Books.
Banerjee, S. (1977). Audio cassettes: The user medium. Paris: United Nations Educational, Scientific and Cultural Organization.
Bangs, L. (1987). *Psychotic reactions and carburetor dung*. New York: Alfred A. Knopf.
Barthes, R. (1977). *Image, music, text*. New York: Hill and Wang.
Batten, J. (1956). *Joe Batten's book*. London: Rockcliff.
Begun, S. J. (1949, September). Science on the march. *Scientific Monthly*, p. 195.
Bell, B. (1987, June 9). [Personal interview with the author]. Unpublished raw data.
Benjamin, W. (1969). The work of art in the age of mechanical reproduction. In H. Arendt (Ed.), *Illuminations* (pp. 217-251). New York: Schocken Books.

Bennett, H. S. (1990). The realities of practice. In S. Frith and A. Goodwin (Eds.), *On record* (pp. 221-237). New York: Pantheon Books.

Benoit, E. (1984, August 13). Music's black box. *Forbes*, p. 102.

Bereza, A. (1983). Home recording. In G. Martin (Ed.), *Making music*. New York: Quill Books.

Berman, M. (1982). *All that is solid melts into air*. New York: Simon & Schuster.

Bettig, R. (1990, August 5). *Critical perspectives on the history and philosophy of copyright*. Paper presented at annual conference of the Association for Education in Journalism and Mass Communication annual conference, Minneapolis, Minn.

Bielecki, B. (1987, April 1). [Personal interview with the author]. Unpublished raw data.

Bill to copyright new electronic sounds. (1955, March 16). *Billboard*, p. 1.

Biocca, F. (1985, August). *The pursuit of sound: Aural media, perception, and the composer in the early twentieth century*. Paper presented at the Association for Education in Journalism and Mass Communication annual convention, Memphis, TN.

Blaukopf, K. (1982). *The Phonogram in cultural communications*. Vienna, Austria: Springer-Verlag.

Block, A. B. (1986, November 3). Digital dream, digital nightmare. *Forbes*, p. 206.

Block, D. G. (1991, August 14). Dig copyright bill agreed on. *Pro Sound News*, pp. 1, SR14.

Boehm, G.A.W. (1958, August). Stereo goes to market. *Fortune*, pp. 110, 165.

Branscomb, A. W. (1990). Technological rips in the seams of intellectual property law. *The Annual Review*, pp. 85-130.

Brown, P. (1979, January). A bedroom not for sleeping. *High Fidelity*, p. 107.

Brush sound mirror, The. (1947, December). *Consumers' Research Bulletin*, p. 25.

Butterworth, W. E. (1977). *Hi-Fi*. New York: Four Winds Press.

Camras, M. (1985, April). Origins of magnetic recording concepts. *Journal of the Acoustical Society of America*, 1314-1319.

Carey, J. W. (1989). *Communication as culture*. Boston: Unwin-Hyman.

Carr, R., & Tyler, T. (1978). *The Beatles: An illustrated record*. New York: Harmony Books.

Chambers, I. (1985). *Urban rhythms*. New York: St. Martin's Press.

Chambers, I. (1988). Contamination, coincidence, and collusion: Pop music, urban culture, and the avant-garde. In C. Nelson and L. Grossberg (Eds.), *Marxism and the interpretation of culture* (pp. 607-611). Urbana: University of Illinois Press.

Chapple, S., & Garofalo, R. (1977). *Rock 'n' roll is here to pay*. Chicago: Nelson-Hall.

Chew, V. K. (1967). *Talking machines 1877-1914*. London: Her Majesty's Stationery Office.

Chris Cutler, pt. 1. (1987, January/February). pp. 27-29.

Christensen, D. (1987, April 1). [Personal interview with the author]. Unpublished raw data.

Cioe, C. (1982, July). The Power Station states the art. *High Fidelity*, pp. 67-69.

Classified Ads. (1987, April). *Keyboard*, p. 141.

Cohen, S. (1991). *Rock culture in Liverpool*. Oxford: Clarendon Press.

Colgrass, U. (1988). *For the love of music*. New York: Oxford University Press.

Coon, C. (1979). *1999*. London: Proteus.

Coppola, V. (1979, January 29). Now, digital records. *Newsweek*, p. 65.

Copyright Act of the United States of America (1976), 17 USC 101, paragraph 26.

Cox, S. (1987, June 5). [Personal interview with the author]. Unpublished raw data.

Culshaw, J. (1981). *Putting the record straight*. New York: Viking Press.

Curley, T. (1987, June 5). [Personal interview with the author]. Unpublished raw data.

Cutler, C. (1985). *File under popular*. London: November Books.

Cutler, C. (1986, March). Skill: The negative case for some new music technology. *ReRecords Quarterly*, p. 27.

Dark, S. (1987, May/June). That which cannot be spoken of. *OPtion*, pp. 30-33.

Davies, H. (1978). *The Beatles*. New York: McGraw-Hill.

Davies, R. (1987a, February). Father of invention. *Music Technology*, pp. 28-30.

Davies, R. (1987b, October). Todd Rundgren. *Music Technology*, pp. 43-46.

Diliberto, J. (1986a, September). Harold Budd. *Music Technology*, pp. 74-76.

Diliberto, J. (1986b, December). Pierre Schaeffer and Pierre Henry: Pioneers in sampling. *Electronic Musician*, pp. 54-59.

Dixon, R., & Godrich, J. (1970). *Recording the blues*. New York: Stein and Day.

Doerschuk, B. (1987, May). Jam & Lewis. *Keyboard*, pp. 74-85.

Dorian, F. (1942). *The history of music in performance*. New York: W. W. Norton.

Drukker, L. (1976, February). Audio-video playback. *Popular Photography*, pp. 110-115.

Dryden, D. (1987, April 1). [Personal interview with the author]. Unpublished raw data.

Eargle, J. (1976). *Sound Recording*. New York: Van Nostrand Reinhold.

Eargle, J. (1979, March). Disc mastering today. *High Fidelity*, pp. 57-60.

Edison, T. (1878a, May/June). The phonograph and its future. *North American Review*, p. 527.

Edison, T. (1878b). *Recording and reproducing sounds*. London: British Patent Office.

Edison's new phonograph. (1888, January 7). *Electrical World*, p. 3.

Eisenberg, E. (1987). *The recording angel*. New York: McGraw-Hill.

Eisenberg, N. (1965, November). High fidelity newsfronts. *High Fidelity*, p. 46.

Ellul, J. (1964). *The technological society*. New York: Knopf.

Ernst, D. (1977). *The evolution of electronic music*. New York: Schirmer Books.

Fabbri, F. (1987, April 4). [Personal interview with the author]. Unpublished raw data.

Fantel, H. (1973). *The true sound of music*. New York: E. P. Dutton.

Feldman, L. (1978, July). Digital hi-fi recording. *Radio Electronics*, pp. 57-59.

Fikentscher, K. (1991). Supremely clubbed, devastatingly dubbed: The nature of mixes on 12-inch dance singles. *Tracking: Popular Music Studies, 4*(1), 6-12.

Form SR. (1976). U.S. Copyright Office, Washington, DC.

Fox, T. (1986). *In the groove*. New York: St. Martin's.

Frith, S. (1981). *Sound effects*. New York: Pantheon.

Frith, S. (1985). *Towards an aesthetic of popular music*. Unpublished manuscript.

Frith, S. (1986). Art versus technology: The strange case of popular music. *Media, Culture and Society, 8*, 259-278.

Frith, S. (1987a). *Copyright and the music business*. Unpublished manuscript.

Frith, S. (1987b, Nov/Dec). In praise of learning. *The Catalogue*, pp. 5-6.

Frith, S. (1987c). The industrialization of popular music. In J. Lull (Ed.), *Popular music and communication* (pp. 53-77). Newbury Park, CA: Sage.

Frith, S. (1988). *Music for pleasure*. New York: Routledge.

Frith, S., & Horne, H. (1987). *Art into pop*. London: Methuen.

Gaisberg, F. W. (1942). *The music goes round*. New York: Macmillan.

Gambacurta, T. (1987, March 8). [Personal interview with the author]. Unpublished raw data.

Gammond, P., & Horricks, R. (Eds.). (1980). *The Music goes round and round*. London: Quartet Books.

Gelatt, R. (1954). *The fabulous phonograph*. New York: Appleton-Century.

George, N. (1985). *Fresh*. New York: Random House/Sarah Lazin Books.

Glass, P. (1987, March 10). [Personal interview with the author]. Unpublished raw data.

Gleason, H. (1988, January). The Nashville cowboy. *Home & Studio Recording*, pp. 59-62.

Gold, S. (1991, September). Sound off. *Home & Studio Recording*, pp. 16-21.

Goodwin, A. (1990). Sample and hold: Pop music in the digital age of reproduction. In S. Frith and A. Goodwin (Eds.), *On record* (pp. 258-274). New York: Pantheon.

Goodyer, T. (1986, August). Peter Gabriel. *Music Technology*, pp. 18-25.

Goodyer, T. (1987a, January). Dawn of a new age. *Music Technology*, pp. 28-34.

Goodyer, T. (1987b, January). How men are now. *Music Technology*, pp. 68-75.

Greene, B. (1974). *Billion dollar baby*. New York: Atheneum.

Grossberg, L. (1984). Another boring day in paradise: Rock and roll and the empowerment of everyday life. *Popular Music, 4*, pp. 225-260.

Grossberg, L. (1986). Is there rock after punk? *Critical Studies in Mass Communication, 31*, 58-74.

Grossberg, L. (1987). Remarks at the International Communication Association Convention, Montreal, Canada.

Guralnick, P. (1971). *Feel like goin' home*. New York: Random House.

H.R. 2911. (1985). Home Audio Recording Act. U.S. House of Representatives.

Harrington, R. (1986, September 8). RIAA moving to Washington. *Washington Post*, p. C2.

Hebdige, D. (1987). *Cut 'n' mix*. New York: Methuen.

Hi-Fi that's just for the trade. (1954, July 10). *Business Week*, pp. 162-165.

Hodges, R. (1978a, February). The cassette: A short history. *Stereo Review*, pp. 26-28.

Hodges, R. (1978b, February). The digital countdown and other timely matters. *Popular Electronics*, p. 15.

Hoover, C. (1971). *Music machines—American style*. Washington, DC: Smithsonian Institution Press.

How it feels to sing for the phonograph. (1924, May 10). *Literary Digest*, pp. 28-29.

Hubert, P. G., Jr. (1889, February). The new talking machines. *Atlantic Monthly*, pp. 256-258.

Hughbanks, L. (1945). *Talking wax*. New York: Hobson Book Press.

Hughes, D. (1964). Recorded music. In D. Thompson (Ed.), *Discrimination and popular culture* (pp. 152-175). Baltimore: Penguin Books.

Illich, I. (1973). *Tools for conviviality*. New York: Harper Colophon Books.

Ingarden, R. (1986). *The work of music and the problem of its identity*. Berkeley: University of California Press.

Innis, H. A. (1950). *Empire and communication*. Toronto: University of Toronto Press.

Innis, H. A. (1951). *The bias of communication*. Toronto: University of Toronto Press.

Jacobson, L. (1987, March). Digital forum: Southern style. *Mix,* pp. 58-64, 69.

Jarvie, I. C. (1972). Technology and the structure of knowledge. In C. Mitcham and R. Mackey (Eds.), *Philosophy and technology* (pp. 54-61). New York: Free Press.

Jaynes, J. (1976). *The origin of consciousness in the breakdown of the bicameral mind.* Boston: Houghton Mifflin.

Johnston, R. (1987, April 1). [Personal interview with the author]. Unpublished raw data.

Jones, G. G., & Rahn, J. (1981). Definitions of popular music: Recycled. In G. Battcock (Ed.), *Breaking the sound barrier* (pp. 38-52). New York: E. P. Dutton.

Jones, S. (1981, March 11). Recording session, Faithful Sound studios, Champaign, IL. [Unpublished raw data].

Joy Division/New Order, Part 2: A history in cuttings (No publication date given). No publisher given.

Jungleib, S. (1987, June 8). [Personal interview with the author]. Unpublished raw data.

Kaar, I. J. (1944, February). Talking wire finds new uses. *Science Digest,* pp. 89-90.

Kagan, S. (1990). The compact disc and its effect on contemporary music. *Popular Music & Society, 14,* 1, 13-18.

Kealy, E. (1974). *The real rock revolution: Sound mixers, social inequality, and the aesthetics of popular music production.* Unpublished doctoral dissertation, Northwestern University, Evanston, IL.

Kealy, E. (1982, Fall). Conventions and the production of the popular music aesthetic. *Journal of Popular Culture,* 98-114.

Korner, A. (1986, December). Aurora musicalis. *Artforum,* pp. 76-78.

Krishef, R. (1962). *Playback: The story of recording devices.* Minneapolis: Lerner Publications.

Kurzweil 150. (1987, May). *Electronic Musician,* p. 18.

Laing, D. (1985). *One chord wonders.* Milton Keynes, England: Open University Press.

Lane, A. P. (1931, July). Home radio records are now easy to make. *Popular Science Monthly,* p. 75.

Lawrence, H. (1955, April). About music—The composing machine. *Audio,* pp. 10-11.

Le Caine, H. (1963, Spring). A tape recorder for use in electronic music studios and related equipment. *Journal of Music Theory,* 69-87.

Leary, T. (1987, April). Cyberpunks. *Spin,* pp. 87-92.

LeBel, C. J. (1958, October). Stereo . . . tape or disc? *Radio and Television News,* pp. 40-41.

Lehrman, P. (1987, March 30). [Personal interview with the author]. Unpublished raw data.

Lewisohn, M. (1988). *The Beatles: Recording session.* New York: Harmony Books.

Lipsitz, G. (1990). *Time passages.* Minneapolis: University of Minnesota Press.

Loneliness of the electronic composer, The. (1966, July). *Audio,* p. 50.

Lowe, J. (1955, March). Tape recorder spurs new interests for audio-minded home owners. *Musical America,* p. 21.

Magnetic wire recorder. (1943, November 1). *Life,* pp. 49-50.

Manufacture of Edison phonograph records, The. (1900, December 22). *Scientific American,* p. 390.

Marsh, D. (1979). *Born to run.* Garden City, NY: Doubleday.

McLuhan, M., & Carpenter, E. (1970). *Explorations in communication*. London: Jonathan Cape.

Men behind the microphones: Makers of music for millions. (1952, September 8). *Newsweek*, p. 57.

Mendenhall, N. E. (1979, January). How to make good records. *Stereo Review*, pp. 76-78.

MIDI & music. (1987, June). *Keyboard*, pp. 32-38, 54-57.

Miller, F. (1978, February). The fifty-eighth AES convention: Digital is here. *High Fidelity*, p. 112.

Miller, J. (Ed.). (1980). *The Rolling Stone illustrated history of rock & roll*. New York: Random House.

Miller, J. (1984, September 10). The wizards of sound. *Newsweek*, pp. 67-68.

Miller, M. (1987, September 1). High tech alteration of sights and sounds divides the arts world. *Wall Street Journal*, p. 1.

Mitcham, C., & Mackey, R. (1972). Introduction: Technology as a philosophical problem. In C. Mitcham and R. Mackey (Eds.), *Philosophy and technology* (pp. 1-32). New York: Free Press.

Monforte, J. (1984, December). The digital reproduction of sound. *Scientific American*, pp. 78-84.

Moog, R. (1987, March 31). [Personal interview with the author]. Unpublished raw data.

Mumford, L. (1934). *Technics and civilization*. New York: Harcourt, Brace & World.

Music maker for the masses. (1968, February 24). *Business Week*, pp. 108-109.

Natural sound. (1954, July 17). *New Yorker*, p. 27.

New Horizons. (1986, October). *Music Technology*, p. 2.

1989 Update. (1988). Washington, DC: Recording Industry Association of America.

On the right tracks. (1968, September 2). *Newsweek*, p. 45.

Ong, W. J. (1982). *Orality and literacy*. London: Methuen.

Oren, D. (1987, June 5). [Personal interview with the author]. Unpublished raw data.

Pareles, J. (1987a, May 1). Record-it-yourself music on cassette. *New York Times*, p. C13.

Pareles, J. (1987b, May 31). Twenty years ago today. *New York Times*, sec.2, p. 18.

Paul, L. (1991, August). Home alone. *EQ*, pp. 38-42, 89.

Peter Wolf. (1987, October). *Music Technology*, pp. 30-36.

Peterson, I. (1983, March 12). Analog "apples" and digital "oranges." *Science News*, p. 172.

Pictures that talk. (1923, January). *Scientific American*, p. 19.

Pines, J. (1987, March 17). [Personal interview with the author]. Unpublished raw data.

Pleasants, H. (1978, December). Exploring the digital frontier in Watford and Tooting. *Stereo Review*, p. 44.

Pollock, B. (1986). *Interviews with great contemporary songwriters*. Port Chester, NY: Cherry Lane Books.

Pollock, S. (1985, March). Is digital next? Is analog a thing of the past? *Theatre Crafts*, p. 82.

Powers, R. (1987, November). Nam Chic. *Gentleman's Quarterly*, p. 170.

Proceedings of the 1890 convention of the local phonograph companies. (1974). Nashville: Country Music Foundation Press.

Ramone, P. (1983). Producing records. In G. Martin (Ed.), *Making music* (pp. 278-283). New York: Quill Books.

Read, O., & Welch, W. L. (1976). *From tin foil to stereo* (2nd ed.). Indianapolis: Howard W. Sams.

Recording in Italy. (1957, July 29). *Time*, p. 68.

Reich, S. (1987, January 5). [Personal interview with the author]. Unpublished raw data.

Repka, C. (1977, August). Resurrecting the Beatles: Star club to stereo. *High Fidelity*, pp. 101-109.

Results are in, The. (1987, November/December). *Synthony Update, 45*, pp. 2-4.

Reynolds, S. (1990). *Blissed out*. London: Serpent's Tail.

Rimmer, D. (1985). *Like punk never happened*. London: Faber and Faber.

Robinson, D. C., Buck, E. B., & Cuthbert, M. (1991). *Music at the margins*. Newbury Park, CA: Sage.

Rubel, M. (1984, June). [Personal interview with the author]. Unpublished raw data.

Sarser, D. (1955, March). Tapes, discs and coexistence. *High Fidelity*, pp. 44-46.

Schaffner, N. (1978). *The Beatles forever*. New York: McGraw-Hill.

Senior, J. (1987, June 5). [Personal interview with the author]. Unpublished raw data.

Shannon, C. E., & Weaaver, W. (1949). *The mathematical theory of communication*. Urbana: University of Illinois Press.

Shepherd, J. (1991). *Music as social text*. Cambridge: Polity Press.

Sound goes magnetic. (1949, December 12). *Newsweek*, p. 87.

Speirs, B. (1950, April). ABC uses magnetic tape for delayed broadcasts. *Radio & Television News*, pp. 41, 134.

Stanley, M. (1978). *The technological conscience*. Chicago: University of Chicago Press.

Sterling, C. (1978). *The mass media*. New York: Praeger.

Stokes, G. (1976). *Starmaking machinery*. New York: Bobbs-Merrill.

Sutherland, S. (1977, June). Peter Asher—Producer, power and a touch of class. *High Fidelity*, p. 110.

Swedien, B. (1987, March 25). *Performing Artists Network interactive electronic conference.*

Talking machine review. (1969, December). *1*(1).

Tankel, J. D. (1990). The practice of recording music: Remixing as recoding. *Journal of Communication, 40*(3), 34-46.

Tape for the networks. (1948, May 3). *Newsweek*, p. 52.

Tapeworms. (1967, December 25). *Newsweek*, p. 74.

The, L. (1986, January). The music connection. *Personal Computing*, pp. 89-90.

Tobler, J., & Grundy, S. (1982). *The producers*. London: British Broadcasting Corporation.

Toop, D. (1984). *The rap attack*. Boston: South End Press.

Transmission by tape. (1938, September 26). *Newsweek*, p. 27.

Truax, B. (1984). *Acoustic communication*. Norwood, NJ: Ablex Publishing.

Turner, F. (1986, November). Escape from modernism. *Harper's*, pp. 47-55.

U. S. Congress, Office of Technology Assessment. (1989). *Copyright and home copying: Technology challenges the law, OTA-CIT-422*. Washington, DC: Government Printing Office.

Ussachevsky, V. (1980, April). Notes on "a piece for tape recorder." *Musical Quarterly*, pp. 205-206.

Van De Voorde, A. (1988, January 3). Teenmania. *Eau Claire Leader-Telegram*, p. C1.

Wale, M. (1972). *Voxpop*. London: George G. Harrap.

Wallerstein, E. (1976, April). Creating the LP record. *High Fidelity*, pp. 56-61.

Wallis, R., & Malm, K. (1984). *Big sounds from small peoples*. New York: Pendragon Press.

Weiner, N. (1948). *Cybernetics; or, control and communication in the animal and the machine*. New York: John Wiley and Sons.

White, P. (1987, November). The Visconti file. *Home & Studio Recording*, pp. 31-34.

White, R. M. (Ed). (1985). *Introduction to magnetic recording*. New York: Institute of Electrical and Electronics Engineers.

Wickersham, R. (1969, September). Multichannel recording for creating the "New Sound." *Electronics World, 823*, pp. 38-39, 77.

Willis, P. E. (1978). *Profane culture*. London: Routledge & Kegan Paul.

Wilson, J. S. (1959, June 21). How no-talent singers get "talent." *New York Times Magazine*, p. 14-18

Wire for sound. (1943, May 17). *Time*, p. 58.

Wire recorder. (1947, May). *Popular Mechanics*, p. 95.

Woram, J. M. (1981). *The recording studio handbook*. Plainview, NY: ELAR Publishing Company, Inc.

Wortman, L. (1954, July). Magnetic recording 1888-1954. *Radio and Television News*, pp. 59-61, 124.

Wyatt, S. (1987a, May 14). [Personal interview with the author]. Unpublished raw data.

Wyatt, S. (1987b, May 27). [Personal interview with the author]. Unpublished raw data.

Wyatt, S. (1987c, May 29). [Personal interview with the author]. Unpublished raw data.

Wyatt, S. (1987d, June 12). [Personal interview with the author]. Unpublished raw data.

Wyatt, S. (1987e, July 24). [Comments during recording session at Private Studios, Urbana, IL]. Unpublished raw data.

Index

About the Author

Steve Jones is Assistant Professor of Communication at the University of Tulsa, Oklahoma. He has published extensively in the fields of popular music, popular culture, and mass communication. Jones received a doctorate in 1987 from the Institute of Communications Research at the University of Illinois, and taught for several years at the University of Wisconsin-Eau Claire. He has been active in the music business since 1983 as a record producer, recording engineer, and performer, with numerous album and performance credits. Jones edits *Tracking: Popular Music Studies*, the journal of the International Association for the Study of Popular Music (IASPM)/ USA, and has held offices at IASPM's national and international levels. He is also active in a number of scholarly organizations, including the International Communication Association, Association for Education in Journalism and Mass Communication, Society for the Study of Symbolic Interaction, and the Society for Philosophy of Technology.